Study
Guide

The American Polity
Everett Carll Ladd

Second Edition

Study
Guide

The American Polity
Everett Carll Ladd

Second Edition

by David B. Magleby
Brigham Young University

W. W. Norton and Company
New York   London

Copyright © 1987, 1985 by W. W. Norton & Company, Inc.

All rights reserved.

Printed in the United States of America.

ISBN 0-393-95593-1

W. W. Norton & Company, Inc., 500 Fifth Avenue, New York, N.Y. 10110
W. W. Norton & Company Ltd., 37 Great Russell Street, London WC1B 3NU

1 2 3 4 5 6 7 8 9 0

Contents

Acknowledgments

This study guide reflects my views on what students should learn in an introductory American government course and how they can apply political science in their studies and everyday lives. My ideas about these subjects have been influenced by colleagues and students at the University of California, Berkeley, the University of Virginia, and now Brigham Young University. Gary Bryner, Keith Melville, and Dick Vetterli, my colleagues who also teach American government at B.Y.U., have provided useful comments and criticisms on parts of this book. Several of the ideas contained in the new section on writing research papers stem from my colleague Stan Taylor and from an excellent essay on writing in political science by Tom Cronin, "The Write Stuff," *News For Teachers of Political Science* (Spring 1986): 1–4.

The second edition of this study guide benefits from the feedback of students who used the first edition. I am especially grateful to Nancy Prescott who read and critiqued the first edition, and to Rob Eaton who provided numerous suggestions, especially with the new section on writing research papers. Others who assisted with the first edition were Kim Alsop, Peter Christensen, Jamie Cook, Scott Edgley, Greg Johnson, George Landrith, Rick Malmgren, Earl Marshall, Debbie Owen, and Murray Snow. I am grateful for their ideas about how a study guide can help students more effectively use a major college text. Dean Martin Hickman of the College of Family, Home and Social Sciences at B.Y.U. has been most supportive of this endeavor. Don Fusting of Norton edited the manuscript and provided helpful suggestions about its format and content. The typing and retyping of this manuscript was done quickly and efficiently by the Faculty Support Center of the College of Family, Home and Social Sciences at B.Y.U. Finally, taking on an extra project like this imposes additional burdens on family. I appreciate the support of my wife and children.

To the Student: Reading the text, understanding data, and taking exams

This study guide is intended to assist you in studying American politics and government. It will not only help you learn and retain the material in *The American Polity*, but will give you suggestions about where to go for additional information, as well as for ideas about how to conduct research. Toward these ends I have provided chapter overviews, outlines, and four different kinds of review questions, as well as additional readings and research projects for each chapter.

I agreed to write the study guide to accompany Everett Carll Ladd's *The American Polity* because I was impressed with the author's approach to the subject. Ladd's focus is on what actually happens, the dynamics of governance, not just on the institutions and their structures. The American government course can be one of the most lively, useful, and surprising that a student will encounter in college.

The subject is lively because it is timely and concerns topics on which there is often no "right" answer. The subject is useful because in a democracy we need to call upon our government and effectively participate in it. For many this is difficult because they lack the basic understanding acquirable in this course. American Government is surprising because most students start out thinking they already know about the subject from their high school civics courses. But at the college level we pursue the subject in greater depth. Topics like bureaucracy, interest groups, and ethnicity are areas of American government most students know little about. The subject is also surprising because students tend to generalize from their own viewpoint and experience, but later discover that many people have differing backgrounds and perspectives. After reading *The American Polity*, you will better understand how a land with such social, economic, and political diversity has survived for so long despite major disruptions like wars, assasinations, and a presidential resignation.

Using this Study Guide

Most students who take American government begin the course thinking they will have little need for a study guide. Some are right; most are not. The intellectual tools you will be asked to employ while taking this course are reading, analytic thinking, and writing. The scope of the course and textbook make comprehension and retention a challenge. The study guide will assist you with reading by allowing you to evaluate your own comprehension and retention. These skills improve with practice, and many students will benefit from the kind of exercises provided in this study guide. In addition, the study guide will help you review for examinations, especially final examinations, whether they include completion, multiple choice, true/false, or essay questions. Finally, the study guide will help you think by asking you questions that require you to apply the information you have learned from the book. Because writing skills are such an important part of a college education and are, perhaps, the single most important foundation of a successful professional career, I have devoted an entire section to it on pages xxv–xxxiii of this study guide.

Like reading, writing improves with practice. The first step in writing is to get ideas, and the study guide should help you pursue some of the ideas presented in the textbook, as well as some that may go beyond the lectures or text. If you will be writing research papers, the suggested readings and application at the end of each chapter should prove useful.

To use the guide most effectively you should use it as a companion to the basic text. Each study guide chapter corresponds to a chapter in the text. Before reading each chapter in the text, read the chapter overview and the list of key terms and concepts provided in the study guide. Effective performance in a course like American government is enhanced by staying current in the reading. If you are confused about something in the reading, you can ask about it during a class period. If you wait to read the text or study guide until just before examinations, you will not benefit from the insights your professor and classmates could have provided.

Each chapter of the study guide consists of six sections: Overview, Key Terms and Concepts, Chapter Outline, Review Questions, Further Investigation, and Applying Political Science. Here is how each section can help you.

OVERVIEW

Before you read each chapter in the text, read the chapter overview in the study guide. It will alert you to the major themes and issues addressed in the chapter. The overview is short and does not pursue ideas in depth; that is the function of the chapter in the textbook. After reading the overview you will sense how the chapter fits together and what major themes will be addressed. This information should help you be a more careful reader. Be attentive to how the author supports his points, how the points relate to one another, and what the implications are for American government.

KEY TERMS AND CONCEPTS

Before reading the chapter, examine the list of key terms and concepts. These are important to understanding the subject as well as the vocabulary of political science. After reading each chapter you should be able to define and state the significance of each term and concept. The definition will be quite easy; it will come with the introduction of the concept in the text and can also be found in the glossary at the end of the text.

Understanding the significance of the concept is a different matter. Here you need to know why the term is important to an understanding of American government and politics. An example may help. In the chapter on Congress, the committee system is discussed. *Standing committees* is one of the key terms. A definition of standing committee would be: a subgroup of Congress whose membership is stable, subject area fixed, and whose task is to consider bills and conduct the day-to-day work of Congress. But there is more than just this definition: standing committees routinely organize into subcommittees, where the legislative process begins. Subcommittee and committee chairmen have important legislative powers. The significance of standing committees is that they are the workshops of Congress. They are based on the principle of specialization secured through division of labor.

It is more likely you will learn the significance of the key terms and concepts if you are on the lookout for them. Therefore, before you read the chapter I suggest you list the key terms and concepts on a sheet of paper; then, as you encounter them in the text, note the definition and significance of each. This will also prove useful when you are taking lecture notes. As your lecturer discusses these concepts, you can add additional insights to your study materials. Finally, when you are reviewing for examinations, you will be able to review quickly the major themes of the book and the course.

CHAPTER OUTLINE

The chapter outline will assist your study in two ways. First, after you have read the chapter, go to the chapter outline and read the topic headings. They are written in a way intended to jog your memory. For example, if you just finished reading the chapter on the presidency and come to the heading in the chapter outline "The institutional presidency," ask yourself the following: Could I answer a question on that topic? Do I remember what the institutional presidency is? If not, return to that section of the chapter and review the material.

Second, the chapter outline will enable you to review for examinations. Use the outline headings in this phase of your study just as you did after reading the chapter for the first time. Chapter titles and major headings provide you with concepts and values the author thinks are important. When you anticipate essay questions, for instance, these headings often become clues to what will appear on the exam. Again, if you are unsure of what the book said about one or another of the headings, turn to that section of the book and review the material.

REVIEW QUESTIONS

After checking your memory with the chapter outline, it is time to test yourself with the review questions. Each chapter in the study guide has four different types of questions: completion, true/false, multiple choice, and essay. Exams typically include some of each type of question, so practice each type. As with the chapter outline, I would suggest you use these exercises at least twice; so do *not* write your answers in the study guide. Go through the review questions a first time immediately after reading the chapter. If you have trouble answering the question, go on to the next question until you complete all of the review questions. Then check your answers against the answer key provided at the end of the chapter. For the questions you answered incorrectly, go back to the text and find the correct answer. To help you correct your answers, each question is followed by the page number on which the topic is discussed. Go through the review questions a second time when you are reviewing for an exam. This time write in the answers. As with the initial review, be sure to follow up on the questions you could not answer or answered incorrectly.

FURTHER INVESTIGATION

A glance at the contents of *The American Polity* reveals the wide array of topics covered in its twenty chapters. Because the book introduces so many subjects and builds a foundation for more advanced work in American government, it cannot go into any of the subjects as deeply as you might like. In the Further Investigation section of the study guide, I suggest several sources from which you may learn more about subjects that specifically interest you. The citations are briefly annotated, and the books are likely to be in your college bookstore or library.

APPLYING POLITICAL SCIENCE

For many, the American government course is their first course in political science. The text and lectures will introduce you to the kinds of questions political scientists ask and how they go about answering them. Where appropriate, I suggest some ways you can test the ideas presented in the book in a local setting or can apply to a research question that is presented in the chapter. Many of the other courses college students take require students to spend time in a laboratory. While that is not typical of political science, the study guide will give you ideas of how to use your community, library, and classmates as a type of political science laboratory.

Using Your Textbook

Before you start reading your first assignment, take a few minutes to get to know the text and how it is organized. Textbooks like this one have headings and subheadings in color that highlight the points the author thinks deserve attention. Also look for the ways the author and publisher use graphs, diagrams, photographs, boxes, summaries, marginal side notes, and other aids intended to help you understand and remember the material.

Read the preface and the table of contents. Students often skip over the preface, but it can give the reader insights into how the book is organized, how the author intends to approach his subject, and whether the author has a distinctive point of view. Scanning the table of contents will give you a sense of how topics are related and the relative weight given to each.

The textbook also features study aids in the back. The index will help you locate subjects or names of information you wish to review. You will find also a copy of the Declaration of Independence, the Constitution, and its Preamble and Amendments. Finally, a glossary of essential terms and concepts is presented in the text. The glossary and index will be valuable tools as you review for examinations.

Improving Reading Retention

A large proportion of the work college students do involves reading. Important to retaining the material you read is reading in the right atmosphere. Because you will want to take notes on your reading and minimize the distractions, I suggest you read the text and use the study guide in a quiet area where you have room to work. The college library is ideal, and it has the added benefit of containing the additional readings suggested in the study guide.

Any good textbook should broaden the student's vocabulary. Don't miss the opportunity to learn the definitions and usages of new words. Have a dictionary nearby. Increasing the number of words you understand and can use correctly will enhance the thinking and writing skills you will carry with you well beyond this course.

Reading a text is different from other reading you will do in that you are reading to learn material you will later be examined on. So read with questions in mind and attempt to find answers. Reading the chapter overview and key terms and concepts presented in this study guide will give you things to look for in your reading. Do not hesitate to make marginal notations or underline key passages. If confused about something, make a note of it; if it is not clarified later in the chapter, bring it up in class. Approach each topic and chapter systematically, using the aids provided in the study guide. Your retention and understanding will improve.

Reading Charts and Graphs

One of the distinguishing features of Ladd's *The American Polity* is its extensive use of charts and graphs. This stems from the author's uncommon access to survey and other kinds of data. Professor Ladd is the director of the Roper Center, which houses one of the largest collections of social and political data in the world. The data presented by Professor Ladd in your text have been gathered by a wide variety of organizations, public and private. Ladd's access to and use of these data help us to understand past trends and give reasonable predictions for the future. The book's charts and graphs are useful in helping us visualize and therefore understand what the data mean.

Even though there is much truth to the adage that "a picture is worth a thousand words," it is also true that pictures can be used to present an exaggerated or distorted impression to the viewer. This is especially the case with charts and graphs. Therefore, you should read all graphical presentations of information carefully. This caution should not reinforce the common tendency of students to simply skip over graphical presentations in their textbook. If the author and editors have chosen to present information in charts and tables, it is important and merits your careful attention. Here in outline form are some important things to remember when reading graphs and charts:

WHEN READING GRAPHS

1. Carefully read the graph's title, captions, legend and source notes. The *title* will tell you what the author thinks the graph is about. The *captions*, usually printed along the vertical and horizontal axes, tell you what is being measured. The *legend* is a short explanation of the symbols that might be employed in a graph. Finally, as a careful consumer of graphical information you will want to know where the data in the graph came from. That information will be found in the source note at the bottom of the table.
2. Study the grid, or format, of the table. What are the intervals on each axis of the table? Are they the same on both the horizontal and vertical axes? What is the range of the data on both the vertical and horizontal axes?
3. Examine the configuration of the line on the graph. When and where does it change? Think about why.

WHEN READING TABLES

1. As with graphs, carefully read the table's title, captions, legend, and source note.
2. Inspect each column and row. Tables are organized horizontally (row) or vertically (column). You can tell which way the table is organized by looking to see in which direction the percentages add up to 100 percent. When examining the table, look for differences and similarities in the data. Typically, tables are constructed to permit comparison of this sort.

Two basic types of data are presented in your text: numerical and categorical. The two are distinguished by whether the unit of analysis (what we are studying) is a number or a word. For example, if a person is asked in a survey about his age, height, or income, his response would be numerical, such as 35, 6 feet, or $25,575. But if a person is asked his religious preference, he could respond by referring to a particular religion or say he has no religious preference at all. This is considered a categorical response. The exception to this is when we break numerical data down into categories, such as putting age into categories like: under 18, 18–24, 25–29, and so forth. Understanding the difference between numerical and categorical data is important because the type of chart or graph used depends heavily on what type of data is being analyzed.

The most common graphs used for categorical data are bar graphs and pie charts. For example, below we have a duplicate of the bar graph found on page 23 of the text, comparing persons 20–24 years of age enrolled in higher education across six nations.

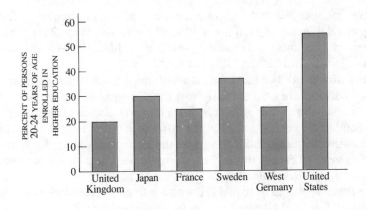

The different categories (nations in this case), are listed across the horizontal axis while the percentage values are listed on the vertical axis. Vertical bars are constructed above each category with their heights corresponding to the percentage of 20–24 year olds enrolled in higher education for each country. The bars represent the actual frequency for each country at the time the survey was taken. The percentage for each country is relative to its own population of 20–24 year olds, so that differences in population size will be taken into consideration.

Another way to look at the percentages for categories is with a pie chart, such as these below. These divide the work force into three main groups and show what percentage of the work force is in each category for each country.

To permit you to compare a pie chart with a bar graph we have reproduced both below, using the same data on employment in the United States.

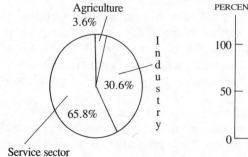

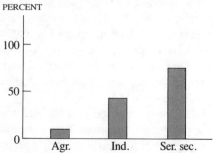

Both pie charts and bar graphs are effective ways to present categorical information. What determines the size of the slice of the pie or the length of the bar is the *relative frequency* for that category in the data set, the term relative frequency is used because we are comparing the frequency for that category relative to the total population of the study. Sometimes the actual frequencies or counts from the surveys are given, although this is less common because it often makes the table harder to read.

When numerical data has been gathered, most often a histogram or a frequency polygon are used to help show the distribution of the data. Histograms are similar to bar graphs because they are also usually created on a horizontal and a vertical axis. But the difference is that the data is sectioned into continuous numerical intervals on the horizontal axis and a frequency tally is given for each interval. For example, we will take the turnout percentage for all fifty states for the 1984 election.

Our first step would be to divide the data into continuous intervals of equal length, say five, and take frequencies (simply count up the number) for each interval.

35-39.9	I	1
40-44.9	IIII II	7
45-49.9	IIII II	7
50-54.9	IIII IIII I	11
55-59.9	IIII IIII IIII	14
60-64.9	IIII I	6
65-69.9	IIII	4
70-74.9	I	1

Then a histogram is created to visualize the distribution of the data.

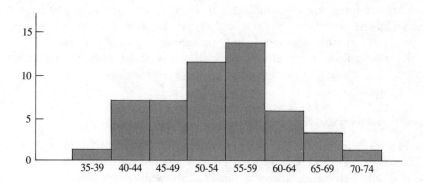

A frequency polygon is made by connecting the midpoints of the histogram with lines, as follows:

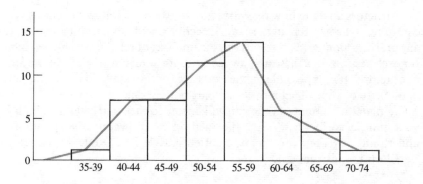

Frequency polygons are popular for monitoring trends over intervals of time.

Preparing for and Taking Exams

A major purpose of this study guide is to inprove your exam grades. Using the review questions, going back over the chapter summary and outline and quizzing yourself on the key terms and concepts will give you confidence in getting ready for that first midterm and the eventual final examination. I have already discussed how to use the study guide for this purpose. The one point I wish to underscore is that it will be most helpful if used at the time you read the chapter; followthrough—going back over information you did not assimilate the first time—is also crucial. Systematic review is perhaps the most effective (and most neglected) study technique a student can use.

Because college examinations, especially essay examinations, are often intimidating to students, let's explore some ways to improve performance on the exam.

LEARN THE FACTS ABOUT THE EXAM

The most important part of exam taking is learning the material. But different types of exams call for different strategies. Here are some questions you should be able to answer about how you will be examined:

1. What type of examination question will be asked: objective, essay, or both essay and objective?
2. Which material, readings, and lectures will the exam cover?
3. Is there a penalty for guessing incorrectly?
4. How much time is allowed for the exam?

PAY CAREFUL ATTENTION TO DIRECTIONS

Instructors differ in how they structure an exam, so follow directions very carefully. Read and reread the exam directions, and pay careful attention to any oral directions given. Most exams include a set of relative weights or points for each section. Use these as a device to apportion your time. If fifty of the one hundred points possible on the exam are for the essay, do not spend only one-fourth of your time on the essay part of the exam. Before you begin the exam, plan the amount of time you will devote to each part, and then budget your time accordingly. Verify the method of answering the question—underlining, circling, checking the correct answer, etc., unless it is clearly stated on the instructions.

STRATEGY FOR OBJECTIVE TESTS

For each chapter in the study guide, I have included a set of objective questions that will help you refine your test-taking skills. I will discuss here some important strategies for taking objective tests which you can apply as you complete the review questions in this study guide.

In an objective exam find out in advance if there is a penalty for guessing. If only correct answers are counted and there is no penalty for wrong answers, you have nothing to lose by guessing. If, however, one-quarter or one-half of a point is subtracted for each incorrect answer from the total number you answer correctly, then you may do well to pass over questions you cannot answer. Sometimes your score on an objective exam will be the number you answer correctly minus the number you answered incorrectly; this also imposes a penalty for guessing. Before you begin to answer questions, check to make sure your exam has all of the questions and that the pages are in the correct order. Because objective tests often are several pages long, it is possible that one page was omitted when your exam was collated or that the pages are not in the correct order.

Perhaps the most important strategy for taking objective exams is reading each question carefully. Many students read things into questions. Others skip over key words or phrases. Objective exam questions sometimes include words like never, only, all, or always, which significantly modify their meaning. Look for double negatives and questions that are only partly correct. (This is especially a problem in true/false questions.) Read all of the alternatives before answering the question, because more than one of them may be correct. Ask yourself, what is the point of the question? If the answer is not obvious, start to exclude the answers that are clearly incorrect. If there is a penalty for guessing but you can exclude one or more of the options, you are probably wise to answer the question by choosing the most likely alternative.

If the correct answer is not apparent on the first reading, you should then eliminate the incorrect answers. You can do this by looking for alternatives that are inconsistent, illogical, or meaningless. Be alert to the fact that test items often will sound good, but in fact be incorrect. Sometimes one of the choices may make sense and even be true but is not an answer to the question. These and other problems are best understood in light of a few examples from this study guide. For each type of question, a short comment follows on the correct and incorrect answers.

FACTUAL QUESTION

Democracy in America was originally written in
    a. French
    b. English
    c. German
    d. Italian
    e. none of these

This straightforward question requires simple recall of a fact — you either know it was written in French or you don't. You might be able to narrow it down to French and English if you recall that Tocqueville was a Frenchman who wrote about America (as the title of his book implies). On such questions it is often best to mark the answer that feels best and then move on, since prolonged contemplation will not likely help you determine the answer. In fact, the longer it takes to think about the question, the greater your chances of missing the correct answer are. The rule is: Read slowly and carefully but answer quickly. If you do not know the answer, go on to the next question.

If time is at a premium you will then be answering the questions you know best, and if time is not at a premium you can go back to the questions you have skipped.

APPLICATION OF PRINCIPLE

Z feels bad that A, who lives on her block, is always cheating B. She files suit against A on B's behalf. The court refuses to hear the suit because
    a. it is not justiciable.
    b. Z has no standing.
    c. there is no real controversy.
    d. Z has failed to fulfill the requirements of a class action suit.
    e. A has not broken the law.

Obviously, this specific question was not addressed in the text. The principles needed to answer it were, however. Justiciability deals with whether the issue is appropriate for judicial review. Since cheating is presumably against the law, the case is justiciable and *a* is incorrect. To attain standing, a party must show that he or she has sustained, or is being threatened with, real injury. Since Z has observed only A's cheating of B, Z has no standing in the court and the court will therefore refuse to hear the suit. Therefore *b* is the correct answer. *C* is incorrect because there is real controversy; *d* is incorrect because a class action suit does not apply to this situation; *e* is incorrect because A has indeed broken the law by cheating.

LOGICAL ELIMINATION

Sometimes you can answer a question you know little or nothing about simply by logically eliminating false answers.

Synonymous answers

The so-called establishment region was the
    a. South.
    b. West.
    c. Sunbelt.
    d. Northeast.

As is often the case, this question includes two possible answers that mean virtually the same thing. Since the South (*a*) and the Sunbelt (*c*) describe essentially the same region, neither can be correct, since you would have to choose between them. The West, you might reason from your general knowledge of American history, was the last region to be settled and could hardly be considered the establishment region. By default, your answer is *d*, the Northeast.

Contradictory answers

In appointing predominantly conservative judges, Reagan has

a. offended members of his own party in Congress.
b. acted similarly to his predecessors.
c. violated the independence of the judicial branch.
d. behaved differently from any presidents before him.
e. none of the above

Careful examination of this set of options reveals two options that contradict each other: *b* and *d*. Not only do they contradict each other, they are totally exhaustive, that is, Reagan behaves either similarly to or differently from his predecessors, so you can forget options *a*, *c*, and *e*. Once you've narrowed it down to two, it requires knowledge to know that the correct answer is *b*.

CONSISTENCY

The Commission on National Elections did not study which of the following issues?

a. length of presidential campaigns
b. high cost of campaigning
c. party procedures for nominating candidates
d. why more people don't vote
e. possibility of a proportional system.

Notice the word *not* in the question, making the answer an exception. From the title of the commission, you know that their work dealt primarily with elections. The first four questions all deal with election problems of a similar nondrastic nature. The fifth option, the "possibility of a proportional system," involves a massive overhaul, going far beyond any of the other issues in scope. By exclusion, (*e*) is the correct choice.

DANGEROUS MODIFIERS

The views of the president appointing federal judges are always to be reflected in the decisions handed down by those jurists.

a. true
b. false

This true or false question is extracted from the text verbatim, with the exception of one word, which has been changed. "Likely" became "always," and what was a true statement became false. It is a rare case in which events "always" or "never" happen a certain way; the odds are with you when you guess against the truthfulness of statements including these words. Similar all encompassing or extremely limiting adjectives are *all*, *only*, and *any*.

After you have completed the other parts of the exam, if time permits, go back to the objective section and make use of information in other test items.

STRATEGY FOR ESSAY TESTS

Often more than half the total points on an exam will be for the essay. Despite the importance of essay questions, most students do not prepare adequately for them. Here are some suggestions to help you improve your performance on essay examinations.

Practice writing timed essays

Writing an essay is in some ways similar to writing a short paper: an essay exam should have a thesis, use supporting evidence, and clearly present the main point. But an essay exam is also different from writing a short paper — you will work against a time limitation, and the exam typically is "closed book" (meaning you may not read from your notes or any other sources while writing the essay). These elements often create anxiety. One way to reduce that anxiety is to practice writing essays under conditions like those you will face in the testing situation (i.e., closed book and with a thirty-minute limit). The study guide provides practice essay questions for each chapter, but you should supplement these with questions that reflect the content of lectures and the emphases of the professor. Make friends with another student in the class, and at the end of each week's lectures, exchange essay questions on that week's materials. Wait to read the question until you are ready to practice, then open the question and write on it for thirty minutes. A day or two later read over your essay as if you were grading it and assess its strengths and weaknesses.

Anticipate questions

When you review for the exam, go back over major subject headings in the lectures or text, search for themes that tie the material together, think of questions you would want to read answers to if you were the professor. Use your list of possible essay questions as a review device and prepare scratch outlines for the most likely questions.

If you have studied the material correctly, you probably will not be surprised by the essay questions asked on the exam.

Read the directions and questions carefully

Often you will be given a choice of which essay questions to answer; if so, be sure to answer only the specified number of questions. Before you start to prepare your outline, read all of the questions through once. Once you decide the question you want to answer, read through it again, circling key words and phrases. Pay careful attention to the kind of writing you are being asked to do and to the clues the question gives you about what is important.

Prepare a brief outline of your answer

Even when time is limited, it is useful to prepare a brief outline of the major points you want to cover in your essay. Sometimes the question itself suggests an outline (be sure you cover all the required topics). Other times you will need to formulate the thesis and plan the topics you want to cover.

The brief outline allows you to write better transitions, helps you to integrate the supporting evidence, and gives your thesis paragraph a sense of direction. If you start the outline before you answer the objective part of the exam, you can use this part of the exam to help you with ideas or examples for your essay. The outline will also help you to gauge your time. If you have only covered one-quarter of your outline in half your time, you know you will have to move more briskly to cover the necessary material.

Begin your essay by stating your thesis

The first few sentences may be the most important ones. After preparing the short outline and deciding the points you want to make, use the first paragraph to state your thesis and introduce the main themes in your argument. Do not waste time copying the essay question or merely restating it. Instead, assert your command of the material.

Stay on the subject

Because you will have spent several hours preparing for the exam, there is an understandable desire to tell the professor everything you have learned, even if it is not related to the question. Avoid this urge. Instead, use the outline and a crisp writing style to lay out your answer to the question asked.

Support your argument

The evidence you present to support your argument will be one of the most important things the reader will look for. Your reading and the lectures will have provided examples that support your case. Where appropriate, use them. The essay is a means to determine whether you have integrated the material and can explain it *in your own words*. It is important that you differentiate between major points and relatively minor ones. Here as well, the brief outline will help you remember the main points and their relation to subordinate points. Do not hesitate to underline them or otherwise call attention to them. You can be sure that the reader will be looking for your thoughts on them.

Write legibly

While all agree that the purpose of an essay question is to determine what you have learned and how effectively you can communicate that knowledge, it is also true that poor handwriting will interfere with effective communication. You may wish to write on every other line of the exam book or to print rather than write longhand. Students often regret they have to write quickly to get everything down. Speed is often associated with poor handwriting. If the tradeoff is illegible scribbles, then you may be better served by writing less and making it legible. This is one of the things you can improve with practice. After you have taken some of the practice essays in the study guide, ask a friend whether he or she can read your handwriting. If not, then you will know the task at hand.

Writing Research Papers

In many courses where *The American Polity* is assigned you will be expected to write a research paper. These may vary from shorter "think piece" kinds of writing to more extensive term papers where you will choose a topic, do research, and then write a paper. Regardless of the kind of paper you are assigned, the process of writing and rewriting is one of the most important parts of your education. Writing is hard work. Effective writing and research require discipline, planning, and a willingness to seek criticism from your peers and professor. Learning to write well, however, is going to be one of the most important skills you will acquire.

This section of the study guide gives you some practical suggestions about how to approach the task of writing papers in your American government course. Much more could have been said. Beyond this brief overview you will want to acquire a style manual, a thesaurus, and most important, a dictionary. To assist you in thinking about topics to research, each chapter has a section called "Applying Political Science," which suggests research questions related to that chapter. Many of these topics could lead to interesting research and a thoughtful term paper.

Choosing the Topic

One of the most important steps in writing is selecting a topic. (The research question is the specific focus of our study within a broader topic area; when rephrased as a statement, it is a hypothesis or thesis.) Nothing makes producing a paper more unpleasant than an unsatisfactory topic — one which does not interest the student, has already been thoroughly researched, or is irrelevant anyway. You might ask yourself three things when you choose research questions: Does it interest you? is it original? and is it relevant?

WHAT INTERESTS YOU?

Students who are bored with their research and annoyed at the thought of writing a paper have failed to recognize that political science is a marvelously broad and interesting field. At the end of each chapter of the study guide is a section called "Further Investigation." The topics presented here are intended to help you think of research questions which emerge from the material covered in this chapter. For each of your professor's lectures there are bound to be additional research questions you might want to explore. What is the effect of nuclear testing on the surrounding environment? How do presidents choose new supreme court justices? What considerations are given to environmental impact when planning roads?

Brainstorming with other students is often an effective way to find a good research topic. Don't limit yourself as you begin to consider potential topics. If a question has always puzzled you or a professor's assertion seems questionable, think about it, discuss it with others, and then write about it. Research papers motivated by genuine curiosity are both more enjoyable and more effective than papers begrudgingly done to fill the required number of pages on an arbitrarily selected topic. If the topic does not interest you, it is not likely to interest your reader.

An important phase of almost all research is the narrowing of the topic once you have chosen it. Often the initial question, after some digging, is found to be much more expansive than you originally thought. It is important, therefore, to think carefully about how you can narrow and focus your question to one that is manageable and still interesting. Nothing will bring greater frustration to a research effort than a topic that is too broad. Can you imagine trying to do a ten-page research paper on "Civil Rights in America"? Anyone who begins a research paper with that title must be prepared to complete a multivolume project. However, a paper on "The Civil Rights of Vietnamese in New Hampshire in the 1980s" is much more manageable and will be more enjoyable to research and write.

Sometimes your professor will prefer to assign you a topic or ask you to write a more focused paper or book review. Yet even when professors assign a topic, rarely do they expect or desire the same approach from each student. As noted in the section on essay questions, read the question carefully, decide upon a thesis, and state it clearly; support your thesis with data and argument, and stay on the subject. If you are sure you have answered the question, do not be afraid to put your own twist on the topic. It not only makes researching and writing the paper more enjoyable for you, it makes reading it more enjoyable for your professor.

IS IT ORIGINAL?

Students in an introductory American government course are often unsure about their ability to think of good questions. Yet one reason professors enjoy teaching the introductory course is that beginning students often ask good questions. Advanced degrees and long-term familiarity are not prerequisites to insight and understanding. In fact, political scientists may be limited by their own traditional ways of thinking. The challenge and excitement of scholarship is to venture out onto virgin territory or to approach an already conquered mountain from a new angle.

Creative and original scholarship does not mean that you ignore the findings of those who have already studied a topic. To ignore existing literature and merely blast away shotgun-style at a topic is not innovative, it is lazy. However, while a student should be familiar with what experts have concluded, he need not accept their conclusions as ultimate truth.

Naturally, original research will be difficult for the average undergraduate. Even if you can only draw from existing research, you can still be innovative. The best insurance against stale summaries of other people's work is to select a question to which you don't already know the answer. Many students fall victim to stagnant ideas because they find the research question and answer in the same source. If this is the case, you may as well give your professor your list of references. When you really need to dig to find answers, you are bound to make some discoveries yourself.

Thus far we have talked about originality and creativity in the context of what it will do to your intellectual development. Another reason to do your own work is that to copy another person's work is dishonest. It is contrary to the norms of scholarship to use another person's words or ideas without attribution. In most universities, plagiarism — quoting from someone else's work without attribution — is grounds for academic probation or dismissal. Students sometimes think they can "cut and paste" long quotes from other sources together and thereby produce a paper. This form of plagiarism is likely to be caught by your professor and penalized, but more importantly you will have denied yourself the opportunity to learn to write for yourself. An equally serious offense is to purchase a term paper from one of the "term paper factories" around the country.

IS IT IMPORTANT?

It is possible, however, to dig so far that you discover something which truly doesn't matter. You will be spending a lot of time reading, thinking, and writing about the topic you choose. Is it sufficiently important to merit this much time and effort? Can you defend the relevance of the topic to a group of bright but uninformed friends? Finally, as noted above, narrow your topic so that it is manageable yet relevant. Be realistic, yet ambitious. Know what you can do with the resources available to you (including time), and then stretch yourself within those limits.

Get Started Now

The sooner you determine your research question, the better. If you choose your topic long before your deadline, you can ask your professor about it. It gives you time to change your question if the data isn't there to answer it or if you find something even more interesting while researching. The principle of not procrastinating holds true throughout the process. Make a schedule for yourself, listing key points in the research and writing process and the dates you plan to be at those stages. A little discipline throughout the semester will help you produce a much better paper.

If you start your research soon enough, you will have time for people to send you helpful materials. Make your term paper an actual term-long project and the quality of it will improve. It is difficult, if not impossible, to research interesting and relevant offshoots of your question if you have procrastinated until the last week of the semester to do your research. Getting an early start is especially important if you are going to do your own research, as contrasted to a library paper. One student of mine in Virginia wanted to study a U.S. Senate election in South Dakota. Had he not gotten an early start he would neither have been able to arrange for interviews in that state nor to make arrangements with both campaigns to mail him campaign materials.

Researching the Question

If you have a question about which you are excited, research takes on a whole new meaning. But even with this excitement and a good question, you need a logical plan of attack to make your research effective.

THE PLAN OF ATTACK

The main focus of your paper will be your thesis, the answer to your research question. It might be descriptive: What was the actual intent of the founders with the First Amendment? You probably should also apply your findings. For example, you might include a short section on how the intent of the founders compares with interpretations of the courts today. Your question might be analytical (most are): How do election-day surveys by the media affect the results of elections? Here your focus is on explaining, rather than describing and applying, a phenomenon. Finally, your question might be prescriptive in nature, i.e., how can Congress best balance the budget? Most prescriptive questions are rather complex and speculative; they necessarily include an understanding of the background of the problem and an analysis of your own solution. Most research questions involve, to at least some degree, a combination of these three levels.

Outline Your Paper

It is easy to spend hours in the library only to realize that you are not any closer to writing a coherent research paper than you were when you began. Outlining gives direction to your research and coherence to your paper. If you have already learned to outline, you have probably already enjoyed improved results. Without an outline, students wander aimlessly through documents and toss together a hodgepodge of analysis the day before the paper is due.

You probably have enough knowledge about your question to prepare a scratch outline before you begin the official research of your paper. (See the section on the importance of an outline to essay questions.) It may change as you discover unexpected elements while digging deeper, but that will only make your paper better.

Read With a Purpose

One trap many students fall into is that they read too much before they start writing. On many questions you are interested in there will have been enough written that you could spend months simply reading it all. Once you have read for several weeks you will have forgotten important parts of what you read initially. To avoid this trap, force yourself to start writing before you are through reading. If you read something that changes your views after you have already written them, you can revise them, but you will not have fallen prey to the mistake of reading without a purpose.

Be smart. Don't put in more effort than you need to. Many students spend much more time than is necessary on research (although more shortchange themselves and their professors). Here are some suggestions for effective research.

Choose Your Sources Carefully

You need not digest all that has been written in the general topic area of your paper in order to be able to write about it well. Compile lists of books, journal articles, and other documents that might be relevant, and start reading. Your reference librarian can help you learn to use the numerous indices in the library that will help you find the books, articles, and government documents relevant to your topic. Begin with a few good general background sources, then begin tossing out material that does not apply to your question. This is where the outline is extremely helpful: You know what you're looking for.

If you are accustomed to using only magazines for research papers, it is time to introduce yourself to the more substantive journals in the field. Guides, such as the *Social Science Citation Index*, can lead you to dozens of relevant articles by experts on your subject.

Government documents may be somewhat more difficult to penetrate than journal articles and periodicals, but if you break the barrier and learn how to find relevant government publications in your library, you will have gained an invaluable resource. Congressional committees and special commissions provide researchers with some of the best, yet least used information available.

Particularly if you are researching a historical event, a good place to begin your research is with the accounts of a good daily newspaper, such as *The New York Times*, which your library is likely to have on microfiche, and which is well indexed. It can provide you with much of the background information you will need.

Two of the most useful tools of research are footnotes and bibliographies from relevant articles. Finding an article pertinent to your research question is often like knocking over the initial domino, since it usually opens the way to many other related articles and books. Be careful, however, not to rely only on one school of thought for your research.

Computer research services are becoming increasingly common among university libraries. Find out what your library has and how you can use it. Unlike the sources listed above, however, many forms of computer research can be expensive. Talk to a librarian to see if your library has something that might fill your needs.

In addition to the library data, we are surrounded by experts. Professors and others can often recommend several sources you might not otherwise find. Don't be afraid to gather your own data, as most of the "applying political science" sections of this study guide suggest. Interviews with judges, state legislators, county officials, journalists, lawyers, and others can add an original and timely aspect to your paper. It is surprising how many people you can get through to on the phone if you speak with a confident voice. You have nothing to lose; your paper has much to gain.

Read Critically

Compare sources — not all sources are equal. Who wrote the article? What were his qualifications? His motives? When did he write it? Was it published by a reputable publisher? If sources disagree, that might be significant to your paper. Be careful who you cite for key arguments. Make sure that they are authoritative and contemporary. As you are reading, be sure to integrate what you read into your overall outline and update what you have already written to incorporate what you have just learned.

Use note cards rather than notebooks and copy machines. Often students attempt to postpone the real mental work by simply transferring material *en masse* from journals and books into spiral binders. Why wait? Start the thinking process in the library and copy down only the essential ideas onto cards. Digest the stuff as you go to avoid the massive indigestion that comes from trying to consume it all the day before the paper is due. Besides, you won't want to use too many actual quotes anyway. Your paper should not be a collection of quotes glued together by your transitions, but rather your analysis supplemented by occasional and essential quotes. Save yourself all the nickels and notebook paper.

Organize your cards according to your outline and the source. If you indicate on the card, as you make the card, to which idea it applies (use the outline number), it will be easy to group related ideas and quotes together when you're ready to make the first draft. You will also want to devise some simple system by which you note the source on each card without having to write out the entire reference each time. If you use cards, limit each card to one significant idea and then phrase that card (even if it contains a direct quotation) in the context of your own research effort.

What Do You Think?

Do not be afraid to do analysis for yourself. If you are studying the Cuban Missile Crisis and how it affected Kennedy's outlook on foreign policy, you need not rely solely on someone else's analysis. Read Kennedy's speeches, before and after the event, for yourself. If you want to compare deficit spending under different presidents, it is quite simple to find the actual figures, which you can then analyze. You will be amazed to find what an abundance of data, both qualitative and quantitative, is available in a university library, from congressional votes to national expenditures on arms to the number of flush toilets in Pakistan. School librarians are experts in these sources and are happy to introduce you to information relevant to your topic.

You will obviously find much more than you will ever be able to use in your paper, but avoid bringing the library home to your typewriter or computer. Start the weeding-out process by selecting an appropriately narrow topic, then find the relevant material and abstract only essential ideas and quotes.

Writing Your Paper

Plan on writing several drafts. Far too often students submit their first draft fresh from the typewriter to their professor. As a goal for your first draft, you might just want to empty the thoughts from your head onto paper. Like a puzzle, it's easier to work with the pieces if they are in front of you in concrete form. It is probably most effective if you aren't too picky for this draft — just write. Perfect it later.

In your second draft you can smooth out the rough spots and clarify your thoughts. You will also think of better ways to organize the paper and find places where you have been redundant. Don't hesitate to make your writing more concise, that is one of the positive features of rewriting.

After you have completed a second draft you will probably need to take a break from the paper for a while. This is a good time to ask a friend to read and critique it. You are not asking your critic to revise or rewrite your paper, but simply to give you feedback on clarity, organization, analysis and mechanics. With these comments in hand you are ready to revise and polish again. Many scholars repeat these steps until they have completed five or more drafts. This revising and polishing proces serves to make writing better. You can see, however, that if you have procrastinated the research or writing phases you will end up with not enough time to do them. Even if you are unable to complete three or four drafts, it is very important that you proof your paper before you submit it. Professors become very annoyed if they are expected to be a proofreading service. If you have not bothered to check for spelling, grammar, clarity, pagination, etc., you have failed the writing assignment in important ways.

BE ORGANIZED

The term paper you submit to your professor should be well organized. It should clearly state the question or issue in the beginning and use headings and subheadings to orient the reader to its content. The final product should reflect what you know about the issue, not the steps by which you learned it. Often students feel they have to take their reader through everything they read or asked to impress him with the amount of work they have done. Do not fall prey to this mistaken assumption. Rather, present your findings in a logical and organized manner, omitting all the false turns and unimportant sources you have pursued.

CONDENSE

As you write subsequent drafts, revise and condense. Students often tend to ramble on needlessly particularly when trying to reach page quotas. Most of us would have more powerful prose if we would reduce our initial drafts by 25 percent or more. But one caution: Don't sacrifice accurateness for brevity. Many things can be explained well in short sentences, but some things can't. If a phenomenon needs explaining, don't be afraid to use the necessary space to do it.

BE YOURSELF

Most undergraduate rambling comes from a desire to fill up pages and sound more sophisticated than one is. Refreshing prose which is simple yet thoughtful will always sound better to a professor than an imitation of William Buckley. Avoid the use of jargon. It is an insecure and inept writer who hides behind the facade of buzzwords, hoping that he will look professional and informed. A good rule of thumb is to write as if for an intelligent but uninformed reader. A paper flows best when the writing is natural.

Master the Mechanics

The psychological impact of nicely typed (or printed) paper, complete with a centered title page, subheadings, and proper style cannot be overstated. It pays to invest an hour reading a good stylebook, such as Turabian's, *A Manual For Writers of Term Papers, Theses, and Dissertations*, to find out how to format your paper. There you can find out how to paginate, do footnotes, bibliographies, and nearly anything else necessary for a good research paper. Increasingly in political science, students and professors write in a style that incorporates many bibliographic and source references in the text. The style, often called the American Psychological Association Style, is a topic you should discuss with your professor. A short description of this reference style is available from the American Political Science Association in Washington, D.C.

Writing good prose may be a gift — one which can be developed — but correct spelling and grammar are mostly the results of work. There is no excuse for misspelled words and incorrect grammatical constructions. If you're not sure about something, look it up. Don't be humiliated because you need to use a dictionary — your professor does too. *The Random House Handbook*, or similar English usage books, will be helpful in improving your grammar. Careful proofreading makes for a lower number of errors and a higher grade.

Conclusion

Government and politics are subjects well suited to student writing. There are scores of interesting topics which will permit you to learn research skills, improve your ability to analyze information and expand your capacity to write clearly and intelligently. The benefits of this hard work will stay with you well beyond this particular course or your college experience.

Note: Some of the ideas presented in the section on objective examinations were obtained from "Taking Objective Exams," a document prepared by the Learning Resource Center at Brigham Young University. Many college campuses have a similar center to assist students with their studies. The section on essay examinations uses some of the ideas of Frederick Crews; see his *Random House Handbook* 4th ed. (New York: Random House, 1984), pp. 460–62. This is an excellent resource book for all aspects of writing.

1 | The American Polity: Continuity and Change

Overview

Alexis de Tocqueville, a French journalist, studied American society in the 1830s. His book, *Democracy in America*, published in 1835, commented on American beliefs, social institutions, and governmental arrangements. Tocqueville noted that American society valued individualism, social equality, and political democracy. He concluded that these trends were likely to continue and would probably be successful. History has shown that Tocqueville's predictions were accurate: individualism, equality, and democracy persist as the central values in American society.

Massive social changes within American society have divided our history into four sociopolitical periods: the rural republic, the industrializing nation, the industrial state, and the postindustrial society. Each period has brought change to American political institutions; this textbook will trace these changes.

Key Terms and Concepts

individualism
equality of opportunity
popular sovereignty
democracy

sociopolitical periods
industrialism
postindustrialism
political reform

Chapter Outline

Tocqueville and American society
  Democracy in America was published in 1835.
  Tocqueville tried to see the system as a whole.

1

He saw a strong interaction among beliefs, social institutions, and governmental arrangements.

He also tried to see where American society was headed and why.

He noted the rise of three principles: individualism, social equality, and political democracy.

Individualism meant a society built around the individual, providing him basic rights.

Social equality meant the collapse of the aristocratic society.

Political democracy followed naturally from the first two principles.

Tocqueville predicted the success of trends in America but not elsewhere.

Continuity

Strong currents of individualism are still present in the United States.

Equality of opportunity is still a powerful force.

Americans are still strongly committed to popular sovereignty (democracy).

The ideals noted by Tocqueville still form the frame of the American system.

Social change

Massive social developments due to changes in technology, economic life, demographic makeup, etc. have changed American political institutions.

Underlying social and economic demands have persisted.

American history can be divided into four sociopolitical periods.

1780s-1860s: rural republic, preindustrial society.

Big business did not exist/agricultural society.

There was no large federal government.

1870s-1920s: industrializing nation.

Population was centered in cities.

Great technological advances were made.

Government expanded, mostly at state and local level.

1930s-1960s: industrial state.

Organized labor acquired significant political influence.

Government greatly expanded, especially at federal level.

1970s-present: postindustrial society.

Review Questions

COMPLETION

1. _____ wrote *Democracy in America*, a book which has been considered the most insightful book ever written about American society and politics.

2. To understand a country's government, one must study the interaction between _____, _____, and _____.

3. The ascendent principles in American society noted by Tocqueville are _____, _____, and _____.

4. Government should rest on _____.

5. Persistence of underlying social and economic relationships over time constitute a _____.

6. The four sociopolitical periods in American history are _____, _____, _____, and _____.

7. The industrializing nation phase resulted in an increase in _____ and _____.

8. The great depression resulted in American _____ losing power.

TRUE/FALSE

1. Tocqueville, the French commentator, came from a working-class background.

2. While Tocqueville's book was well received at the time, it is now considered to lack substance.

3. Tocqueville believed that understanding a country's government required more than looking at governmental institutions.

4. Individualism is built around the idea of such rights as life, liberty, and a full chance to pursue happiness.

5. At the time *Democracy in America* was written, Western society was not undergoing much change.

6. The American experience with democracy was presumed to be unique.

7. Equality of opportunity necessarily means equality of result.

8. During the rural republic it took weeks of arduous travel to get from Maine to South Carolina.

9. The population of the United States doubled between 1870 and 1920.

MULTIPLE CHOICE

1. *Democracy in America* was originally written in
   a. French.
   b. English.
   c. German.
   d. Italian.
   e. none of these

2. One factor which contributed to vigorous democracy in America was
   a. the native American culture.
   b. a rejection of British culture.
   c. the Pilgrims' religious beliefs and institutions.
   d. none of these

3. In the American and French revolution equality replaced
   a. autocracy.
   b. aristocracy.
   c. democracy.
   d. all of the above
   e. none of the above

4. The New World differed from the Old World in
   a. the people who colonized America.
   b. the power of revolutionary ideas.
   c. that once it had achieved its revolution it became conservative.
   d. all of the above

5. During the rural republic, which sector of the country was most important in commerce and manufacturing?
   a. South
   b. Midwest
   c. Northeast
   d. Rocky Mountain states

6. The industrializing nation phase in U.S. history resulted in
   a. the United States becoming the leading industrial nation.
   b. the United States lagging far behind European countries in industrial capacity.
   c. the United States coming close to some European countries in industrial capacity.
   d. no real change in industrial output.

7. In the industrial state, _____ gained power and recognition.
   a. the South
   b. organized labor
   c. governors
   d. the Interstate Commerce Commission

ANSWER KEY

Completion

1. Alexis de Tocqueville   p. 3
2. beliefs and values of a people; their social institutions; their political system   p. 4
3. individualism; social equality; and political democracy   p. 6
4. popular sovereignty   p. 8
5. sociopolitical period   p. 10
6. rural republic; industrializing nation; industrial state; post-industrial society.   pp. 10–11
7. scale; interindependence   p. 14
8. business   p. 15

True/False

1.	F	p. 3	6. T	p. 6
2.	F	p. 3	7. F	p. 8
3.	T	p. 4	8. T	p. 12
4.	T	p. 6	9. F	p. 13
5.	F	p. 6		

Multiple Choice

1.	a	p. 3	5. c	p. 11
2.	c	p. 4	6. a	p. 12
3.	b	p. 6	7. b	p. 15
4.	d	p. 6		

ESSAY QUESTIONS

1. A foreign observer can sometimes see things others take for granted. What features of American society did Tocqueville identify which help us understand American society and politics?
2. Professor Ladd identifies four sociopolitical periods of American development. Identify each of these periods and explain what distinguishes each and how each period changed politics and society.

Further Investigation

Bryce, James. *The American Commonwealth*. New York: Macmillan, 1912.
Bryce, like Tocqueville, writes about America for a primarily foreign audience. His focus is more exclusively on government, but his observations in many ways reinforce the French observer Tocqueville.

Reeves, Richard. *American Journey: Traveling with Tocqueville in Search of Democracy in America*. New York: Simon and Schuster, 1982.
In a recent book, journalist Richard Reeves retraces Tocqueville's steps and writes of an America in the 1980s.

Tocqueville, Alex de. *Democracy in America*. New York: New American Library, 1956.
As the text indicates, a classic examination of American life and politics. The framework adopted by Tocqueville in the 1830s is equally useful today.

Applying Political Science

1. After reading Tocqueville's descriptions of town meetings, churches, or civic associations, choose one of these in your community (e.g. PTA, zoning commission, utility commission) and compare what happens there to what Tocqueville described over 150 years ago.
2. From what you now know about the four phases of American society, identify other countries that are presently in each of these phases of development.
3. Observers of American society from Tocqueville to Reeves have commented on the peculiar nature of American society, a nature which has allowed democracy to fluorish. What makes democracy possible in the United States? To answer this question read about two or three countries which do not have democratic governments and compare their social structures to that of the United States.

2 | Postindustrial Society

Overview

Postindustrialism is a transformation in economic and social structures that has arisen over the last quarter-century in the United States and other developed countries. Five major developments marked the creation of postindustrial society.

First, technological developments, resulting from the systematic application of science, made increased output possible and created new industries. Second, a knowledge base was developed because the population, through higher education and actual experience, was trained to apply the new technology. Third, postindustrialism brought about a shift of American workers from the agricultural sector to the service and white collar sectors. This increased government responsibility toward providing health, education, and welfare services. Fourth, technology has been applied to economic production, which has made the United States and other postindustrial countries affluent in a world of scarcity. Finally, social class distinctions have become less important, so that the union-oriented working class is now part of America's middle class, thus perpetuating the historically weak class divisions in the United States.

A nation built on immigration, the United States is usually diverse ethnically and religiously, and this fact has left and continues to leave its mark on national life. Even today the United States is experiencing the effects of immigration as large numbers of Hispanics immigrate to the United States.

Many Americans take pride in the ethnic and religious diversity of their country. But they also want a unity in the diversity. Within white America, historic ethnic group differences in socioeconomic standing have been greatly reduced in recent years. However, blacks and Hispanics are still in inferior economic positions.

Americans also have strong regional identities. These identities have been reinforced by the differing economies, immigration patterns, and political orientations of the regions. The most prominent sectional differences were once those between the North and South. Today, however, regionalism is much less divisive than it was a century ago.

Economic opportunity, and the resulting social mobility, are part of the American dream. Even among those who are poor, the belief in upward mobility is important. The idea that any person can work his or her way up the economic scale is central to the American ethos. Even people questioned during the Great Depression believed that economic opportunity remained.

Another aspect of mobility is social mobility, the ability to acquire a higher social status. Studies indicate that Americans experience a large proportion of upward mobility both educationally and occupationally.

Key Terms and Concepts

postindustrial	frostbelt
advanced technology	bicoastal liberalism
knowledge base	melting pot
service economy	regionalism
mass affluence	sunbelt
class relationships	immigration
ethnocultural makeup	race
social mobility	social class

Chapter Outline

A new era
    The present era is known as *postindustrial*.
    Like other eras, this one has affected American politics.
        There has been a shift in the makeup of the work force to professional and service occupations.
        The mass communications system has also changed our politics.
    Daniel Bell describes *postindustrial society* as being organized around knowledge.
    The five key developments of this era are advanced technology, the knowledge base, occupations in a service economy, mass affluence, and new class relationships.
Advanced technology
    Postindustrial society uses technology for practical ends.
    Technology contributed greatly to increased industrial output.
    Almost all major industries were the result of inventors.
    Business and technology have become intertwined.
        Vast economic resources were committed to research and development.

Technological innovation requires large commitments of resources.
Federal research and development expenditures have steadily increased.
The knowledge base
Advanced technology created a highly trained and educated work
force.
The number of college graduates has increased tremendously since
1960.
Expenditures for education have soared.
Occupations: The service economy
Industrialization moved Americans from the farms to service and
white collar jobs.
Growth of service workers reflected societal demands for health, edu-
cation, and welfare.
Government provided a larger array of services, therefore govern-
ment bureaucracy expanded.
Professional and technical employment increased greatly.
The development of administrative bureaucracies in all sectors of the
economy created millions of jobs.
The wealthy nation
The United States is a wealthy society in a world of scarcity.
This is primarily a result of applied technology to economic
production.
Since World War II, the median income of American families has
doubled.
Consumer goods were made available to most of the population.
United States per capita GNP has surpassed other advanced
democracies.
Class relationships
Social class or status reflects both income and cultural outlooks.
American class divisions are historically weak.
Working-class people gained greatly from the New Deal.
The union movement gained strength.
Since World War II, there have been fewer blue collar workers.
This has meant a gradual decline in union strength.
The working class has moved up the socioeconomic ladder.
Higher education has created an upper-middle class.
Ethnocultural makeup of the United States
Ethnic and religious diversity has been a source of social conflict.
Immigration contributes to this diversity.
The present ethnic makeup includes whites, blacks, Hispanics, and
others.
Religion is an important element.
The present makeup includes Protestants, Catholics, Jews, and
those who have no religious preference.

Americans still show strong religious attachments despite being highly developed economically.

Socioeconomic differences exist.

The fabled melting pot has greatly reduced old ethnic differences in socioeconomic status.

Blacks and Hispanics are still in inferior economic positions.

The principal ethnocultural groups seem more alike now than at any point in U.S. history, including similarity in political stands.

John F. Kennedy's election signaled the closing of a once great divide between Protestants and Catholics.

Regionalism

The differing resources, ethnic makeup, and economic development in major geographic areas of the U.S. have resulted in distinct political regions.

The Northeast — once the "establishment" region — is now labeled the Frostbelt, while the South has been renamed the Sunbelt.

Although the South is still the least affluent, it has narrowed the gap.

Social and political regionalism exist as well.

Generally, the coastal regions are more socially liberal than the heartland regions.

Overall, however, American regionalism has lost much of its divisiveness.

Opportunity and mobility

Horatio Alger's "Ragged Dick" exemplifies the American ideal of economic opportunity.

Even in difficult times, most Americans still believed that opportunity exists.

Social mobility

An exceptionally large proportion of Americans are educationally upwardly mobile.

They are also very mobile occupationally, especially upwardly.

Inequality

The top forty percent of all families in the U.S. gained over two-thirds of earnings, while the bottom forty percent received under one-sixth of national income.

Socioeconomic determinism?

As important as the socioeconomic attributes described in this chapter are, they are only part of the political environment.

Review Questions

COMPLETION

1. The United States is a _____ in a world of scarcity.

2. The unionized labor force has moved up _____.

3. America's class distinctions have been historically relatively

_____.

4. Mass affluence is brought about by using advanced technology for

_____.

5. The use of advanced technology demands a population with a

_____.

6. The _____ is still the least affluent part of the country.

7. The election of _____ as president signaled the end of a political cleavage between Protestants and Catholics.

8. Today we speak of those who rise spectacularly in social position

through personal initiatives as living an _____.

9. In most _____ societies people work in the same jobs as their parents.

10. In the 1980s, the United States is experiencing immigration from

_____.

11. American _____ has lost a lot of its historic divisiveness.

12. The most striking finding about income equality is the _____

_____ that prevails from one country to another.

TRUE/FALSE

1. Agriculture was the main occupation of Americans until the late 1950s.
2. Administrative bureaucracies are a major factor in the growth of a service economy.
3. Economic success has dampened class tensions.
4. Post-World War II brought moderate growth in family incomes.
5. Postindustrialism is organized around knowledge.
6. The greatest wave of immigration took place between 1879 and 1900.
7. The principal ethnocultural groups of the United States seem to be less dissimilar now than at any point in U.S. history.
8. There has been some decline in church attendance, but Americans still show strong religious attachments.
9. The fabled melting pot has had no effect on the socioeconomic status of Americans.
10. The major geographic regions of the United States are rarely at odds politically, even though they have had different experiences with immigration and so forth.

11. The idea that any person can work his or her way up in economic and social status is central to the country's self-image or conception.

12. Religious beliefs and values are unimportant to most Americans.

MULTIPLE CHOICE

1. Christopher J. Matthews argues that television news networks
   a. trivialize politics.
   b. have liberalized the views of American voters.
   c. have absorbed many traditional party functions.
   d. are responsible for greater awareness of international affairs.
   e. sensationalize politics by concentrating on personalities rather than issues.

2. Which of the following is *not* a key development defining the post-industrial era?
   a. The exponential growth of science
   b. The creation of systematic research through research and development budgets
   c. The rise of a new intellectual technology
   d. The increase in multinational corporations
   e. The codification of theoretical knowledge

3. Large increases in industrial productivity in the nineteenth century were due to which of the following?
   a. The development of heavy industry
   b. The technological advances in communication
   c. The invention of new methods of transportation
   d. All of the above
   e. None of the above

4. What has made possible the attainment of higher education among the population?
   a. Increased mechanization of industry
   b. Increased productivity
   c. Increased national wealth
   d. All of the above
   e. None of the above

5. Union membership has
   a. declined in the 1960s and 1970s.
   b. risen in the 1980s from the 1940s and 1950s.
   c. become proportionately more agricultural.
   d. All of the above
   e. None of the above

6. Among Protestants, Baptists are by far the largest group, making up about _____ percent.
   a. 20
   b. 30
   c. 15
   d. 24

7. The so-called establishment region was the
   a. South.
   b. West.
   c. Sunbelt.
   d. Northeast.

8. Regional differences remain striking with issues such as
   a. sexual norms, religious tax-
      ation, and employment.
   c. sexual norms, abortion,
      and religious taxation.
   b. sexual norms, employment,
      and the role of women.
   d. sexual norms, abortion,
      and the role of women.

9. During the Great Depression _____ percent of the public thought economic opportunity still existed.
   a. 66
   c. 83
   b. 72
   d. 40

10. Four percent of today's professionals had fathers who worked in _____ occupations.
    a. clerical
    c. farming
    b. blue collar
    d. unskilled labor

ANSWER KEY

Completion

1. wealthy   p. 28
2. the socioeconomic ladder
   p. 34
3. weak   p. 33
4. economic production   p. 28
5. highly trained and educated
   labor force   p. 22
6. Southern "Sunbelt"   p. 43
7. John F. Kennedy   p. 41
8. Horatio Alger story
   pp. 45–46
9. aristocratic   p. 47
10. Latin American countries
    p. 38
11. regionalism   p. 43
12. broad similarity   p. 50

True/False

1. F   p. 25
2. T   p. 27
3. T   pp. 31–32
4. F   pp. 29–30
5. T   p. 18
6. F   p. 38
7. T   p. 41
8. T   pp. 39–40
9. F   p. 40
10. F   pp. 41–42
11. T   pp. 45–46
12. F   p. 39

Multiple Choice

1. c   pp. 17–18
2. d   p. 18
3. d   p. 20
4. d   p. 22
5. a   p. 34
6. a   p. 39
7. d   p. 42
8. d   p. 43
9. b   p. 47
10. a   p. 48

ESSAY QUESTIONS

1. Much of what has been written about postindustrial society implies that it constitutes progress over industrial society. Do you agree? Why or why not? What impact will postindustrial society have on American political life? Why?
2. America is a land of tremendous social and economic diversity. Identify the most important social and economic divisions in American society and explain their political relevance.
3. Religious differences can be among the most important ones in a society, and in many countries they have resulted in civil wars. What religious differences exist in America? What is the relationship between those religious differences and politics? Finally, why have religious differences resulted in less violence in America than in many other countries?

Further Investigation

Bell, Daniel. *The Coming of the Postindustrial Society: A Venture in Social Forecasting*. New York: Basic Books, 1973.
  Bell's book defines postindustrialism as an idea. It has become the central book in this area.
Gastil, Raymond D. *Cultural Regions of the United States*. Seattle: University of Washington Press, 1975.
  Examines cultural regions of the United States in terms of religious affiliations, political behavior, national origins, etc. An excellent treatment of regionalism in its social manifestations.
Glazer, Nathan, and Moynihan, Daniel. *Beyond the Melting Pot*. Cambridge: MIT Press, 1963.
  Examines the distinct ethnic groups of New York and how they have kept their distinctive identities.
Kirkpatrick, Jeane J. *Political Women*. New York: Basic Books, 1974.
  Professor Kirkpatrick, former ambassador to the United Nations, presents her research on women career politicians. She attempts to explain how they achieved political success and the social and political hurdles they overcame.
Sale, Kirkpatrick. *Power Shift: The Rise of the Southern Rim and Its Challenge to the Eastern Establishment*. New York: Random House, 1975.
  The thesis of the book is that over the past quarter century there has been a shift of population, industry, money, and political power from the Northeast to the "Southern Rim."
Thurow, Lester C. *The Zero Sum Society: Distribution and the Possibilities for Economic Change*. New York: Basic Books, 1980.

Argues that we have entered an era of no economic growth and explores the social consequences should this prove true.

Toffler, Alvin. *Future Shock*. New York: Random House, 1970.
One of the better known books on the impact of profound change on society.

Applying Political Science

1. One of the implications of the advent of the computer age is the potential loss of privacy. To what extent is this a problem in your community? How has government responded? What should government do to protect privacy? Select a local government agency, the local office of the state highway department, or your college or university registrar, and interview them about how they use identification numbers and computers. What safeguards do they impose for privacy? What public policies, if any, would you propose to protect privacy?

2. Considerable attention has been directed to educational reform. One of the most noted study commissions, the National Commission on Excellence in Education, concluded that our nation was at risk because students were not being adequately trained. What are the most important skills for the "postindustrial" generation? With rapid change, what skills will not become quickly obsolete? How is your local school system dealing with these questions? To what extent does your college education prepare you for the future?

3. Choose a group that represents one of the social or economic groupings discussed in this chapter and visit one of their meetings. Examples could include a senior citizens' organization, a local chapter of the National Organization of Women, or the National Association for the Advancement of Colored People. Look for ways the group builds identity and cohesion and attempts to influence politics.

4. Choose some area of the national budget—defense spending, highway construction, or agricultural subsidies—and then ask your librarian to help you find the data that will allow you to compare expenditures by state and region. Given what you have learned in this chapter, look for shifts in spending toward the Sunbelt and toward politically powerful states.

3 | The American Ideology

Overview

Americans are strongly committed to an ideology or set of beliefs called classical liberalism. Some corporate executives feel responsible for abolishing poverty, as was the case at times with Henry Ford. His firm commitment to democratic capitalism inspired him to increase wages while at the same time lowering prices. Democratic capitalism makes it possible for the general population to increase their standard of living constantly. This is capitalism committed to democratic and egalitarian ends.

The American ideology is acquired through the socialization process. Its roots can be traced to seventeenth and eighteenth century political philosophy known as classical liberalism. This view embraces the ideas of individualism, freedom, equality, private property, and democracy. The United States is held together by a common commitment to these ideals. In America, classical liberalism has taken the place of a common ethnic heritage.

Classical liberalism originated in Europe as a protest against aristocratic society. The continued growth of the middle class gave the philosophy power to develop. The birth of the United States drew strength from the middle class, and its intellectual core was classical liberalism. The ideas of liberalism have been formalized in the great documents that form the backbone of American government. America's lack of experience with anything but classical liberalism has insulated it from some European conflicts and has shown up in its foreign and domestic policies. It is the firm commitment to these ideals that accounts for the lack of socialism in this country.

America is a nation founded on a creed: classical liberalism. The ideal is so widely accepted that few dare to challenge its legitimacy. Indeed, our political and economic successes are founded in classical liberalism.

16

Key Terms and Concepts

ideology

classical liberalism

democratic capitalism

aristocratic society

socialism

egalitarianism

political socialization

individualism

"fragment society"

Chapter Outline

Henry Ford and democratic capitalism

    A maverick, Ford raised real wages 150 percent in one day while simultaneously lowering the price of cars.

    He wanted to build a lasting foundation.

    His actions proved to be good business.

    As wages rose and prices fell, people were able to buy more cars.

    Ford took these steps because he believed in "democratic capitalism."

    Although Ford's actions were unusual, they were consistent with democratic capitalism and American ideology.

The role of ideology

    An ideology is a set of related political beliefs and values.

    Through socialization we absorb fragments of American political ideology.

    As we grow up, we are introduced to the underlying beliefs and values of our society.

    The beliefs are loosely organized.

    Socialization occurs through various media, subtly and directly.

Roots: Classical liberalism

    The core of classical liberalism is:

    Individualism—society exists to fulfill individual rights.

    Individual freedom.

    Equality—each person is worth the same as another.

    Private property.

    Popular choice.

    Limited government.

Europeans and the origins of classical liberalism

    It began as a protest against aristocracy.

    Aristocracy justifies permanent subordinate status for most of the populace.

    The growth of the middle class challenged aristocracy.

    People are equal in natural capabilities.

    It is their environment that determines what they can do.

    Aristocrats had better environments, not more natural capabilities.

The economic expansion of the sixteenth and seventeenth centuries encouraged liberalism.

Life was more than a struggle for survival.

During the seventeenth and eighteenth centuries, people began to demand their rights.

Society became more heterogeneous — the middle class was stronger than ever.

Enter America

America was able to develop liberalism quickly.

There was no longstanding social structure.

America formed a "fragment society" broken off from the Old World.

In America, classical liberalism became Americanism.

America was built on an ideology.

Political disagreements were within liberalism.

Liberalism created a common bond.

The legacy of liberalism

Classical liberalism is embodied in the Declaration of Independence, the Constitution, the Gettysburg Address, etc. Although sometimes liberalism was ignored (slavery), the ideas have had a profound effect on American social and political life.

American ideological blindspots

American liberalism opens doors to minorities.

It also creates a certain intolerance — people not embracing the philosophy are labeled "un-American."

America's ideological world has been insular.

America has been removed from European conflicts concerning the overthrow of aristocracy.

American isolationism stemmed from insularity.

Why no socialism?

Liberalism has strongly influenced America's approach to economic questions.

Socialism has never been strong in America.

The strongest was in 1912, when Debs won 6 percent of the total vote for president.

No socialist has ever carried a single state.

American egalitarianism undercuts the appeal of socialism.

The foundation of American political institutions

America's political institutions are founded on classical liberalism.

The strength and endurance of the Constitution stem from economic success and high social mobility.

Review Questions

COMPLETION

1. Henry Ford, in 1914, raised his employees' wages by _____ percent in one day.

2. An _____ is a set of political beliefs and values that are constrained, or tied together.

3. American political ideology finds its roots in _____ _____.

4. Liberalism began as a protest against _____.

5. _____ developed the idea that the brain works through inputs and outputs, similar to a machine.

6. The demand for equality and the destruction of the aristocracy was launched by the _____ class.

7. There has never been a _____ movement in the United States.

8. American liberalism often _____ rather than _____ doors to those previously on the outside.

9. The United States is usually _____ to the efforts of other peoples attempting to replace authoritarian regimes with some form of popular government.

10. America's political institutions and their rationale and legitimacy were molded by the influence of _____.

TRUE/FALSE

1. The development of American capitalism and the development of the American as capitalist are indistinguishable.

2. American politics are both nonideological and highly ideological.

3. Classical liberalism includes the modern notion of conservative and liberal as used in everyday discussion.

4. In the aristocratic societies of Europe, the nobility and peasantry were considered equal in natural abilities.

5. During the sixteenth, seventeenth, and eighteenth centuries, people began to challenge fundamental aristocratic premises.

6. Liberalism was not made in America.

7. The ideas of classical liberalism are recorded in the documents of American political life.

8. Socialism has never been strong in America.

9. There were no political disagreements among those who created the new American government.

10. Systems of hereditary privilege are rejected by classical liberalism in the name of *equality*.

MULTIPLE CHOICE

1. Henry Ford raised the minimum wage in 1914 because
   a. the unions pressured him to do it.
   b. the employees demanded it.
   c. the other executives persuaded him that it would create greater profit for the company.
   d. he was committed to raising the standard of living for the general population.
   e. competing industries were doing it.

2. To abolish poverty is the aim of
   a. a purely socialist economic system.
   b. a purely capitalist economic system.
   c. a mercantilist economic system.
   d. all nations, regardless of their economic system.
   e. none of the above.

3. Political socialization takes place through the medium of
   a. books.
   b. participation.
   c. family communication.
   d. television.
   e. all of the above.

4. Which of the following is not included in the classical liberalism philosophy?
   a. Freedom
   b. Private property
   c. Capitalism
   d. Democracy
   e. Equality

5. For the early American settlers, liberalism
   a. provided a springboard to capitalism.
   b. was a common bond.
   c. was hotly disputed.
   d. was not yet a concept.
   e. none of the above.

6. Aristocratic values defended all of the following except
   a. legal and social inequality.
   b. economic freedom.
   c. the class structure.
   d. an arbitrary government.
   e. none of these; all are part of aristocracy.

7. Sometimes American ideology has been ignored, as in the case of
   a. the Vietnam War.
   b. Watergate.
   c. slavery.
   d. the New Deal.
   e. capital punishment.

8. In a study conducted in 1981, the percentage of people rejecting the idea of an income ceiling was
   a. 50.
   b. 25.
   c. 75.
   d. 60.
   e. 40.

9. Those who created the new American government
   a. disagreed within tight boundaries.
   b. represented several opposing ideologies.
   c. feared the potential ineffi-ciency of the separation of powers.
   d. were unified in their wish to create a decentralized democracy.
10. The strength and endurance of the Constitution stems from
   a. its never having been challenged.
   b. the brilliance and originality of its authors.
   c. a clause within it which prevents it from being replaced.
   d. classical liberalism.
   e. the religious freedom it guarantees.

ANSWER KEY

Completion

1. 150   p. 56
2. ideology   p. 58
3. classical liberalism   p. 59
4. aristocratic society   p. 60
5. Newton   p. 60
6. middle   p. 61
7. "liberal"   p. 62
8. opens; closes   p. 64
9. sympathetic   p. 65
10. classical liberalism   p. 68

True/False

1. F   p. 56
2. T   p. 58
3. F   p. 59
4. F   p. 60
5. T   p. 61
6. T   p. 61
7. T   p. 64
8. T   p. 66
9. F   pp. 62–63
10. T   p. 59

Multiple Choice

1. d   p 56
2. a   p. 57
3. e   p. 58
4. c   pp. 57, 58
5. b   p. 63
6. b   p. 60
7. c   p. 64
8. c   p. 67
9. a   p. 63
10. d   p. 68

ESSAY QUESTIONS

1. Why has socialism never taken root in America?
2. What is the intellectual relationship between classical liberalism and democratic capitalism? Is one more important than the other to the American ideology? Why?

Further Investigation

Hartz, Louis. *The Liberal Tradition in America.* New York: Harcourt, Brace, 1955.
  Examines the impact of classical liberalism on American history. This book traces the ideas of liberalism to some of their origins and then applies them in different contexts, including the New Deal and foreign policy.

Lipset, Seymour Martin. *Political Man.* Garden City, N.Y.: Doubleday, 1960.
  Lipset examines the social bases of politics.

McClosky, Herbert and John Zaller. *The American Ethos: Public Attitudes Toward Capitalism and Democracy.* Cambridge: Harvard University Press, 1984.
  Examines American attitudes and behavior with respect to capitalism, free markets, political freedom and democratic institutions.

Oakun, Arthur. *Equality and Efficiency: The Big Tradeoff.* Washington, D.C.: Brookings Institution, 1975.
  Examines the contradictory tendencies of the political and economic systems. The political system seeks to foster equality, while the economic system wants to maximize efficiency.

Reich, Robert B. *The Next American Frontier: A Provocative Program for Economic Renewal.* New York: Penguin, 1983.
  Stresses the need for increased cooperation among business, labor, and government, and an emphasis on high-quality, high-technology industries.

Schumpeter, Joseph. *Capitalism, Socialism, and Democracy.* New York: Harper & Row, 1950.
  As the title of the book suggests, this book compares three of the most important social and political ideologies. The book is especially interesting in its comparison of socialism and capitalism and in its assessment of the strengths and weaknesses of democracy.

Verba, Sidney and Gary R. Oren. *Equality in America: the View from the Top.* Cambridge: Harvard University Press, 1985.
  Examines American attitudes towards political and economic equality, as well as the importance of the ideal of equality to American life.

Applying Political Science

1. Identify a business in your community that has a profit-sharing plan and interview workers and managers in the business to see how this program affects their view of the firm. Contrast these atti-

tudes to those of workers and managers in a firm with a more traditional approach.

2. In an effort to understand why socialism has never taken root in America, make a list of attitudes you think would be consistent with a "socialist" perspective and then review public opinion polls about American attitudes on those kinds of issues. A good place to look for information is in the "Opinion Roundup" section of *Public Opinion* magazine.

3. In 1972 George McGovern proposed a major inheritance tax increase. The idea was very unpopular, even with poor people. Why do you think this was the case? Construct a set of questions that relate to economic and social mobility and ask them of people in your community in an effort to understand better how Americans view these subjects.

4 | The Constitution

Overview

The American Constitution has proven to be remarkably durable. It was written by men who believed in classical liberalism and were convinced that America was a nation chosen to be an example to the world.

The Articles of Confederation, the first form of national government adopted at the time of the revolution, were seriously flawed. Under the articles, sovereignty remained with the states, robbing the national government of the initiative necessary to govern postrevolutionary America. Men such as Washington, Hamilton, and Madison led the movement in favor of a stronger national government and provided prestige and political leadership.

In 1787, delegates came to Philadelphia to modify the Articles of Confederation, but quickly decided to write a complete constitution. They generally agreed that the powers of the national government in the new constitutional system would need to be enhanced and that certain state powers would need to be restricted. But they disagreed over how the states would be represented in the new national government. Populous states wanted representation by population; small states felt that representation should be equal by states. The impasse was resolved by the Great Compromise, whereby the House of Representatives would be apportioned by state population and the Senate would equally represent the states. In a second compromise it was decided that for purposes of representation and taxation, slaves would count as three-fifths of all other persons.

Delegates at the Constitutional Convention feared centralized government power. To blunt that possibility, they created a federal system, with divided power at the national level and with some shared powers, allowing each branch to check the others. Madison, the architect of this plan, expected that individual ambition within the system of checks and balances would prevent the concentration of power and, at the same time, preserve the ability of government to function.

After the Constitution was written and approved by the delegates, it needed to be ratified by the states. Persons in favor of the new Constitution formed a political party to aid ratification and called themselves Federalists. Those opposed were known as Anti-Federalists. All of the thirteen states ratified the Constitution, although at times by narrow margins.

The same men who were the most central characters in the drafting of the Constitution were also important in its implementation. Washington, as president, was cautious yet assertive. His decision after two terms to step down voluntarily created an important precedent for future presidents. Hamilton, as secretary of the treasury, was instrumental in reestablishing confidence in America's credit, in stimulating local manufacture, and in establishing a national bank. Madison, who was the first speaker of the House, was instrumental in the creation of the national judiciary, in the passage of the Bill of Rights, and in the creation of the president's cabinet.

Throughout the course of American history, the Constitution and its founders have been subject to various interpretations. Charles A. Beard, in *An Economic Interpretation of the Constitution of the United States*, argued, for instance, that the founders wrote the Constitution in order to advance their personal economic interests. His thesis has since been challenged by others who argue that the dominant spirit in Philadelphia in 1787 was public spirit and not economic self-interest. Although the Constitution is not perfect, it is for the most part what the founders intended it to be—"a standard to which the wise and honest can repair."

The Constitution is continually being changed, both by formal amendment and by judicial reinterpretation. It has proven to be a document elastic enough to withstand the trials of two centuries of American government and definitive enough to shape the institutions and processes of our national and state governments.

Key Terms and Concepts

American exceptionalism
Articles of Confederation
federal system
the Virginia Plan
the New Jersey Plan
the Great Compromise
the three-fifths compromise

separation of powers
checks and balances
individual ambition
Federalists
Anti-Federalists
Bill of Rights

Chapter Outline

Introduction
  The Constitution of the United States has proven unusually durable.

The Constitution has survived partly because it is based on the foundation of classical liberalism.

To understand the Constitution and how it came to be written, approved, and implemented, we study political beliefs and objectives of the document's authors.

Washington takes office

When Washington arrived in New York to take his oath of office, he was received by an overwhelming display of gratitude.

He was hailed as the father and savior of his country.

American exceptionalism

In the eighteenth and nineteenth centuries, many Americans believed their nation had special virtues that gave America a special mission: to make America an example of self-government to the world.

An abundance of fertile land, independent property owners, and the absence of European aristocratic institutions permitted Americans to experiment with new forms of government.

Translating the ideological consensus

On July 4, 1776, the Continental Congress adopted the Declaration of Independence, written by Thomas Jefferson with the assistance of John Adams and Benjamin Franklin.

The Declaration was written in the liberal tradition of individual rights made familiar by John Locke and affirmed in the American experience.

American independence took seven years to win, but American ideological independence had long been a reality.

The Articles of Confederation

Under the Articles of Confederation the sovereign power of government rested in the states.

The national government's inability to levy taxes on the states without their unanimous consent made it unable to deal with postwar debts.

The government also lacked sufficient power to deal with British and Spanish encroachments on U.S. territory.

State governments printed their own currency and forced their citizens to accept it in payment of state debt.

Shay's Rebellion is an example of the dissatisfaction caused by the economic chaos that existed under the Articles of Confederation.

Under the Articles, a strong national government was impossible.

The move to a strong national government

Not all Americans were dissatisfied with the Articles.

Seaport merchants, tired of the state tariffs and regulations, supported the "Continentalists"—such men as Washington and Hamilton, who were supportive of a stronger national government.

The biggest barrier to the adoption of a strong national government was the fear of concentrated governmental power.

Three who made a revolution

The three men who played a leading role in the adoption and implementation of the Constitution were George Washington, Alexander Hamilton, and James Madison.

Washington's support gave the constitutional effort respectability.

Hamilton and Madison provided the energy and practical political imagination necessary to bring about a new government.

Called to the Annapolis convention to consider the financial woes of the states, Hamilton and Madison achieved a more dramatic solution—a convention to significantly revise the Articles.

Philadelphia, 1787

Although the delegates assembled at the Constitutional Convention were comparatively young (average age forty-two), they were mature and accomplished.

The delegates shared many ideas common to classical liberalism, such as the belief in the individual rights of man (Locke) and the separation of powers (Montesquieu).

The making of the Constitution

The delegates quickly chose to go beyond their assigned task of revising the Articles to create a new constitution.

The delegates disagreed about the ability of the citizens to govern themselves, but agreed that a constitution should minimize the risk of self-government while maximizing citizen participation.

The decisive intellectual leader at the convention was Madison, who is known as the father of the Constitution.

The delegates agreed that the national government would be granted the power to levy and regulate taxes, regulate foreign and interstate commerce, and raise and maintain an army and a navy, and that states should not coin money, make treaties, or tax imports.

Large states' delegates supported the Virginia Plan, which called for representation to the new national congress based on population.

Small states supported the New Jersey Plan, which called for equal representation for each state.

In the Great Compromise, the delegates agreed to have members of the House of Representatives apportioned by population and members of the Senate apportioned by state.

Slavery also required some compromise.

For taxing and representation, slaves were counted as three-fifths "of all other persons."

Final resolution of the slavery problem was delayed.

The delegates fashioned a national government that would consist of a bi-cameral legislature, an executive branch, and a national judiciary.

Key provisions

A federal system dividing authority between national and state governments was designed.

A system of checks and balances was established.

Power was also divided among the three branches of government.

In Europe, the idea of separation of powers meant that each class of society received separate representation.

In the U.S. Constitution, it meant that the executive, legislative, and judicial branches were independent from each other.

The delegates also overlapped the powers of the three branches so that one branch could not dominate the others.

To Madison, individual ambition would prevent the concentration of governmental power.

Ratification

The founders required the Constitution to be ratified by state convention.

Federalists supported the ratification of the Constitution, while anti-Federalists opposed it.

Although they disagreed on this question, the two parties were unified on many essential issues.

By the following year the Constitution had been ratified by the required nine states.

New York ratified later due to the work of Alexander Hamilton.

Putting the new institutions in place

The implementation of the Constitution was as important as its contents.

Washington, Madison, and Hamilton were also important in this phase.

Washington was a strong yet cautious president.

Madison was instrumental in the creation of the president's cabinet, the federal judiciary system, and the passage of the Bill of Rights.

Hamilton secured the new nation's financial credit, encouraged internal manufacture, and encouraged the creation of a national bank.

Assessing the framers' work

Charles A. Beard views the founders as "plutocrats" who were engaged in nothing more than seeking their own economic benefit, a view that has generally been discredited.

Martin Diamond sees liberty and democracy as the fundamental values of the revolutionary generation, the Declaration of Independence as a statement of those values, and the Constitution as a practical embodiment of them.

The Constitution in American governmental practice
  Its longevity is largely attributable to its provisions dealing only with
    structure and procedure rather than policies.
  It shapes governmental institutions.
  It has changed through amendment and court interpretation to meet
    changing conditions.

Review Questions

COMPLETION

1. The name of the document that constituted the first national

   government of the United States was _____.
2. The classical liberal tradition of individual rights was popularized
   by John Locke and was incorporated by Thomas Jefferson into

   _____.
3. The biggest drawback to a strong national government from a

   classical liberal standpoint was _____.
4. A governmental system made up of both national and state

   governments is known as a _____.
5. The strongest advocate of a national bank in the early history of

   the United States was _____.
6. *An Economic Interpretation of the Constitution of the United*

   States was written by _____.
7. The political party opposed to the ratification of the Constitution

   was known as the _____.
8. For the Constitution to be successfully ratified it had to be ap-

   proved by _____ of the thirteen states.
9. The first speaker of the House in the history of the United States

   was _____.
10. The idea that each separate function of government should
    operate independently within its own branch is known as

    _____.

TRUE/FALSE

1. Charles Pinckney wrote the New Jersey Plan.
2. The Articles of Confederation were responsible for the economic
   chaos which led to Shay's Rebellion.

3. American exceptionalism was fundamentally the idea that the continent could not be shared with Britain and Spain.
4. The factors that united the Federalists and the anti-Federalists were less significant than those that divided them.
5. Farmers were more likely than seaport merchants to be dissatisfied with the Articles of Confederation.
6. The Great Compromise temporarily decided the controversy involving the spread of slavery in the union.
7. The New Jersey Plan was supported by the larger states.
8. The delegates to the Constitutional Convention were originally convened only to revise the Articles of Confederation.
9. James Madison is known as the father of the Constitution.
10. The Constitution's longevity can be attributed largely to the founders' restricting its content to structure and procedure.

MULTIPLE CHOICE

1. The concept that gives the president the legislative power to veto legislation and gives the Senate the executive power to refuse presidential appointments is known as
   a. the federal system.
   b. the bicameral legislature.
   c. checks and balances.
   d. the separation of powers.
   e. American exceptionalism.

2. The difference between the concept of the separation of powers in Europe and in America is that
   a. in Europe the sovereign had all the power and in America there was no sovereign.
   b. in Europe there was a middle class of nobles and lords, which separated the powers of the state and in America most men were independent property owners.
   c. in Europe each class was represented separately and in America the different functions of government were separated.
   d. in Europe bourgeois classes had arisen and overthrown their government and in America governmental change was accomplished peacefully.
   e. in Europe the state was not allowed to have the economic power of a national bank, but in America no such restriction existed.

3. The Constitution can be changed in which of the following ways?
   a. By a majority vote of Congress
   b. By executive order
   c. Through a reinterpretation of its meaning by the Supreme Court
   d. By a referendum vote
   e. By a majority of state legislatures

4. Probably George Washington's most significant act as our first president was to
   a. step down after two terms.
   b. appoint Jefferson as secretary of state
   c. appoint Hamilton as secretary of the treasury.
   d. give the directions he gave America in his farewell address.
   e. keep us out of a war with France.

5. It was necessary that New York ratify the Constitution because
   a. our nation's first capital was New York City.
   b. Alexander Hamilton was a citizen of New York.
   c. it was a populous and strategic state.
   d. the number of free states had to equal the number of slave states.
   e. New York's population was wealthier than the populations of other states.

6. The three-fifths compromise decided that
   a. at least three-fifths of the thirteen states had to ratify the Constitution before it could become the law of the land.
   b. at least three-fifths of the delegates present at the convention had to sign the Constitution before it could be presented to the states.
   c. no more than three-fifths of the states in the union could permit slavery at any one time.
   d. three-fifths of the seats in Congress would be chosen by state population.
   e. for purposes of taxation and representation, one slave would count as three-fifths of a person.

7. Madison said in the fifty-first *Federalist Paper* that, given our constitutional system, the insurance against the dominance of faction or the centralization of governmental power was
   a. the separation of powers.
   b. the ambition of individuals.
   c. the court system.
   d. public virtue.
   e. severe penalties for such infractions.

8. The Articles of Confederation proved insufficient because
   a. they required a national government that was too strong.
   b. they permitted states to have their own legislatures.
   c. they established a national militia.
   d. they were the work of inferior statesmen.
   e. they did not permit the national government enough power to deal with its problems.

9. The constitutional draft written by Madison and presented at the convention was called
   a. the Madison Plan.
   b. the New Jersey Plan.
   c. the Great Compromise.
   d. the Virginia Plan.
   e. A Modest Proposal.

10. The founders probably provided that the Constitution should be ratified by state convention rather than by state legislature because
    a. they thought they could "pack" the conventions with Federalists.
    b. they feared the legislatures would resent their loss of power under the Constitution.
    c. they desired the Constitution to be ratified quickly.
    d. it was a requirement of the Articles of Confederation.
    e. they wanted the public to elect representatives to consider this important issue separately.

ANSWER KEY

Completion

1. the Articles of Confederation p. 75
2. the Declaration of Independence p. 75
3. fear of centralized governmental powers p. 78
4. federal system p. 80
5. Hamilton p. 86
6. Charles A. Beard p. 87
7. Anti-Federalists p. 83
8. nine p. 84
9. Madison p. 85
10. the separation of powers p. 82

True/False

1. F p. 81
2. T p. 77
3. F pp. 71–72
4. F pp. 83–84
5. F p. 77
6. F p. 81
7. F p. 81
8. T p. 80
9. T p. 81
10. T p. 90

Multiple Choice

1. c p. 82
2. c p. 82
3. c p. 91
4. a p. 85
5. c p. 84
6. e p. 81
7. b p. 83
8. e p. 75
9. d p. 81
10. b p. 83

ESSAY QUESTIONS

1. What were the major weaknesses of the Articles of Confederation and how were they corrected in the Constitution?
2. Some have argued that the Constitution is simply a bundle of compromises. What are the major compromises found in the Constitution and why were they necessary? Is the Constitution more than

the sum of these compromises? Is there an underlying theory of government found in the document?

Further Investigation

Brown, Robert E. *Charles Beard and the Constitution*. New York: Norton, 1965.
   A frequently cited response to Charles A. Beard's theory.
Burns, James MacGregor. *The Power to Lead: The Crisis of the American Presidency*. New York: Simon and Schuster, 1984.
   In the tradition of his earlier books, Burns finds fault with the separation of powers and other impediments to action.
Cutler, Lloyd. "To Form a Government." *Foreign Affairs* 59, no. 1 (Fall 1980): 126–43.
   From his vantage point as counsel to President Carter, Cutler was frustrated by the separation of powers. In his view it limited our power and influence around the world and our ability to govern at home.
Epstein, David F. *The Political History of the Federalist*. Chicago: University of Chicago Press, 1984.
   Excellent treatment of the politics of the founding and the impact of *The Federalist Papers*.
Fairfield, Roy P., ed. *The Federalist Papers*. 2d ed. Baltimore: Johns Hopkins University Press, 1981.
   Fairfield provides a useful summary to the documents in his introduction. Students will want to read especially numbers 10 and 51. The index will allow you to find information readily on other topics.
Jensen, Merrill. *The Making of the Constitution*. New York: D. Van Nostrand, 1964.
   An excellent history of the convention, its primary actors, and some of the reasons it produced the document it did.
Levy, Leonard. *Essays on the Making of the Constitution*. New York: Oxford University Press, 1969.
   An excellent compilation of essays on the founding and the Constitution.
Rossiter, Clinton. *Seedtime of the Republic*. New York: Harcourt, Brace, 1953.
   Provides an insightful overview of the period and the events that influenced the convention.
Sorenson, Theodore. *A Different Kind of Presidency*. New York: Harper & Row, 1984.
   Argues that the system designed by the founders needs fundamental

reform because it is ineffective and prone to gridlock. Sorenson's solution is something he calls coalition government.

Wills, Gary. *Inventing America: Jefferson's Declaration of Independence.* New York: Vintage Books, 1979.

An inciteful book on the Declaration and Jefferson.

Applying Political Science

1. Obtain a copy of a state constitution. In what ways is it different
   from the U.S. Constitution? Select an article or issue in the U.S.
   Constitution and then see how your state constitution addresses the
   same topic.
2. While James Madison is called the father of the Constitution, he
   would probably have fathered quite a different version than the one
   that finally passed, had he had his way. What might our country
   be like today if the Virginia Plan had passed?
3. It is likely that a constitutional convention will be called to consider adoption of a federal balanced budget amendment. Some contend that the convention will only consider the balanced budget
   issue, while others believe that the convention could change any
   part of the Constitution. What do you think? What has been the
   experience of recent state constitutional conventions? Do you think
   these are comparable?

5 | American Democracy

Overview

Throughout history, democracy has been far from universally accepted, and most of the world's governments have not been democratic. But democracy is central to American political thought, and for many Americans it is unchallenged as the best form of government.

Our thinking about democracy has been influenced by the Greek democracy of the fifth century B.C. Athenians used the term democracy to refer to government by the many, as contrasted to oligarchy (rule by a few) or monarchy (rule by a monarch or king). Aristotle enlarged the concept of democracy by combining two distinct elements: popular sovereignty and minority rights. He called this system that successfully combined these elements a constitutional government or "polity." Aristotle saw a contradiction between constitutional government and democracy, because democracy had a potential for "mob rule," which could endanger minority rights and interests.

The framers of the U.S. Constitution incorporated much of Aristotle's philosophy in their design of institutions that would make democracy a practical form of government. They also feared democracy would degenerate into mob rule because it lacked institutions able to curb self-seeking interests and assure individual liberty. Their solution was "republicanism," or representative democracy.

Democracy in America is sometimes called liberal democracy, which places equal emphasis on realizing popular sovereignty and protecting individual and minority rights. These two objectives are sometimes in conflict, when majorities take actions that minorities think violate their essential rights as citizens. Two such recent examples of this conflict are seen in racial segregation and school prayer. The American constitutional tradition holds that majority rule must be superseded in cases where majority actions infringe on essential rights of citizenship, such as those articulated in the Bill of Rights. But as the country's experience shows, the most fundamental of minority rights have sometimes been denied nonetheless. There has never been agreement

35

among experts or the public at large on where the democratic requirement of majority rule must surrender to the competing democratic requirement of respect for individual rights.

Ideally, democracy asserts that ultimate political authority rests with the general public. Not only must the people be allowed to vote, they must also be able to exercise authority over the "big decisions" of their country's political life. Direct democracy reforms, including the use of initiatives and referendums, are an attempt to allow more direct participation. A common criticism of American democracy is that power is concentrated in the hands of certain "elites," thereby limiting popular sovereignty. The standard rebuttal contends that the "Madisonian system" has generally succeeded in preventing great concentrations of power. While not disputing the fact that some individuals and corporations have more political resources, they don't agree that these elites have been a unified force opposing majority preferences. Rather the American system is pluralistic, with political elites in competition with one another for general public support. Finally, elections give the public an important resource for determining national leadership and basic policy direction.

Some argue that there are social requisites for democracy, conditions not present in most countries. Indeed, in a study done by one sociologist, fewer than thirty nations could be considered democracies. But where it is present, it flourishes.

Key Terms and Concepts

democracy (direct and representative)
monarchy
oligarchy
majority rule
minority rights
classical liberalism

polity
referendum
initiative
pluralism
direct primary
power elite

Chapter Outline

America and democracy
  While the Constitution remains the foundation of American government, it does not solve all problems.
  Frustration over the national election process has led to many suggestions for reform.
  But although it can be frustrating, Americans still believe democracy to be the best form of government.
  Democracy should be judged by performance, not ideals.

It is inherent in the U.S. Constitution and American ideology.

Historically, democracy has not been universally accepted.

Observers assert that the U.S. government is flawed by democratic standards.

What is democracy?

The term "democracy" is derived from two Greek terms:

Demos, meaning people, and kratis, meaning authority.

It connotes government by the many as contrasted to oligarchy and monarchy.

Aristotle's idea of democracy

He outlined three basic forms of government and their corresponding corruptions:

Kingship—tyranny/interest of the monarch.

Aristocracy—oligarchy/interest of the rich.

Constitutional government—democracy/interest of minorities.

He observed none of the three above governed with regard to interests of the community.

He saw a contradiction between constitutional government and democracy.

Democracy was the perverted form.

Aristotle opposed extreme direct democracy or "mob rule," which lacked structure for protecting minority rights.

He did favor majority rule and laws upholding public interest and individual rights.

He felt democracy was impossible in most social settings.

In democracy, elites have privileges over the masses.

A large middle class is necessary, along with an even distribution of property.

Political administration is best handled by the middle class because of balance and consistency.

An idea a long time coming

Aristotle was ahead of his time.

Not until the seventeenth and eighteenth centuries did political inquiry advance beyond Aristotle.

Classical liberalism was nurtured in the seventeenth century.

Rights and freedom of the individual are its key principles.

Democracy is conducive to this because it gives individuals the power to govern themselves.

Social conditions conducive to individualism would make democracy a practical possibility.

Madison's idea of democracy

His plan for representative (democratic) institutions was developed in the Federalist Papers, which argued for "republicanism."

The people are sovereign but cannot and should not govern directly.

Representative institutions would be within the governmental
structure of defined and dispersed powers.

Separation of powers and checks and balances would protect
minorities and curb narrow interests that are not in the public
good.

The Constitution would give equal weight to popular sovereignty
and individual rights.

Majority rule versus minority rights

The two objectives conflict, as exemplified by the case of school
prayer.

Experts do not agree about when majority rule should be suspended
because of respect for individual rights.

School prayer was ruled unconstitutional in 1962 in *Engle v. Vitale*.
The ruling generated much opposition.

Efforts to amend the U.S. Constitution to allow school prayer
failed in 1966 and in 1984.

Public opinion on school prayer was overwhelmingly positive—as
recently as 1985, 67 percent were in favor of it.

In 1985 the Supreme Court struck down as unconstitutional an
Alabama law which authorized a minute of silence in schools for
"meditation or voluntary prayer."

The Court held that such a law violates the principle of government neutrality toward religion.

Chief Justice Burger dissented, insisting that such a stance
actually "manifests not neutrality but hostility toward religion."

Attempts to pass an amendment failed again in both the House and
Senate in 1985 and 1986.

Direct democracy versus representative democracy

Direct democracy proponents want more frequent and direct public
participation in government.

Progressives were also advocates of this.

They wanted the direct primary, where nominees are selected by
rank-and-file party supporters. They also urged the use of
referenda and initiatives.

Do we have a proper balance between direct and representative
democracy in the United States?

Democracy cannot exist without the expression of wishes of the
public.

Bypassing the representative institutions, however, may weaken them
too much.

Direct democracy was first practiced in New England town meetings.

How democratic is American democracy?

Who governs?

Some people have much more political influence than other people.

Unequal power in a democracy has implications.

Elites do exist.

    C. Wright Mills maintained that the leaders of major corporations, the heads of armed forces and defense industries, and the executive branch of government really run America and preclude the possibility of true democracy.

Most political scientists disagree with Mills.

    The "Madisonian system" of separation of powers and checks and balances prevents elitism from obstructing popular sovereignty because power is widely dispersed.

    Pluralism has resulted in highly fragmented political power.

Money talks.

    Campaign contributions by corporations and individuals can influence elections and public policy.

Elections and popular sovereignty

    The majority still rules.

    Critics argue that American political parties are so similar that they allow no real choice.

    Does the public desire major change?

Conditions needed for democracy

    Lipset believes that a stable representative democracy requires a certain mix of social conditions.

    Once democracy is in place it sustains these conditions.

    Aristotle argued that a large middle class was necessary to assure a stable polity.

    Liberal democracy does require much of the public and its social institutions.

Democracy in the world arena

    According to one sociologist, fewer than thirty countries fit into the range of reasonable democracy.

    Most were economically advanced.

    Although democracy is not flawless, it is popular with the public.

Review Questions

COMPLETION

1. The representative democracy sought by the founding fathers gave equal weight to _____ and _____.

2. A conflict in majority rule and minority rights was displayed in the case _____.

3. Voters, by signing petitions, may require policies to be put to popular vote through _____.

4. The earliest American institution for direct democracy was called the _____.
5. Aristotle argued that a _____ was essential to a stable polity.
6. To the Greeks, democracy was a term referring to government by the _____.
7. Even though democratic theory was fairly developed by the eighteenth century, until 1787 the _____ through which constitutional democracy could operate, had not been developed.
8. In the 1830s the primary political unit was the _____ government; now it is the _____ government.
9. Although the framers opted for _____ democracy, the idea of _____ democracy has continued to find support in the United States.
10. C. Wright Mills's power elite is composed of people who have _____ interests and act together coherently to dominate policy on the major issues of national life.

TRUE/FALSE

1. Democracy has traditionally been accepted throughout history.
2. Aristotle saw democracy as a perverted form of government.
3. Classical liberalism places little value on individual rights.
4. Madison argued for republicanism, saying the people should not govern directly.
5. Two-thirds of the people polled in 1985 favored a constitutional amendment allowing school prayer.
6. The Progressives were avid supporters of representative democracy.
7. North Dakota was the first state to provide for the initiative in 1898.
8. In 1985, the Supreme Court ruled that government must pursue a course of complete neutrality toward religion.
9. The initiative amendment has received strong support from the House and Senate.
10. Pluralism is the notion that political power is highly fragmented and competitive.
11. Polls show the American people feel dissatisfaction toward the capitalist economic system.
12. The Bollen measure concludes that there are fewer than thirty countries within the range of reasonable democracy.

MULTIPLE CHOICE

1. Aristotle's general "pure" forms of government did not include
   a. kingship.
   b. democracy.
   c. aristocracy.
   d. constitutional government.
   e. any of the above

2. In *The Power Elite*, C. Wright Mills maintains that America is run by a narrow group of people drawn from three institutions, which does not include
   a. private business corporations.
   b. government.
   c. religion.
   d. military.
   e. All of the above are part of the power elite.

3. Political elites are generally sharply divided on
   a. defense spending issues.
   b. political contribution issues.
   c. separation of church and
   state issues.
   d. foreign policy issues.
   e. all of the above

4. When an amendment to permit school prayer came to vote in 1966 and 1984,
   a. a majority was unfavorable in the House of Representatives.
   b. a majority, but not the necessary two-thirds majority, was favorable in the Senate.
   c. public opinion was distinctly unfavorable to the amendment.
   d. three-quarters of the states failed to ratify the amendment.
   e. lobbying was fairly mild on both sides of the issue.

5. How power is distributed is of _____ to democratic government.
   a. no concern
   b. great importance
   c. some importance
   d. little importance
   e. none of the above

6. In order for the United States to strike a proper balance between the direct and representative dimensions of democracy,
   a. heavy demands are made on intermediary institutions.
   b. parties must not influence the governing process.
   c. executive leadership can
   have little effect on policy making.
   d. legislators can operate without general public consent.
   e. all of the above

42

7. Unequal distribution of power is a reality of democratic government but is acceptable because
   a. leaders will always have power over those they lead.
   b. modern communication allows some people more influence over the lives of others.
   c. special interest group competition accomplishes the ends of democracy.
   d. all of the above
   e. none of the above

8. The Commission on National Elections did not study which of the following issues?
   a. length of presidential campaigns
   b. high cost of campaigning
   c. party procedures for nominating candidates
   d. why more people don't vote
   e. possibility of a proportional system

Completion

1. popular sovereignty; individual rights   p. 98
2. *Brown v. Board of Education of Topeka*   p. 98
3. initiatives   pp. 101–103
4. town meeting   p. 104
5. large middle class   p. 96
6. many   p. 95
7. mechanism   pp. 97, 98
8. local; national   p. 105
9. representative; direct   p. 101
10. common   p. 108

True/False

1. F   p. 94
2. T   p. 95
3. F   p. 97
4. T   p. 98
5. T   p. 100
6. F   p. 102
7. F   p. 103
8. T   p. 101
9. F   p. 104
10. T   p. 109
11. F   p. 112
12. T   p. 114

Multiple Choice

1. b   p. 95
2. c   p. 108
3. d   p. 110
4. b   p. 101
5. b   p. 105
6. a   p. 104
7. d   pp. 105–107
8. e   p. 93

ESSAY QUESTIONS

1. Elections and popular sovereignty are often considered essential to democracy. Why? Are elections inherently democratic? Present examples to support your argument.

2. What are the major differences between representative democracy and direct democracy? In contemporary American history, select two examples of each type of democracy and assess the strengths and weaknesses of that approach to government.

Further Investigation

Barber, Benjamin. *Strong Democracy: Participatory Politics for a New Age.* Berkeley: University of California Press, 1984.
    Advocates substituting participatory forms of politics for representation as a cure for what ails American government.
Magleby, David B. *Direct Legislation: Voting on Ballot Propositions in the United States.* Baltimore: Johns Hopkins University Press, 1984.
    How the initiative, referendum, and ballot questions generally work in the United States, with comparisons to other democracies.
Margolis, Michael. *Viable Democracy.* New York: Penguin Books, 1979.
    Highly critical of the prevailing acceptance among political scientists of the state of democracy. Proposes reforms to make democracy more viable.
Pitkin, Hanna Fenichel. *The Concept of Representation.* Berkeley: University of California Press, 1972.
    Reviews the alternative definitions of representation and their relationship to democracy and government.

Applying Political Science

1. How do elected officials incorporate public opinion into their decisions? Select a set of elected officials in your town, county, or state and ask them whether they worry about public opinion when deciding upon public policy. When they have a conflict between their beliefs about what to do and what they sense the majority of the community desires, which course do they follow? Why? Finally, if public opinion is important to them, how do they measure it?
2. The idea of greater participation in politics and government has spread to the economic sector as well. Select a set of local businesses and compare them in the extent to which management decisions are open to employee input. Interview the management about their attitudes concerning the potential uses and abuses of more open decision making. Are these arguments similar or different from those expressed about greater "democratization" of the political process?
3. Identify a direct democracy activity in your community: a recall petition, an initiative or referendum, or merely an effort to organize

a letter-writing campaign. Interview some of the people working in this way and try to learn why they are involved, how they are organized, and whether their efforts will be successful.

6 | Congress

Overview

The first article of the Constitution establishes a national legislature and gives it certain powers. This prominent position in the Constitution reflects the founders' expectation that Congress would play a prominent role in governing the new nation. To understand the role Congress plays in American politics, it is essential to understand Congress as an institution.

The Constitution also provides that the president be separately elected and independent of the legislature. The president cannot dissolve Congress, and Congress cannot easily remove the president from office. This separation of powers also includes generally separate responsibilities and functions for each branch.

Congress is bicameral. The two chambers are more equal in power than are the houses in bicameral national legislatures abroad. Each chamber tends to moderate the other because each one has an absolute veto on legislation passed by the other. Every bill must pass both houses in the same form to become law.

Although the Senate is smaller than the House and generally operates with fewer restrictions, both houses have rules that regulate the legislative process. These rules usually act only as procedural guidelines, but sometimes rules will be used to reach political goals, such as when a filibuster is used to block action on a bill in the Senate.

The workload of Congress during the past several years has meant greater delegation of the work of legislation to committees. There are four common types of committees: standing, special or select, joint, and conference. Each type has its own function, and each is usually divided into subcommittees that have a significant amount of autonomy from their parent committees. The congressional workload has also caused Congress to increase the size of its staff for individual congressmen, for committees, and for congressional agencies. The U.S. Congress staffs itself more extensively, and at a higher cost, than virtually any other legislature in the world.

Although the two-party system is strong in America, party discipline in congressional voting behavior is quite low. It is rare to find an issue that clearly sets the Republicans and Democrats against each other. Only once, around the turn of the century, have the parties voted as blocks against each other, and this rise of party loyalty lasted only a few years. Weak party discipline in America results from structural differences between presidential and parliamentary systems and from most Americans' feeling that strong party leadership is undemocratic.

Eligibility requirements for membership in Congress are relatively nonrestrictive, but most members of the large majority of Congress are white males. Congress has also generally attracted wealthier men and women. Women and blacks have gained significantly more seats in recent years. Congressmen are disproportionately well educated, and most have practiced law.

The founders' expectation that Congress would become the leading branch of government was largely realized during the nineteenth century. First, the House of Representatives dominated behind powerful speakers like Henry Clay, and then the Senate asserted itself behind leaders like Webster and Calhoun. The executive branch displayed powerful national leadership only once throughout most of the 1800s, during the Lincoln administration. But congressional dominance resumed again after the Civil War as Radical Republicans reconstructed the South.

In the early 1900s a wave of social and economic legislation gave the American presidency an opportunity to assert itself. Because complex regulations can be easily administered by the executive branch, strong personalities like Theodore Roosevelt expanded the leadership of the presidency. During much of the twentieth century, the president has been viewed as a strong, progressive force and Congress has been viewed as weak. Recently several influences and events, such as the Vietnam War and the Watergate scandal, have given Congress the opportunity to reassert itself. It has done so in three areas: the power of the purse, legislative oversight, and legislative veto. The Congressional Budget and Impound Control Act of 1974 significantly restructured the budget process.

Congress can fill at least two roles which may not always harmonize with each other: lawmaker and representative assembly. Its critics give Congress higher marks in filling the latter role, and call for reform to help it better fill the former.

Key Terms and Concepts

government by the legislature

bicameralism

filibuster

rules committee

separation of powers

impoundment

congressional oversight

legislative veto

congressional committee
  system
interest groups
seniority system
lawmaking institution
standing committees
select committees
joint resolution

party discipline
legislative-executive power
  balance
representative assembly
cloture
conference committees
joint committees

Chapter Outline

The role of Congress
  While no longer the dominant branch, Congress is still in the middle of things.
Congress and the policy process
  Both Carter and Reagan called for tax reform.
  Nearly every constituency is affected by tax law.
    Most descended on Congress in 1985 when tax reform legislation was proposed.
  Like Carter, President Reagan saw a need for tax reform. In 1985 he proposed such legislation.
    Democratic tax committee chairman Rostenkowski backed the proposal.
      Even with support of leadership in both parties, the bill barely passed the House.
    The bill almost died in the Senate.
      The Senate passed a very different version from the one it got from the House.
    Finally, the conference committee produced a bill which passed both houses and was signed into law by the President.
  Congress is in the middle of the policy process.
    Power in Congress is widely disbursed.
    Party "control" in Congress is now a misnomer.
      Individuals and interest groups are strong.
      Parties are weak.
Organization of the Congress
  Unlike most other democracies, the American executive and legislative branches are separately elected and have separate responsibilities.
  The U.S. legislature is bicameral.
  The framers had different expectations for the House and Senate.
    Because the Senate is smaller than the House, it is less formal and debate is more open.
    Senate rules allow members to filibuster and also provide for the means to end a filibuster (cloture).

The large size of the House necessitates having a Rules Committee to establish guidelines for floor debate.

The increasing workload and weak party discipline led to an increase in the number of congressional committees.

There are four main types of committees in Congress: standing, special or select, joint, and conference.

Standing committees, which are permanent units with continuing membership, are where most of the legislative work takes place.

Joint committees coordinate activities that are the responsibilities of both chambers, such as congressional oversight.

Conference committees reconcile the differences between the House and Senate versions of a bill.

Select and special committees include both those which investigate a particular problem and report to the parent chamber, and those which are composed of just one party.

Committees are divided further into subcommittees.

Until 1970, subcommittees were tightly controlled by parent committees, but in the early 1970s a congressional redistribution of power gave subcommittees a great deal of autonomy.

Congress also restricted the influence any one subcommittee can have.

The number of congressional staff assistants increased dramatically during the 1970s because of two factors: the increasing workload and the members' desire for independence.

Consequently, the cost of operating Congress has also sky-rocketed in the past thirty years.

Party unity in Congress

Less party discipline is found in Congress than in most national legislatures.

Few votes for any issue clearly divide the Republicans and Democrats in Congress.

The American separation of powers removes much of the incentive for party-line voting.

The composition of Congress

The Constitution sets forth few requirements for membership in Congress.

In practice, membership in one of the two major parties is a prerequisite.

Democrats have dominated Congress since the 1930s.

Congressmen are usually well educated, wealthy, and from prestigious occupations, such as law and business.

Congress has traditionally been disproportionately white and male, but more recently, blacks and women have been gaining seats.

Congressional trends

Because of their experience with the British Crown, most Americans had a strong distrust for executive authority in general.

As a result, early state legislatures were given significant power while executives were quite weak.

The Constitution was an attempt to balance power more evenly among the three branches of government, but Congress still dominated national politics during most of the nineteenth century.

During the early 1800s, the House was more powerful than the Senate, but by the 1830s the locus of power had shifted to the Senate.

During the Civil War, congressional supremacy was interrupted briefly as the country looked to the president for strong leadership.

Congress regained its dominant position with the assassination of Lincoln, as Radical Republicans impeached President Johnson and almost removed him from office.

Party discipline reached a high point around the turn of the century, first behind the speaker of the House and then behind the House Democratic caucus.

By about 1915, national leadership shifted away not only from congressional parties but from Congress altogether.

A new era of national leadership opened as the president replaced Congress as the dominant national leader.

One reason the president emerged as a powerful leader is that the executive branch is more suited to administer the complex government regulations that began to appear in the early twentieth century.

Four reasons for a modern congressional comeback

Growing individualism in Congress during the 1960s led to less party discipline.

Unpopular executive decisions, such as the Vietnam War, reduced the appeal of a strong president.

Recent conservative presidents have demonstrated that the presidency is not always a progressive liberal force.

Watergate led many Americans to believe that executive authority was excessive.

Recent assertiveness in Congress

In 1974, Congress passed the Congressional budget and Impoundment Control Act, taking away the president's power to impound funds, also establishing a much more integrated budgetary process.

Congress has reemphasized its oversight powers by expanding the functions of the General Accounting Office and by requiring executive agencies to notify Congress of program changes.

In light of the *Chadha* ruling, Congress has revamped the legislative veto in recent years.

Two congressional roles

Congress can be viewed either as a lawmaking body whose function is to formulate cohesive national policy or a representative assembly whose members must represent the various interests of their constituents.

As a representative assembly, Congress receives public praise, but most Americans feel that Congress is a rather poor lawmaking institution.

Because of the fragmented interests of Congress, special interest groups wield significant power.

Reform is needed but hard to achieve.

Review Questions

COMPLETION

1. President Nixon attempted to expand the president's role in the budgetary process by _____ funds.

2. Most of the work of Congress is performed in _____ because a large assembly like the House would be inundated trying to work out the details of each bill.

3. The framers expected the _____ to be a cool, deliberative assembly.

4. One way senators can delay action on a bill is to extend debate or _____.

5. During most of the nineteenth century, the _____ branch of national government was the dominant leader.

6. A congressional redistribution of power in the early 1970s was called _____.

7. Before their elections to Congress, more congressmen were _____ than any other occupation.

8. The framers provided that the Senate be elected by _____.

9. The _____ is responsible for determining the guidelines for debating each bill in the House.

TRUE/FALSE

1. Decisions made during the Vietnam War damaged the credibility of the presidency in the American people's eyes.

2. The smaller Senate is burdened with less rules than the House.

3. Congressional oversight refers to some undesirable consequence as a result of a misjudgment.
4. In America, Democrats and Republicans tend to vote as solid blocks against each other on important issues.
5. Because most U.S. presidents once served as congressmen, we can say that American executive authority is derived from the legislature.
6. The U.S. House and Senate tend to be more equal than the legislative chambers in other bicameral systems.
7. While the executive agencies have grown almost out of control in recent years, the average congressional staff size has remained about the same.
8. Since 1930, Congress has usually been controlled by the Democrats.
9. During the 1970s, congressional subcommittees have been more involved in the work of legislation but they have also been supervised more closely by parent committees.
10. Because of the House's size, its members tend to be insulated from currents of public opinion more than senators are.

MULTIPLE CHOICE

1. The total cost of operating Congress in 1985 was about
   a. $50 million.
   b. $70 million.
   c. $1.6 billion.
   d. $6 billion.
2. Congressmen are usually _____.
   a. schoolteachers.
   b. better educated than the general public.
   c. more religious than the general public.
   d. wealthier than the general public.
   e. two of the above
3. It is the responsibility of the _____ committee to reconcile different versions of a bill.
   a. conference
   b. joint
   c. select
   d. standing
4. The increasing amount and complexity of legislation has caused Congress to
   a. refuse to legislate in areas where it once passed many laws.
   b. give more power to party leaders.
   c. refer most of its legislative business to committees.
   d. often follow the lead of the majority leaders when voting on noncontroversial bills.
5. Who did *not* favor tax reform?
   a. Jimmy Carter
   b. Ronald Reagan
   c. Dan Rostenkowski
   d. all of the above
   e. none of the above

6. During the Civil War, the _____ was the most powerful arm of the national government.
   a. Senate
   b. House
   c. Congress as a whole
   d. presidency

7. Edmund Burke advocated that legislatures should be
   a. lawmaking bodies.
   b. representative assemblies.
   c. assemblies where members can fight for their constituents' interests.
   d. subservient to the executive.

8. _____ is the provision that enables Congress to overturn executive actions.
   a. Execitive privilege
   b. The new Bill of Rights
   c. Presidential initiative
   d. Legislative veto

9. Congressional party discipline was at a high mark in America
   a. in the first twenty years after ratification of the Constitution.
   b. after the 1980 election of Ronald Reagan.
   c. during the late nineteenth and early twentieth centuries.
   d. just before the Civil War.

10. The House will use _____ to remove a stalled bill from a committee.
    a. suspension procedures
    b. discharge petitions
    c. cloture
    d. unanimous consent agreements

ANSWER KEY

Completion

1. impounding   p. 1
2. committees   p. 131
3. Senate   p. 126
4. filibuster   p. 128
5. legislative   p. 144
6. spreading the action   p. 135
7. lawyers   p. 142
8. their state legislatures   p. 126
9. Rules Committee   p. 130

True/False

1. T   pp. 152–53
2. T   p. 128
3. F   p. 158
4. F   pp. 139–40
5. F   p. 125
6. T   p. 126
7. F   p. 136
8. T   p. 142
9. F   pp. 133, 135
10. F   p. 127

Multiple Choice

1. c   p. 138
2. e   pp. 142–43
3. a   p. 133
4. c   p. 131
5. e   pp. 119–20

6. d   p. 145
7. a   pp. 162–63
8. d   pp. 159–60
9. c   p. 146
10. b   pp. 130–31

ESSAY QUESTIONS

1. Assume you are an Australian journalist writing a short feature article on the U.S. Congress. Your editor asks you to write a short article in which you describe the most important institutional characteristics of the U.S. Congress and their significance for the legislative process.
2. As Professor Ladd notes, Congress has undergone important changes over its history. What are the most important transitions, why did they come about, and what were their consequences?

Further Investigation

Dodd, Lawrence C., and Oppenheimer, Bruce I. *Congress Reconsidered.* Washington, D.C.: Congressional Quarterly Press, 1981.
   Deals with reforms in Congress during the 1970s.
Fenno, Richard F., Jr. *Home Style.* Boston: Little, Brown, 1978.
   How congressmen behave in their home districts. Provides insights into elections and representation.
Fenno, Richard F., Jr. *Congressmen in Committees.* Boston: Little, Brown, 1973.
   Study of the styles of twelve standing committees.
Hinckley, Barbara. *Congressional Elections.* Washington, D.C.: Congressional Quarterly Press, 1981.
   A good place to begin the study of apportionment, redistricting, candidate recruitment, campaigns, voting behavior, and the relationship of congressional elections to public policy.
Jacobson, Gary. *Money in Congressional Elections.* New Haven: Yale University Press, 1980.
   The role of campaign spending in congressional elections and an interesting perspective on federal financing of them.
Malbin, Michael. *Unelected Representatives: Congressional Staff and the Future of Representation.* New York: Basic Books, 1980.
   As the text has pointed out, one of the most important developments in Congress has been the dramatic growth in staff. Malbin analyzes its causes and consequences not only for Congress but for government generally.

Mann, Thomas, and Ornstein, Norman J., eds. *The New Congress*. Washington, D.C.: American Enterprise Institute, 1981.

An excellent group of articles on change in Congress.

Mayhew, David R. *Congress: The Electoral Connection*. New Haven: Yale University Press, 1974.

The idea that legislative behavior is shaped by a congressman's desire to win reelection.

Redman, Eric. *The Dance of Legislation*. New York: Simon and Schuster, 1973.

Redman describes how a bill becomes a law from his vantage point as an intern in a U.S. senator's office. The book provides insights into the formal and informal workings of the Congress.

Schick, Allen. *Congress and Money: Budgeting, Spending and Taxing*. Washington, D.C.: Urban Institute, 1980.

Carefully examines the relationship between budgeting, taxing and spending as well as such issues as the deficit, defense spending, and tax reform.

Applying Political Science

1. Replicate Richard Fenno's research on congressmen in their home district in your congressional district. Arrange to spend one or two full days with the congressman and monitor the way Washington is described to the constituents, how the congressman identifies with the district, etc.
2. Choose a public policy question of interest to you and trace the involvement of Congress in that area. In addition to the government documents section of your library, be sure to read in the *Congressional Quarterly Almanac* or *CQ*'s Congress and the Nation Series. Another well-indexed source on policy questions is *The National Journal*.
3. As your reading has said, much of what a congressman does is casework or constituent service. Visit your congressman or U.S. senator's field office and interview the staff about the kinds of services they provide. Also inquire about how important these activities are to the congressman or senator.

7 | The Presidency

Overview

Much is expected of American presidents, both by themselves and by the public. But even when a president is highly popular, as was Ronald Reagan, he usually sees very limited success in implementing his programs.

The presidency is an office with as many limitations as powers. It differs from any other national executive office in several respects. The president achieves power through election rather than by heritage, party control, or appointment. The actual election of the chief executive, however, is insulated from direct popular vote by the electoral college. The electoral college, originally intended as a deliberative body, now reflects the popular vote winner for each state.

The president's powers are outlined in the Constitution. These include being commander-in-chief of the armed forces, the ability to negotiate treaties, the authority to appoint executive and other officers, and the right to veto acts of legislation. This separation of powers identifies an area of presidential authority. However, the president does not have a free rein; his powers are checked and balanced by the other branches of government, especially the legislative branch. Every basic constitutional grant of authority to the president is also constitutionally limited. Even when the president has mass public appeal, the public continues to support the system of checks and balances outlined by the Constitution. This is illustrated by Franklin D. Roosevelt's experience with his "court packing" bill. A more modern example is the War Powers Resolution. The ultimate check on the executive is the power of Congress to impeach. Although the process of impeachment has been rarely used, its potential use helps keep the executive on the right track.

The founders did not want the presidency to resemble a monarchy, but because of their experience with the Articles of Confederation they also did not want a weak executive without real powers. The system of checks and balances serves to satisfy the demands for strength and limited powers.

The president's leadership roles extend beyond merely serving as an executive: he must also fulfill the public's expectations from his election campaign. To be successful he must effectively communicate with the electorate while campaigning as well as while he serves as president. The president must also work well with other politicians. He must be a good administrator. He must be able to determine what needs to be done and do what must be done in order for his policies to be carried out. Above all, the president must possess strong leadership skills.

The Executive Office of the President is the institutional means for assisting the president. The most important unit within the EOP is the White House staff, which the president chooses and organizes. An effective personal staff can greatly assist the president in performing his job. Two other important offices are the National Security Council and the Office of Management and Budget, which serve in advisory capacities. The vice-president has risen in importance as an aid to the president.

An important skill for a president is the ability to persuade individuals and groups to do what he wants them to do. Different situations require different sorts of leadership and action. In a crisis, typically, public opinion swings toward the president. These shifting criteria have resulted in changing assessments of the president over time. More generally, the public is not afraid to criticize the president, and over time his popularity usually declines. The public has high expectations and sets high standards for the president but also realizes that the job is extremely demanding.

Key Terms and Concepts

Electoral College	institutions
checks and balances	Executive Office of the
separation of power	President
impeachment	White House staff
presidential responsibilities	vice-presidency
and skills	presidential power
policy judgment	assessments of presidents

Chapter Outline

Executive power
  The President is an important leader both symbolically and practically.
    Much is usually expected of him, both by the public and himself.
    There is a frustrating gap, however, between what he wants to do
      and what he can actually accomplish.
    The powers of the office are inherently limited.
      Ronald Reagan, for example, saw only limited success in

implementing his programs, despite tremendous personal popularity.

John Kennedy also experienced the frustration of the gap.

What kind of chief executive?

The founding fathers were breaking new ground.

The office is still essentially unique to America.

A republican executive

American presidents are different from executives in other countries.

They rely on public will rather than heredity.

The office was to be insulated by indirect selection.

The plan with the electoral college had both a mechanical and a philosophical failure.

No distinction was made between electoral votes for president and vice-president.

The Twelfth Amendment rectified the situation.

The electoral college was not a ratification of popular preferences.

Evolution of the process has changed it into one which is virtually a direct election.

Democratization of the presidency strengthened the office.

An independent executive

Executive power comes directly from the Constitution.

His duties are extensive and specific.

A checked and balanced executive

Every basic constitutional grant of authority to the president is also constitutionally limited.

Commander-in-chief is limited by congressional budget powers.

His appointment powers are limited by the Senate's confirmation powers.

The presidency exemplifies American ambivalence toward political authority.

The president has the executive authority but must share his powers.

The system of checks and balances has always been in operation.

Despite FDR's tremendous popularity, his proposal to short-circuit checks and balances by stacking the Supreme Court was soundly defeated.

The system of checks and balances remains strong today.

Changing technology has increased the president's dominance in the role of commander of the armed forces.

The War Powers Resolution reasserts legislative limits over executive action in military intervention.

It has been criticized as an infringement on the executive's powers as commander-in-chief.

It has also been assessed as merely an assertion of Congress's constitutional role.

The ultimate check on the executive is impeachment.

The House impeaches and the Senate tries.

Andrew Johnson is the only president to have been impeached by the House.

The Senate came one vote short of convicting him.

Richard Nixon was never actually impeached but was forced to resign by the threat of impeachment.

The scandal which led to this stemmed from a break-in at Democratic party headquarters at Watergate.

The subsequent coverup attempt included the President.

It created a general distrust of the presidency among the public, who felt that the office had become aggrandized.

The presidency was not intended to be a pompous role.

A vigorous "one-person" executive

The president was not to resemble a monarchy.

A strong president was desired because of experience with the Articles of Confederation.

George Washington favored a strong executive.

Washington's personal virtue helped strengthen the presidency.

The delegates' commitment to checked and balanced power also strengthened the executive's role.

Duties of the president

He has many responsibilities.

He is both the head of government and the chief of state.

As head of government, Americans hold him responsible for the well-being of the economy.

He is the head of the American military.

As such he is responsible for the security of the nation.

He is expected to transcend the narrow partisanship in his leadership roles while also upholding the philosophy and promises that got him elected.

He also needs the skills necessary to fulfill the responsibilities.

First, he must have the external skills.

He must be a durable and effective campaigner.

He must be a good communicator.

Internal political skills are also necessary.

He must have a good professional reputation among the politicians with whom he works.

He must know when to push and when to compromise.

Administrative skills are vital to successfully running the executive branch.

The United States Government is an extremely large business.

Personal staff provide important advice, but the president is responsible for organizing and choosing them.

In addition to all these skills, he must also demonstrate policy judgment.

He needs policies for which he uses his skills.

He need not be an expert, but he must initiate policy to deal with the nation's problems.

With leadership, the whole is greater than the sum of its parts.

Washington, for example, did not display outstanding ability in any of the areas outlined above.

He was in the right place at the right time.

He exercised very good political judgment.

He achieved national unity and democratic legitimacy.

The institutional presidency

It began under FDR with the formation of the Executive Office of the President.

For Roosevelt it consisted mainly of his personal staff and the Bureau of the Budget.

Its size has been steadily increasing.

Some have recommended reducing the size of this staff.

Increased staff size made organization very important.

Some presidents have used a circular style, leaving the door open to many senior assistants.

Others have used a hierarchical arrangement with a chief of staff who wields great authority.

The staff needs to maximize the president's time by bringing only the proper things to his attention.

Power struggles among the staff are inevitable.

The Executive Office of the President

The EOP is really ten offices.

Each reports directly to the president, who appoints top officers.

The National Security Council advises the president on American foreign policy

The Office of Management and Budget helps the president formulate and administer the budget, reviews the organizations structure and management procedures of the executive branch, develops regulatory reform proposals, and assesses program objectives.

The vice president

It is traditionally a low-visibility position.

Succession is its most important function.

He is officially the president of the Senate.

He is a sort of assistant to the president.

Because they were selected to add geographic or ideological balance to the ticket, vice presidents rarely became confidants of the presidents they served.

This has changed over the last thirty years.

Vice presidents have been given increasingly greater responsibilities to prepare them for the possibility of becoming president.

He is also expected to remain loyal to the president.

Presidential power

Some believe that the power of the presidency depends too much on his ability to persuade.

Lloyd Cutler argued that the current system almost guarantees stalemate.

There are contradictory judgments about presidents and their power.

The public is satisfied with the limits on the presidency.

Experts do not agree about whether there is a problem with presidential power.

Some situations warrant a strong president, whereas others do not.

Changing circumstances make it difficult for presidents to know which role is expected of them.

Assessing presidents

Assessments change over time.

As times change, so do the dimensions on which presidents are evaluated.

The presidencies of Hoover, Eisenhower, and Nixon have been interpreted and reinterpreted with time.

It remains to be seen how Reagan will be judged.

In the last couple of decades the character and personality of the president have also become viewed as important.

The public's ratings of presidents also change with time.

Review Questions

COMPLETION

1. The two prevailing methods of organizing the White House staff are the _____ and _____ methods.

2. _____ was the only president to have achieved office without actually campaigning in a presidential campaign.

3. John F. Kennedy characterized the presidency as a gap between what the president _____ and what the president _____.

4. The president of the United States is formally elected by the _____.

5. FDR was unable to pass his "court packing" bill because the public was firmly committed to _____.

6. _____ presides over the impeachment trial in the Senate.

7. There are _____ units within the Executive Office of the President.

8. The vice-president is, in a literal constitutional sense, "a _____ away from the presidency."

9. According to Richard Neustadt, the power of the presidency is depicted too much in terms of formal authority and not enough in terms of _____.

10. The presidents described as having "active-negative" personalities are _____ and _____.

11. When the founding fathers set up the executive branch, they intended the selection of the president to be based on _____ rather than on heredity.

TRUE/FALSE

1. Every state has two electors in the Electoral College.
2. Both houses in Congress must approve all treaties by a two-thirds majority for the treaty to take effect.
3. The War Powers Resolution gives Congress greater power in restricting the commander-in-chief role of the president.
4. The campaigning skill of the president is considered a necessary "external political talent."
5. Policy is something that the president never chooses; rather, he acts upon the guidelines provided to him by Congress.
6. The increase in the size of the White House staff began in the 1930s.
7. The National Security Council is the largest unit within the Executive Office of the President.
8. Within the last three decades, the office of vice-president has become less of a ceremonial post and more of a major responsible position.
9. There is no general agreement among experts as to whether the United States has a problem with regard to the presidential power.
10. In a poll conducted in 1983, Richard Nixon was considered the best president in regard to foreign affairs.

MULTIPLE CHOICE

1. Which one of the following is *not* a responsibility of the president?
   a. Chief diplomat
   b. Voice of the people
   c. Chief of party
   d. Chief presiding officer of the Senate
   e. All of the above are responsibilities of the president.

2. Presidential electors are now selected by
   a. direct popular election.
   b. state legislatures.
   c. the governor.
   d. the parties.
   e. petition.

3. Why was Ronald Reagan unable to implement more of his agenda than he did?
   a. He was a lame duck president.
   b. He was actually not as popular as commonly believed.
   c. There were simply limitations inherent to the office.
   d. He was ineffective in dealing with Congress.
   e. None of the above.

4. Reagan's later staff arrangements can best be described as
   a. traditional.
   b. circular.
   c. hierarchal.
   d. institutional.
   e. departmental.

5. Which of the following is *not* included within the Executive Office of the President?
   a. Council on Environmental Quality
   b. Office of Policy Development
   c. Council of Economic Advisors
   d. Office of Administration
   e. Council of Food and Drug Administration

6. The American political system is almost unique in that
   a. the congressional branch dominates the government.
   b. the executive branch dominates the government.
   c. the executive leadership and the Congress do not necessarily work in concert.
   d. the executive branch and the Congress do necessarily work in concert.
   e. the executive branch and the Congress are always of the same party and philosophy.

7. The popular standing of the president must also be accompanied by _____ in order for him to be successful.
   a. high opinion poll ratings
   b. a good professional reputation
   c. a high education level
   d. large amounts of money
   e. none of the above

8. The executive is unique among other public officials in that he
   a. is elected from a national constituency.
   b. has specific powers that are not outlined in the Constitution.
   c. can appoint his own staff.
   d. has the franking privilege.
   e. all of the above

9. The commander-in-chief role of the president includes also the power to
   a. raise armies.
   b. declare war.
   c. support armies.
   d. make treaties.
   e. commit troops with or without authorization by Congress.

Completion

1. circular, hierarchy   p. 190
2. Gerald Ford   p. 184
3. wants to do, actually does   p. 167
4. Electoral College   p. 172
5. the separation of powers principle   p. 176
6. The chief justice of the Supreme Court   p. 178
7. ten   p. 192
8. heartbeat   p. 194
9. persuasion   p. 197
10. Lyndon Johnson, Richard Nixon   p. 204
11. public will   p. 171

True/False

1. F   p. 172
2. F   p. 174
3. T   p. 177
4. T   p. 184
5. F   p. 187
6. T   p. 189
7. F   p. 193
8. T   p. 195
9. T   p. 198
10. T   p. 206

Multiple Choice

1. d   p. 183
2. a   p. 173
3. c   pp. 168–69
4. c   p. 191
5. e   p. 193
6. c   p. 174
7. b   p. 185
8. a   p. 183
9. d   p. 174

ESSAY QUESTIONS

1. Based upon your reading of Ladd and your lecturer, write a summary of the president's job (responsibilities and roles). Describe the most important elements of the job first and indicate why each element is important. To what extent does the system of presidential elections give voters information about the qualifications of the candidates for these specific parts of the job?
2. It is often argued that the presidency is more than the president. Assess this statement in light of the modern presidency. If you agree with the statement, what implications does it have for American government?

Further Investigation

Barber, James David. *The Presidential Character: Predicting Performance in the White House.* 2d ed. Englewood Cliffs, N.J.: Prentice-Hall, 1977.

Barber's controversial and widely discussed typology of presidential personality and character applies psychological dimensions to the study of the presidency.

Califano, Joseph A. *A Presidential Nation*. New York: Norton, 1975.
Having worked with presidents, Califano traces the development of the modern presidency and proposes ways to keep accountability and power in the office.

Corwin, Edward S. *The President: Office and Powers*. 4th ed. New York: Oxford University Press, 1957.
A look at the historical development of the office of the president.

Cronin, Thomas E. *Rethinking the Presidency*. Boston: Little, Brown, 1982.
Insightful collection of essays on the president and his office.

Edwards, George C., III. *Presidential Influence with Congress*. San Francisco: W. H. Freeman, 1980.
How a president deals with Congress.

Hess, Stephen. *Organizing the Presidency*. Washington, D.C.: Brookings Institution, 1976.
Reviews the organization of presidential offices from Roosevelt to Nixon.

Neustadt, Richard E. *Presidential Power: The Politics of Leadership from F.D.R. to Carter*. New York: Wiley, 1980.
A classic study of how presidents acquire and hold on to power.

Schlesinger, Arthur, Jr. *The Imperial Presidency*. Boston: Houghton Mifflin, 1973.
Watergate and Nixon's fall from grace seemed to undermine Schlesinger's thesis that the presidency had gone well beyond the expectations of the founders. Book remains important because of its commentary on the potential for arbitrary power in the White House.

Applying Political Science

1. Select a recent decision announced by the president and identify as many of the factors that were important to that decision as you can. To what extent did the president appear to consider opposing points of view? How much political capital can the president expect to spend in getting his way with Congress, the bureaucracy, the private sector? Will the decision enhance or diminish his political position?

2. Can the president become the captive of his staff? Select a local executive—mayor (if you have a strong mayoral form of government), city or county administrator, or governor. Interview the staff about how options are presented. Are opposing viewpoints

welcome? Are all options examined? Why? If a local executive is
hard to find, read any of the memoirs of former presidential advisors with an eye to the same set of questions.

3. Why does presidential popularity decline over time? Identify the
patterns of declining popularity in presidents and then attempt to
explain what causes this pattern. Relate the Gallup Poll data to
news stories, major domestic or foreign policy announcements,
successes or failures in Congress, etc.

8 | The Executive Branch and the Bureaucracy

Overview

With roughly 2.9 million civilian employees, the executive branch is by far the country's largest employer and has no easy task in managing itself. Perhaps the case of Donald Devine, the Reagan-appointed director of the Office of Personnel Management, best exemplifies some of the problems that arise between the career bureaucrats and the administration. Devine attempted to implement some ambitious reforms, including some dealing with the retirement system and merit pay, but drew tremendous criticism from the employee unions and Congress. Eventually Reagan succeeded in getting at least one of the sought reforms, but Devine was forced to leave the post.

The executive branch is responsible for administering laws passed by Congress. From the beginning it was clear that the president and his advisers could not possibly administer all of the federal government's programs. As a result, a bureaucracy was formed to assist him with this duty.

In 1789, the State, Treasury, War, Post Office, and Attorney General's departments were formed by an act of Congress, marking the beginning of the federal bureaucracy in the United States. The president nominates the cabinet secretaries and agency heads, and the Senate confirms them through "advise and consent." Since Washington's time additional federal departments or agencies have been formed through legislation.

Since its inception, the federal bureaucracy has grown in size and expanded in scope. As the nation grew, so did the federal bureaucracy. Most of the growth between 1789 and the Civil War occurred in the Post Office. Later the federal government became a "promoter of interests," establishing the Department of Agriculture, the Bureau of Education, and the Department of Labor. These new federal agencies had a following or clientele. They were not designed to regulate or subsidize; those functions came later.

The industrial revolution and the rapid change in business during the latter half of the nineteenth century and the beginning of this century brought about more growth in the federal bureaucracy. The federal government set up regulatory commissions such as the Interstate Commerce Commission and the Food and Drug Administration. Population growth and the administration of new laws passed by Congress also were factors in the larger role for government. The federal bureaucracy today includes thirteen departments, the leaders of which compose the president's cabinet.

It also includes independent regulatory commissions and the federal foundations and institutes. The independent regulatory commissions were designed to be insulated from presidential and political interference. For example, the commissioners who serve on the regulatory boards have lengthy terms, which are staggered or overlapping. This prevents a president from "stacking" a commission for his own purposes. The federal foundations and institutes were established to promote such things as scholarships, the arts, and science.

The bureau is the basic unit of federal administration and policy making. Because presidents serve at most eight years and secretaries or department heads serve an average of less than two years, much of the agency expertise resides with the bureau chiefs, who are typically career "bureaucrats." These individuals generate the policy options and carry out the policy decisions. Bureaus are often powerful in setting policy because they have an ongoing relationship with important interest groups.

Despite their location in the executive branch, bureaus tend to have close working relations with Congress. Congress has the responsibility to oversee each executive agency and bureau and has delegated to each committee and/or subcommittee this responsibility. Over time, the bureau chief and the (sub)committee chairman will develop a close working relationship, which is often mutually beneficial. Bureaus tend to become independent of the president and his appointees because of their relationships with the clientele groups and the Congress. Since the bureau deals with each of the groups extensively, it becomes the "hub" of many policy decisions.

The president has limited power in directing the executive branch. He nominates his cabinet secretaries (the Senate must approve them, however), and may fire or dismiss them. Dismissal of the president's cabinet members and advisers does not require Senate approval as did their appointment. But the commissioners of the independent regulatory commissions do not serve at the pleasure of the president. Likewise, the vast majority of bureaucrats are protected by civil service laws and are not subject to the president's dismissal power. This is why presidents frequently complain that the bureaucracy is dragging its feet and not putting their programs into practice.

Civil service reform removed most federal employees from political patronage. Justifications for this reform were that a great number of the federal employees have nothing to do with policy—they perform blue collar labor or provide services but do not make policy decisions. Secondly, the "spoils system" led to massive turnover when a new party took control.

Under the "merit system," civil servants are now hired on the basis of performance on competitive tests. The first step toward the "merit system" is not totally equal, however, since veterans receive bonus points on civil service exams and other preferential treatment.

To provide a politically neutral pool of managerial talent much like the British bureaucracy, the Senior Executive Service was formed. The SES also has the following goals: (1) to minimize the conflict between the president and the bureaucracy; (2) to develop a group of expert managers who could give the executive feedback and thus avoid costly mistakes; and (3) to develop managers and administrators that could be moved between departments and bureaus as the need might arise.

The bureaucracy plays a very important role in our government. It is involved in the day-to-day workings of legislation and policy. Because society expects more from government, the scope and size of the federal bureaucracy has expanded.

Key Terms and Concepts

departments	foundations
agencies	bureaus
bureaucracy	civil service
clientele	merit system
regulatory agencies	spoils system
cabinet	Office of Personnel
independent agencies	Management
patronage	Senior Executive Service (SES)

Chapter Outline

The executive branch
  It has grown from about 2,000 employees in 1790 to about 2.9 million today.
  It is by far the nation's largest employer.
The battle of OPM
  The office covers roughly 1.7 million of the federal employees.
  Donald Devine served as its director from 1981 to 1985.
  His story exemplifies the nature of the relationship between the executive branch and the bureaucracy.
  Federal workers criticized him while conservatives praised him.
  In an attempt to curb mushrooming costs of retirement pay, the administration and OPM helped pass legislation forcing new federal employees to pay Social Security.
  Federal workers won on other retirement issues.

Devine attempted to create merit pay, replacing automatic pay increases with raises based on job performance.

Employee unions saw it as an attempt to replace the civil service system with political patronage.

The unions finally managed to block the implementation of the policy through the courts.

In 1985 Devine's nomination for a second term faced serious opposition in the Senate, so he withdrew his name.

After Devine's ouster the administration finally got one of the reforms it had sought: a new Federal Employees' Retirement System.

Evolution of the executive branch

Congress creates the agency, and the president appoints the heads of departments with the consent of the Senate.

In 1789, Congress first set up four executive departments: State, Treasury, War (now called Defense), and Office of Attorney General (now called Justice).

Since 1800, nine other departments have been added to the executive branch.

Early executive departments were small in size and limited in scope.

Bureaucratic growth in our first century paralleled population growth.

The Department of Defense is now the largest federal employer.

Before World War II, the defense establishment was small during peacetime.

The government as promoter of interests

After the Civil War, government agencies and bureaus like the Department of Agriculture, Bureau of Education, and Department of Labor were created as a means of dealing with group interests.

These agencies were not intended to regulate, but instead to gather information and to promote progress in their areas.

Over time, the constituencies have used these agencies as advocates to gain benefits from the government.

Concentrated benefits and widely disbursed costs have often helped the interest groups attain their goals.

The growth of industry in the late 1800s led to government regulation of the economy.

The Interstate Commerce Commission, the Sherman Anti-Trust Act, etc. were government responses to economic problems and efforts to promote public objectives.

The expanding scope of the federal bureaucracy has contributed to the growth in its size and expenditures, making the federal government larger than any firm.

The federal executive today

Thirteen departments have cabinet rank.

Independent agencies may be outside of the executive departments, but they are not all independent of the executive.

Foundations and institutes have been set up to promote science and learning.

Independent regulatory commissions were designed to be safeguarded from presidential and political involvement.

Commissioners' terms are long and overlapping.

The president appoints the commission members and can have some influence, especially if he serves two terms.

The bureau is the basic unit of federal administration.

It is important in determining policy.

Bureau heads have more longevity than do presidents or cabinet secretaries.

Bureau constituencies are enduring.

Bureaus and interest groups often share objectives and are able to help each other, establishing a lasting bond between them.

Often Congress and the bureaus also have such a symbiotic relationship.

Congress has oversight for the bureaus.

Executive authority is lessened because of the relationship between Congress and the bureaus.

Bureau chiefs are usually policy-makers in their own right.

They can develop a certain degree of autonomy.

Iron triangles between bureaus, congressional committees, and interest groups are hard to break.

Public-policy formation is very fragmented.

The bureau is the hub of the policy-making wheel.

The president and the bureaucracy

The president can hire and fire only political executives—about 8,000 employees.

The rest are under protection of the civil service system.

Reagan's political appointees at the Environmental Protection Agency drew heavy criticism from Congress and from within the agency.

When they resigned in March of 1983, career staff at the agency acted as if they had been liberated.

Nixon had a particularly adversarial relationship with the bureaucracy.

Organization of the federal civil service

Most civil servants have little to do with policy.

Over ninety percent of federal civilian workers are covered under a merit system.

The old "spoils" system brought on the change.

The Pendleton Civil Service Act of 1883 was the first step to change.

Hatch Acts of the 1930–40s helped bring about the present system.

There is an attempt at objectivity in the hiring process.

The Office of Personnel Management gives examinations to measure applicants' skills.

For higher-level positions no real test is given, only a resume of
sorts is reviewed.

This process is designed to cut down on political favoritism and
base employment on skills.

Is the merit system free of favoritism?

Veterans receive at least five additional points on their examination
scores and are placed first on the eligibility roster.

Firing an employee was made difficult in the civil service to avoid the
ill effects of the spoils system.

However, it is difficult to fire lazy and incompetent people.

Even so, the inefficiency of the bureaucracies may be overstated.

The 1978 Civil Service Reform Act made it easier to dismiss
employees.

The Senior Executive Service (SES)

It was designed to form a mobile and neutral pool of managerial
talent.

It gives feedback to the executive so as to avoid costly mistakes.

The British civil service served as a model for the SES.

It reduces the conflict between the executive and the bureaucracy.

Review Questions

COMPLETION

1. Federal employees' pension checks are raised automatically each
   year by _____.
2. The first four bureaucracies set up were _____.
3. Briefly explain the difference between a cabinet post in the British
   system and our own.
4. Briefly explain the function of government organized foundations
   and institutions.
5. Our federal civil service uses a _____ system in its hiring
   practices.
6. The most obvious exception to the idea of the merit system in our
   present civil service is _____.
7. Why did President Carter want to phase out veterans' privileges or
   advantages in the civil service?
8. What were the two most important pieces of legislation when
   government first began to regulate the economy?
9. What was the model for the Senior Executive Service?
10. Explain why President Nixon had problems with the bureaucracy.

TRUE/FALSE

1. The 2.9 million employees of the executive branch make it by far and away the country's largest employer.
2. Although Donald Devine was too ideological and political for his opponents, they realized that he was sympathetic to employee interests.
3. Opponents of merit pay claimed that it might be used to replace civil service with political patronage.
4. During the first one hundred years of our country, the major growth in the bureaucracy was due to the Post Office's growth.
5. Bureaus or offices are important subsets of the departments and are a key factor in determining policy because of the president's direct influence upon the heads of bureaus or offices.
6. The president's department secretaries must be approved by the Senate.
7. The civil service is an attempt to make government hiring more fair by departing from the spoils system.
8. The president has little or no influence on the independent regulatory commissions.
9. Most of the bureaus of the federal bureaucracy have no real effect on policy matters.

MULTIPLE CHOICE

1. The British civil service is often considered the model bureaucracy because
   a. it is very efficient and wastes very little.
   b. it is politically neutral.
   c. it is fairer in its hiring practices.
   d. it is smaller and still gets just as much accomplished as the American bureaucracy.
2. The Senior Executive Service was designed to do which of the following?
   a. Allow elderly administrators to retire at seventy-two instead of sixty-five, thus relieving the burden on Social Security.
   b. Form a group of politically neutral and mobile managers.
   c. Give the managers or administrators the opportunity to give helpful feedback to the executive.
   d. Cut down on the conflict between the executive and the bureaucracy.
   e. All of the above
   f. b and d
   g. b, c, and d

3. Which of the following are reasons why interest groups have had reasonable success in dealing with the bureaucracy?
   a. The benefits that the bureaucracy deals out are concentrated and the costs are widely dispersed.
   b. Interest groups and the bureaucracy sometimes have similar goals and so they cooperate.
   c. Interest groups force bureaucrats to go along with them on policy decisions.
   d. Interest groups play upon bureaucrats' desire to be reelected.
   e. All of the above
   f. a and b

4. Which of the following is not a way that the independent regulatory commissions have been protected from political involvement by the president?
   a. The commissioners have overlapping or staggered terms of office.
   b. The commissioners have fairly long terms of office.
   c. The commissioners are appointed by Congress.
   d. The membership of the commission is required to be bipartisan.

5. Which of the following was or were motivation(s) to organize a civil service?
   a. Political patronage was seen as unfair.
   b. The bureaucracy was too unstable.
   c. The bureaucracy was too powerful and independent.
   d. The system was seen as too inefficient.

6. Which of the following is false with regard to the influence the president can exert over the bureaucracy?
   a. The president appoints and can dismiss the cabinet secretaries.
   b. The president can dismiss only a small percentage of the administrators in the bureaucracy.
   c. Bureaucrats are under oath to uphold the Constitution and therefore are required to follow presidential recommendations since the president is in charge of the executive branch.
   d. Most presidents in the past forty years have felt that the bureaucracy did a good job of implementing their policies.
   e. a and b
   f. c and d

7. The new Federal Employees' Retirement System provides all but which of the following?
   a. basic Social Security benefits
   b. a governmental employee pension
   c. cost of living increases for retirees under 62
   d. a tax-deferred savings plan
   e. a retirement age of 57

74

8. The chiefs or heads of bureaus are important in determining policy because
   a. they are appointed by the president and try to carry out his programs.
   b. they are well insulated from interest groups and thus can act more independently.
   c. they are usually career civil servants and as such enjoy longevity in their job.
   d. they are tested and examined by the OPM and subsequently trained so that they are well qualified and prepared to make policy choices.

9. The bureau is referred to as the "hub" of policy making because
   a. the administration or executive plays a role in leadership.
   b. various interest groups make their wants known.
   c. the committees in Congress play a role in leadership.
   d. the Supreme Court reviews each major policy decision.
   e. a, b, and c
   f. a and b
   g. a and c
   h. all of the above

10. Which of the following are actual denotative traits of a bureaucracy?
   a. Hierarchical
   b. Formalized rules and procedures
   c. Inefficient
   d. Maintenance of records
   e. Ill-trained staff
   f. All of the above
   g. a, b, and c
   h. a, b, and d

ANSWER KEY

Completion

1. Cost of living adjustment; p. 211
2. State; Treasury; War; Attorney General;   p. 215
3. The British cabinet collectively exercises governmental authority, but in the United States the cabinet has no clear governing role.   p. 220
4. To promote science and scholarship   pp. 224–25
5. merit   p. 241
6. veterans' privileges   p. 243
7. Few women are veterans and thus it hurts their chances for employment.   p. 244
8. the Interstate Commerce Commission and the Sherman Anti-Trust Act   p. 219
9. the British bureaucracy   p. 248
10. Nixon distrusted career federal administrators so he tried various methods, mostly unsuccessful, to gain central control over them. The civil servants resented his innovations. pp. 237–38

True/False

1. T p. 209	6. T p. 234
2. F p. 210	7. T p. 241
3. T p. 212	8. F p. 226
4. T p. 216	9. T p. 230
5. F pp. 231–32	

Multiple Choice

1. b p. 248	6. f p. 234
2. g p. 247	7. c p. 214
3. f pp. 230–31	8. c pp. 231–32
4. c p. 226	9. e p. 233
5. a p. 241	10. h pp. 227–30

ESSAY QUESTIONS

1. More than any other branch of government, the executive branch (federal bureaucracy) reflects the changing scope and direction of government. Do you agree or disagree with this statement? Why? Present examples to support your case.

2. Although the president is nominally the chief executive, he may encounter problems getting the executive branch to implement his policy. Why might this be true? What can the president do about it?

Further Investigation

Downs, Anthony. *Inside Bureaucracy*. Boston: Little, Brown, 1967.
Examines bureaucratic routines, tendencies, and pathologies. Provides a framework in which to compare and study bureaucracy.

Heclo, Hugh. *A Government of Strangers*. Washington, D.C.:
Brookings Institution, 1977.
Examines the relationship between presidential appointees and senior civil servants in the federal bureaucracy. Also examines the tensions between civil servants and the White House.

Mosher, Frederick C. *Democracy and the Public Service*. 2d ed.
New York: Oxford University Press, 1982.
Examines public employees and the public service, including the impact of merit systems, professionalism, personnel practices and procedures, and theories of management.

Nathan, Richard. *The Plot that Failed*. New York: Wiley, 1975.
A review of Nixon's attempt to gain control over the bureaucracy.

Peters, Charles. *How Washington Really Works*. Reading, Mass.: Addison-Wesley, 1980.
  Suggests that politicizing the bureaucracy would make it more responsive and effective.
Ripley, Randall, and Franklin, Grace. *Congress, the Bureaucracy, and Public Policy*. 3rd ed. Homewood, Ill.: Dorsey Press, 1984.
  Examines subgovernments among bureaucracies, Congress, and interest groups.
Rourke, Francis, ed. *Bureaucratic Power in National Politics*. 3rd ed. Boston: Little, Brown, 1978.
  Readings on the federal bureaucracy, administrative agencies, and the branches of national government. Themes include expertise, power, constituencies, and reform.
Seidman, Harold. *Politics, Position, and Power*. 3rd ed. New York: Oxford University Press, 1980.
  An account of relations between the White House and the bureaucracy.
Wilson, James Q., ed. *The Politics of Regulation*. New York: Basic Books, 1980.
  Essays on regulation in various sectors of the economy.

Applying Political Science

1. People complain a lot about big government bureaucracy. What do they mean? Make a list of predictably bureaucratic behaviors and then attempt to determine whether these same behaviors exist at your university or college or in a major private corporation in your community.
2. Choose one program area such as social security, the forest service, or disaster relief. Visit the local office of that agency and attempt to determine how much policy is made locally and how much is made at other levels. What discretion does the local official have? Does he or she feel constrained by policy announcements from above? Does the local mayor, congressman, or other elected official ever ask for assistance?
3. Budgets are one way to determine political influence and power. Choose a unit of government and study its budget and the budgetary process. What predictable behaviors can you observe? If you were to try and make budgeting more sensible what would you do?

9 | The Judiciary

Overview

Chief Justice William Rhenquist has pointed out the paradox of the Supreme Court being able to decide questions arising under the Constitution, while its members are actually appointed by the other two branches. Powerful as the court is, what it says is determined by who sits on it, and the other two branches determine who sits on it.

While federal judges usually share the political philosophy of the presidents who appoint them, some have claimed that Reagan has taken this practice too far, sometimes sacrificing quality for political compatibility. The Justice Department maintains that he has simply been more meticulous than his predecessors. In any case, he has had a substantial impact on the federal courts, having appointed more judges than any other president.

The courts are an influential and unique political institution. They affect policy and law through such methods as judicial review. Judicial review is the power vested in the courts to interpret laws and actions of other branches of government and decide upon their constitutionality. Most scholars argue that the writers of the Constitution intended that the Court should have this power so that it could deal with state legislatures that passed laws contrary to the Constitution. However, it is less clear that the authors of the Constitution intended for the court to review the actions of the president and Congress.

The Supreme Court first claimed this power over its coequal branches of government as early as 1803 in its historic ruling in *Marbury* v. *Madison*. Its importance in American political life was not fully felt until well after the Civil War. Since that time judicial intervention has been much more common. In the period since the 1930s most statutes declared unconstitutional infringed on civil rights or liberties. With the exception of Canada, few other nations have a comparable power of judicial review.

The courts also have substantial power when interpreting the meaning of existing statutes. Judges are political. Consequently, when they are called upon to interpret vague statutes their own philosophical preferences emerge. When a court interprets such a law it is making policy. A court also makes policy by deciding the controversies that come before it. The Court issues its decision in what is known as an opinion, which explains the rationale behind the decision and attempts to convince other political actors of its soundness. Judges on the Court who are not in agreement with the majority decision file what is known as a dissenting opinion, which is a document explaining the reasons of the minority.

In recent years the Courts have signaled major changes in national policy. For instance, in *Brown* v. *Board of Education of Topeka* the Court led the way in race relations by declaring that racially separate schools were in violation of the Fourteenth Amendment. In *Baker* v. *Carr*, the Court forced a redistribution of state representation to ensure equal voting rights. And, in *Roe* v. *Wade* the Court changed national policy regarding abortion by attempting to balance the right of an individual's privacy with the prerogatives of the state.

Judicial activism seems inappropriate to many. One reason that the other branches of government often resent it is that U.S. Supreme Court judges are not required to face elections as are congressmen and presidents. Nor are the judges required to pay the costs of the programs they often insist on. Justices also often deal with rights that are difficult to placate with compromise.

Some justices, sensing the limitations of judicial activism, advocate judicial restraint. Under this approach, unless something in the Constitution specifically restricts the actions of the other branches, they feel that the court should not intervene.

American federalism with its dual governmental system established courts at both the state and the national levels. The Supreme Court of the United States is at the apex of both governmental court systems. The federal court system is made up of district courts (the court of original jurisdiction in most cases), circuit courts of appeal, and the Supreme Court. There are also some specialized courts involving taxes, customs, courts-martial, and civil service appeals. State courts, as exemplified by the California court system, consist of municipal courts for smaller legal matters; superior courts, which in most cases are the courts of original jurisdiction; appellate courts, which handle cases appealed from superior courts; and a state supreme court, which is charged with maintaining uniformity in state law.

In general, all cases involving federal constitutional questions, violations of federal law, bankruptcy, or litigation involving parties in two different states are filed in federal court. All cases involving violations of state law are filed in the state court systems. When a case can be filed in either court, there is a concurrent jurisdiction. When a case must be filed in either a federal or a state court, there is an exclusive jurisdiction.

Cases very rarely arrive at the Supreme Court through its original jurisdiction, but rather on appeal from lower courts. There are two different ways in which appeals can reach the Supreme Court. A party to an action in a lower court can file a writ of certiorari, which is basically a request that a higher court order a lower court to send it the records on a disputed case so that the higher court can review the decision. Four of the nine justices of the Supreme Court must agree to hear the case before a writ of certiorari is granted. Second, in some cases the Supreme Court is obliged to hear the appeal.

The Court refuses to hear cases if they do not meet several criteria. First, parties to suits filed in court must have standing to file their complaints. Second, the suit must be justiciable. Third, the Court refuses to give advisory opinions on hypothetical cases.

The tremendous increase in litigation has led to several suggestions for reform of the American court system. Some of the suggestions that have been endorsed by Chief Justice Warren Burger include the elimination of some cases from federal jurisdiction, abolishing the requirement that judges preside over all probate cases, and the creation of a national court of appeals. Some reforms have already been implemented; for instance, all federal district judges now have professional court administrators and federal magistrates to assist them in their workload.

Most state judges are elected for a certain term on nonpartisan ballots. In the Northeast, most judges are still appointed by the governor and approved by the legislature. Federal district judges are appointed by the president but are really selected through a process known as senatorial courtesy. Judges to the circuit court of appeals are selected by the president from a list made for him by a special commission, which he appoints. Justices to the Supreme Court of the United States are selected by the president with broad policy considerations in mind. The president will generally pick someone of his own party who shares his philosophical convictions. Presidents often use their power of judicial appointment to send political signals.

For the most part, Americans have a high degree of confidence in their Court system.

Key Terms and Concepts

judicial review
judicial activism
judicial restraint
case or controversy
standing
justiciable
majority opinion
dissenting opinion
municipal courts
superior courts
writ of certiorari

Marbury v. *Madison*
Baker v. *Carr*
Roe v. *Wade*
judicial solution
senatorial courtesy
original jurisdiction
concurrent jurisdiction
appellate jurisdiction
advisory opinions
court administration
litigation explosion

Chapter Outline

Political paradox

The Supreme Court has the final say in interpreting the law but the other two branches determine who sits on the Court.

Some say the Court is the most powerful tribunal ever.

Who gets on the courts plays an important role in what the courts decide.

The idea of judicial election becomes a heated question in light of these facts.

Reagan drew particular criticism toward the beginning of his second term for his method of appointing judges.

Some claimed he sought ideological clones to pack the judiciary.

The Justice Department claimed that it was following the traditional process of finding qualified judges who shared the general ideology of the president appointing them.

Remaking the judiciary

By 1986, Reagan had appointed more judges than any president in history.

Federal courts are an important political institution.

Presidents usually appoint judges who share their political views.

Some judges surprise their supporters and critics.

Most do not.

Reagan has been more meticulous in screening the ideologies of his appointees than have past presidents.

Some question if quality is being sacrificed for ideological compatibility.

Most appointees during Reagan's first term were able legal scholars.

Many appointees during his second term have come under fire.

Courts as political institutions

Judicial review is a key part of their role.

It is the Court's power to review legislative and executive acts, interpret them, and determine their constitutionality.

In an 1803 Supreme Court case, *Marbury* v. *Madison*, judicial review was first exercised.

John Marshall, the chief justice, declared that any law passed by Congress that was "repugnant to the Constitution" would be void.

Hamilton had expressed a rationale for judicial review in *Federalist Paper 78*, but it had never been used until the Court claimed the power in *Marbury*.

With time, judicial review has been used more extensively.

Four-fifths of all federal statutes declared unconstitutional by the Court have been struck down since 1900.

In the last fifty years, most of the legislation struck down has dealt with civil rights and liberties.

Judicial review as practiced by the Supreme Court is peculiar to the United States.

Judicial policy-making

Most of the courts' work involves interpreting legislation.

The extent of judicial policy-making through interpretation depends on the scope and precision of the law being interpreted.

The more precise the law, the less the courts can interpret it.

Making policy by deciding cases

Majority court opinion determines the outcome of the particular case and will be applied in like cases.

Through opinions, courts persuade other political institutions.

Brown v. *Board of Education of Topeka* (1954) is the most important Supreme Court decision in recent years.

It signaled a change in national policy regarding race relations by declaring racially separated schools unconstitutional.

The *Brown* decision is an example of checks and balances and the separation of powers.

Baker v. *Carr* was another landmark case.

Prior to 1962, legislative districts were unequal in population.

Although urban areas suffered from malapportionment, they were too underrepresented to achieve reapportionment.

In *Baker*, the Court held that the failure of the states to equally apportion their representatives was unconstitutional.

In contrast to *Brown*, the Court's prescriptions in *Baker* were immediately fulfilled.

Roe v. *Wade* has been one of the more controversial landmark cases of late.

Abortion presented the Court with a conflict that remains controversial long after being decided.

In *Roe*, the Court ruled that the right to privacy of a woman seeking an abortion needed to be balanced against the prerogative of the state to protect human life.

With these competing values, the Court held that the state could not outlaw abortions in the first trimester of pregnancy.

During the second trimester, the state could regulate abortions as long as they did so in view of the health of the mother.

Finally, in the last trimester, states could outlaw abortion except in cases where the life of the mother was threatened.

The Constitution says nothing specifically about abortion, and so if the Court decides to hear the case it is interpreting law, and thus making policy.

The Court is still divided over the issue, with the split having narrowed to 5-4 with the addition of Sandra Day O'Connor.

Recent developments in judicial intervention
  The tremendous increase in litigation in recent years and the expanding role of government have helped increase judicial activism.
Problems with increased judicial intervention
  Courts are not responsible for the costs of their decision, nor are they accountable to the electorate.
  Because the courts often decide among competing rights, compromise is more difficult.
  Some advocate judicial restraint—refraining from intervening on matters where the Constitution is silent.
The court system of the United States
  It is a dual system with the Supreme Court at the apex of both state and national courts.
  Federal courts include three levels: district courts, courts of appeals, and the Supreme Court.
    Circuit courts were established in 1891.
    Special three-judge district courts were established in 1903.
    Other special courts include the U.S. Court of Appeals for the Federal Circuit, Claims Court, Customs Court, Tax Court, and the Court of Military Appeals.
  State courts conduct the majority of American legal business.
    Each state structures its own system.
    California, with its four tiers, provides a good example of a state system.
      Municipal courts have original jurisdiction in cases involving minor criminal or civil matters.
      Each county is divided up into judicial districts, with judges elected on a nonpartisan ballot for six-year terms.
      The superior courts have original jurisdiction for more serious crimes and civil cases involving more than $15,000.
      They also handle matters involving wills, estates, and juvenile matters.
      Each county has at least one superior court with judges elected for a six-year term on a nonpartisan ballot.
      Superior court decisions are appealed to one of the eleven courts of appeals.
        These judges are elected on nonpartisan ballots for twelve-year terms.
      The state supreme court attempts to maintain uniformity among the various judicial districts.
        Justices are appointed by the governor and then approved by a state commission on judicial appointments.
        At the next general election, their appointment must be approved by the voters, after which they serve a twelve-year term.

Jurisdiction

The Constitution indicates which cases can be heard by federal courts.
If the federal courts have jurisdiction, cases usually originate in the
U.S. district courts.

Concurrent jurisdiction means that a case can be tried by either a federal or a state court.

Exclusive jurisdiction means that only the state or federal court has
jurisdiction.
U.S. district courts have exclusive jurisdiction in all cases involving
bankruptcy and violations of federal criminal laws.
In most cases when a violation of state law occurs, state courts have
exclusive jurisdiction.

How cases reach the U.S. Supreme Court

Most cases reach the Court through one of two processes: *writ of certiorari* or appeal.
Writ of certiorari involves the Court requesting a lower court to
send the records of a case to the higher court for review.
The right of appeal is guaranteed in certain cases involving the
constitutionality of a law.

Special procedures in court actions

The Supreme Court only hears cases that clearly meet certain requirements.
These rules limit judicial intervention and are a way the Court
shows respect for the doctrine of separation of powers.
The Court will refuse to hear a case unless the person who brought
it has standing.
The Court will not take the case if it is not a justiciable one.
The Court also refuses to hear appeals if the matter is not a case or
controversy.
The Court will not issue advisory opinions.

Administration of the federal courts

With the increase in litigation, administration of the federal courts
has become more difficult.

Former Chief Justice Warren Burger suggested a set of reforms intended to reduce the case load of the courts.
He recommended getting federal courts out of cases involving
people from different states.
Another suggestion was to abolish the mandatory appellate jurisdiction of the Supreme Court.

Federal courts have adapted slowly to the explosion of litigation.
Professional court administrators have been allowed to assume
much of the administrative burden.
Congress has been slow to act on other recommendations, such as
Burger's proposal for an inter-circuit tribunal which would relieve
the Supreme Court of much of its burden.

Computers have helped to cope with exponential growth in cases, law, and precedents.

Others recommend diverting several types of cases from the federal courts to state courts and special tribunals.

Selection of judges

Most state judges are elected on nonpartisan ballots.

Some judicial elections are partisan.

Most of New England's judges are appointed by the governor and approved by the legislature.

Federal judges are technically appointed by the president and confirmed by the Senate.

In practice, senatorial courtesy is followed.

Judges on the circuit court of appeals are chosen by the president from a list prepared for him by the United States Circuit Judge Nominating Commission, whose members he appoints.

Supreme Court justices are selected by the president and confirmed by the Senate.

Usually he has leeway in whom he chooses, but occasionally the nominees will be rejected by the Senate.

Routes to the judiciary

Federal court appointees typically are members of the president's political party and share his judicial philosophy.

Presidents may use court appointments to send other kinds of political signals.

Jimmy Carter appointed more women and minorities to the bench than any other president.

Public opinion and the courts

The public is generally pleased with the performance of the courts, excepting their treatment of criminals.

Most people believe the courts are not properly punishing criminals.

Review Questions

COMPLETION

1. The belief that judges should let the people do what they want to do unless the Constitution expressly forbids it is known as _____.

2. When either a federal or a state court has the authority to hear a case, there is _____

3. A higher court uses a _____ to order a lower court to send it the records of a disputed case.

4. For a party to bring a suit he must have suffered personal injury. This is known as _____.

5. The major complaint against American courts by the American public is that they _____.

6. The Court's power to determine the constitutionality of congressional, presidential, or state action is known as _____.

7. The nation that has a power of judicial review most similar to our own is _____.

8. The Court issues its decision in a particular case in a document known as _____.

9. The federal court of original jurisdiction is _____.

10. _____ held that separate school facilities were inherently unequal.

TRUE/FALSE

1. The Judiciary Act of 1789 created the federal court system as it still exists today.
2. Senatorial courtesy does not apply to Democrats when there is a Republican president.
3. The New England states persist in electing their state judges.
4. The Supremacy Clause indicates that the Supreme Court will be at the apex of the dual court system.
5. The principle of judicial review is clearly endorsed in Article 3 of the Constitution.
6. *Marbury* v. *Madison* was the first case in which the Supreme Court found a state law unconstitutional.
7. The court's decision in *Baker* v. *Carr* met with surprisingly rapid compliance.
8. The Superior Court is the name of California's highest state court.
9. The views of the president appointing federal judges are likely to be reflected in the decisions handed down by those jurists.
10. The principle of judicial review came from English common law.

MULTIPLE CHOICE

1. In *Roe* v. *Wade* the court decided that
   a. abortions could be restricted at no time by the states.
   b. abortions could be restricted at any time by the states.
   c. abortions could be permitted only in the third trimester of pregnancy.
   d. states could restrict abortions only in the second and third trimester of pregnancy.
   e. states could restrict abortions only in the first and second trimester of pregnancy.

2. Z feels bad that A who lives on her block is always cheating B. She files suit against A on B's behalf. The court refuses to hear the suit because
   a. it is not justiciable.
   b. Z has no standing.
   c. there is no real controversy.
   d. Z has failed to fulfill the requirements of a class action suit.
   e. A has not broken the law.

3. Bob and Charles have invented a game. They cannot decide how they should split the profits should the game prove a success. They decide to file a friendly law suit to let the court decide upon an equitable division. The court refuses to accept the case because
   a. there is no real controversy.
   b. neither Bob nor Charles has standing.
   c. the case is not justiciable.
   d. they have failed to comply with the requirements of a class action suit.
   e. the game would have not made any profits.

4. Justice Burger has suggested that in order to lighten the load on the federal judiciary we might
   a. abolish class action suits.
   b. allow state courts to hear bankruptcy cases.
   c. create forty more federal judicial districts.
   d. eliminate diversity of citizenship cases from exclusive federal jurisdiction.
   e. establish a new federal property court.

5. The U.S. Supreme Court heard a case last term that it did not receive on appeal or from a writ of certiorari. The case must have
   a. involved a constitutional question.
   b. included the U.S. government as a party to the suit.
   c. come from the court's original jurisdiction.
   d. involved two other countries.
   e. been an advisory opinion for the Senate.

6. The Constitution says nothing explicitly about a right to privacy, yet today's courts have interpreted the Constitution to grant such a right implicitly. Such an interpretation might be an example of
   a. judicial passivity.
   b. judicial restraint.
   c. judicial inconsistency.
   d. judicial activism.
   e. judicial rectitude.

7. A conservative president appoints a justice to the Supreme Court who is committed to judicial restraint. Such an appointment would be
   a. consistent with what other conservative presidents have done in the past.
   b. inconsistent with what other conservative presidents have done in the past.
   c. good judicial policy.
   d. a strong signal for affirmative action in the judiciary.
   e. an historical precedent.

8. The state court of original trial jurisdiction for more serious crimes in California is
   a. the municipal court.
   b. the district court.
   c. the superior court.
   d. the state appeals court.
   e. the Supreme Court.

9. In appointing predominantly conservative judges, Reagan has
   a. displayed unusually partisan behavior.
   b. acted similarly to his predecessors.
   c. violated the independence of the judicial branch.
   d. been more meticulous in the ideological screening of judges.
   e. both *a* and *c*.
   f. both *b* and *d*.

10. The majority of American legal business is handled by
   a. federal district courts.
   b. the U.S. Supreme Court.
   c. state courts of original jurisdiction.
   d. U.S. circuit courts of appeal.
   e. federal magistrates.

ANSWER KEY

Completion

1. judicial restraint p. 274
2. concurrent jurisdiction p. 279
3. writ of certiorari p. 280
4. standing p. 281
5. are too lenient on criminals p. 291
6. judicial review p. 258
7. Canada p. 262
8. an opinion p. 263
9. the federal district court p. 275
10. *Brown* v. *Board of Education of Topeka* p. 264

True/False

1. F p. 276
2. T p. 287
3. F p. 286
4. F p. 275
5. F p. 259
6. F p. 260
7. T p. 269
8. F p. 278
9. T p. 256
10. F p. 259

Multiple Choice

1. d p. 270
2. b p. 281
3. a p. 281
4. d p. 283
5. c p. 280
6. d p. 273
7. a p. 274
8. c p. 278
9. f p. 256
10. c p. 268

1. Assess the consequences of the following procedures on American courts: jurisdiction, standing, justiciable case, precedent. How would the federal government be different if the court offered advisory opinions, was not concerned about jurisdiction, etc.
2. Some scholars argue that the courts are the most powerful branch because of judicial review. Define judicial review and assess its importance in American politics.

Further Investigation

Abraham, Henry J. *The Judicial Process.* 4th ed. New York: Oxford University Press, 1980.

A highly respected treatment of the federal courts, how they are organized and function.

Abraham, Henry J. *Justices and Presidents.* New York: Oxford University Press, 1974.

Analysis of the process of judicial appointment.

Auerbach, Jerrold. *Unequal Justice.* New York: Oxford University Press, 1976.

Critical study of the legal profession's lack of concern for securing equal justice.

Cardozo, Benjamin N. *The Nature of the Judicial Process.* New Haven: Yale University Press, 1921.

Landmark book on judicial thinking.

Cox, Archibald, ed. *The Role of the Supreme Court in American Government.* New York: Oxford University Press, 1978.

Essays on the role of the Supreme Court in American government.

Jacob, Herbert. *Justice in America: Courts, Lawyers and the Judicial Process.* 3rd ed. Boston: Little, Brown, 1978.

An examination of the judicial process at all levels, incorporating research from sociology, psychology, and political science.

McCloskey, Robert G. *The American Supreme Court.* Chicago: University of Chicago Press, 1960.

A history of the Supreme Court and its impact on America.

Woodward, Bob, and Armstrong, Scott. *The Brethren: Inside the Supreme Court.* New York: Simon and Schuster, 1979.

Two investigative reporters report on their extensive interviews with those who have worked in and around the court. Although not scholarly in focus, the book does discuss how the court functions as a political institution.

Applying Political Science

1. One form of political participation that is rarely studied is jury service. How are jurors selected in your community? By what means are they enpaneled? Why are some jurors removed from the jury? What impact does jury duty have on participants? To answer these questions you will need to interview the clerk of your local court system, the local prosecutor and defense attorneys, and perhaps even some jurors.
2. Generally speaking, only attorneys can be judges. Is this a good idea? What aspects of legal training or experience can be cited as reasons for the exclusion of nonlawyers from judicial service? To answer these questions visit your local law school and/or interview recent law graduates or practicing attorneys.
3. Attend court and observe a trial or proceeding. You can choose anything from a small claims court to a major felony or civil trial. How is the proceeding conducted? Why? What does the judge do? Why? If possible, interview some of the participants afterward to determine their thoughts on the process.

10 | Separation of Powers

Overview

The separation of powers is unique to American democracy. In parliamentary democracies, such as Britain's, there is no division between the executive and legislative branches. Instead, the executive derives its authority from the legislative.

Because of the separation of powers, American government has a large number of officials who can influence policy-making. This dispersement of power accounts for the fractious and decentralized nature of policy-making in the U.S., as exemplified by the seven-month-long battle of the budget in Congress during 1986. Such a battle demonstrates the continual need for compromise in a system with separation of powers.

Critics have been pointing out the weaknesses of this system for a century. Modern advocates of reform claim that the system's inadequacies are especially detrimental in an age of big government. They have offered various proposals aimed at reducing the autonomy of the executive and legislative branches and increasing the ability of the government to cope with complex problems in a coherent manner.

Others acknowledge that the current system has its weaknesses, but claim that would-be reformers exaggerate the flaws. While some change may be necessary, they argue, tampering with such an intertwined array of institutions is bound to have more than just the intended effects. The American public in general seems very hesitant to sacrifice some of the safeguards provided by the separation of powers, so radical departure from the present system seems unlikely.

Key Terms and Concepts

separation of powers
parliamentary democracies

lowest common denominator
political accountability

budget process   individualism in Congress
lines of influence   role of the cabinet

Chapter Outline

Separation of powers
  The Constitution separates the three branches of government in
    significant ways, yet still requires them to work together.
The federal budget: separation of powers in action
  The budget process is an excellent case study for examining the effects
    of the separation of powers.
    Separating powers results in an enormous dispersement of power
      among officials.
    There is a huge number of independent actors involved in
      policy-making.
    Other countries usually have just a few such officials.
Policy-making in Britain
  There are some similarities between the process in Britain and in
    the U.S.
    In both countries public opinion and interest groups (via lobbying)
      play a role.
  There are many more differences.
    In Britain, power is concentrated in a small group of party leaders.
      They exercise tight discipline over party members in the House of
        Commons, which has official responsibility for the budget.
      If the prime minister and her cabinet remain unified, they can
        pass almost any measure just as they have drafted it.
The making of the budget in the United States, 1986
  While both the U.S. and Britain are stable democracies, their budget
    processes differ drastically.
  In Britain, direct authority and control are highly concentrated.
  In the U.S., power is so dispersed that the system is enormously
    complex.
Act 1: the president proposes
  On February 4, 1985, Reagan sent his budget to Capitol Hill.
    The message was only 3,000 words.
    The budget was five volumes.
    It basically continued the trends of the previous four years,
      including a $180 billion deficit.
  The administration's budget must reconcile competing claims of the
    various departments and agencies.
Act 2: Congress reacts
  Legally, the president's budget proposals are nothing more than
    suggestions.

They still carry much weight.

Congress didn't particularly like Reagan's 1986 budget, especially the large deficit.

Democrats were especially upset about proposed cuts in domestic programs.

Act 3: House Democrats' uncertain call

By virtue of their large majority, House Democrats were assured a major role in the 1986 budget process.

Divergent views and lack of discipline within the party made it impossible for Democrats to agree on an alternative.

Reagan was no longer able to call upon the coalition of Republicans and conservative Democrats that passed the budget in 1981.

Democrats attempted to simultaneously curb government's growth and protect domestic programs.

Act 4: Senate Republicans scramble

With a majority in the Senate, the White House and Senate Republicans tried to cooperate.

They formed a working group to resolve differences.

Still they disagreed on some significant issues.

Senate Republicans disagreed among themselves.

Their budget plan came apart on the Senate floor.

Act 5: Senate Republicans agree . . . barely

On May 10, 1986, the Republicans finally passed their budget by a one-vote margin.

Act 6: House Democrats pass their budget resolution

Their bill, guided through by Rep. William Gray, provided for the same deficit but in a different way.

More was cut from defense and less from social programs.

Act 7: On to conference

House and Senate negotiators disbanded in anger on June 25.

Even after reconvening they remained deadlocked.

Act 8: "Ron" and "Tip" agree

After a month's impasse, Reagan and O'Neill struck a deal that infuriated Senate Republicans.

The compromise called for adopting the House's approach to Social Security and the Senate's approach to defense spending.

Act 9: The House/Senate split

Even after the deal had been made, legislators remained split—along House/Senate lines.

Act 10: Agreement on a budget resolution

The final budget, adopted on August 1, found the "lowest common denominator" in all of the different proposals.

It made everyone somewhat unhappy.

The case for reform
   Separation of powers creates a frustrating, though not necessarily
      bad, situation.
   Critics over the last one hundred years, including Woodrow Wilson,
      have noted the shortcomings of the separation of powers.
   Critics today make similar observations.
      They argue that the system does not demand political accountability.
         The high federal deficits of the 1980s are an example of this,
            since they persist despite the opposition of virtually all
            politicians.
         The politicians all blame each other—with some degree of
            justification.
      They also argue that it hinders the president's ability to lead
         the country.
         Lloyd Cutler, an aide to President Carter, contrasted the ability
            of Margaret Thatcher to legislate her program with Carter's
            inability to do the same, despite larger margins of support in
            Congress.
      Critics point out how difficult the separation of powers makes it to
         develop coherent policies.
         Coherent policies are essential, insist critics, given the size and
            scope of our government today.
   Separation of powers refers primarily to the independence of the
      executive and legislative branches.
      It also applies to division within the legislative branch itself.
         Congressional reforms of the late 1960s and 1970s have enhanced
            the individuality of members of Congress.
Proposals for change
   Critics have looked longingly at parliamentary government,
      particularly as it is found in Great Britain.
   No one urges a complete replacement of the present constitutional
      system
   Such a change is virtually a political impossibility.
   Separation of powers is an important American tradition.
   Critics advocate moderate reforms.
      Some propose that, in presidential years, voters be required to vote
         for a president, vice president, and member of the House from
         the same party.
      Others simply propose that representatives be elected only every
         four years, at the same times as the president.
         While such proposals would undoubtedly remove some of the
            independence in congressional/presidential relations, they
            might also force voters to choose candidates they otherwise
            would not have picked.

Another proposal would amend the Constitution to require the
president to appoint fifty percent of his cabinet from among his
party's members of Congress.

Another proposal would give the president power to call for new
congressional elections once during his term.

This would give him power to break impasses, but it also poses
many technical difficulties.

Another proposal would give an extraordinary majority in Congress
the ability to call for new presidential elections.

Another odd combination of two different systems, this proposal
also poses many difficult problems.

The Committee on the Constitutional System has reviewed these
proposals.

Obvious problems

The issue is not whether or not the present system is perfect.

All the actors involved get frustrated periodically.

Gramm-Rudman-Hollings was an effort by Congress and the
president to overcome problems inherent to the separation
of powers.

The Supreme Court struck down one of the law's key provisions
as unconstitutional, calling it a violation of the separation of
powers.

The question is not whether or not anything should be done, but
whether or not the Constitution should be amended.

Separation of powers blocks unwise action

When FDR proposed packing the Supreme Court in 1937, his plan
was defeated even by a heavily Democratic Senate.

This is one of the best examples of the advantages provided by the
separation of powers.

Arthur Schlesinger argues that our problem is not a lack of ability to
implement good solutions, but rather a lack of good solutions.

He claims that the delays often caused by our system are beneficial.

Much has been done

Given the accomplishments of government in the last fifty years, it is
difficult to believe that it is a helpless giant paralyzed by the
separation of powers.

Reformers sometimes exaggerate the weaknesses of the U.S. system
and the strength of parliamentary systems.

A responsive system

The president is far from feeble.

In Britain the prime minister must be concerned about the approval of
his cabinet but not Parliament.

In the U.S., the president must be concerned about the approval of
Congress but not his cabinet.

The separation of powers has made Congress the most powerful
legislature in the world.

It is a democratic phenomenon.

Proceed with caution

The constitutional system has served us well for over two
hundred years.

It is an integrated set of institutions based on a sweeping political
philosophy.

It is difficult to tinker with certain parts of such a system without
affecting others.

Americans should proceed with caution.

Some minor changes might be beneficial.

We might amend the Constitution so as to *allow* the president to
appoint cabinet members from the ranks of Congress.

Another proposal would be to make former presidents members
of the U.S. Senate *ex-officio*.

We should at least agree with Woodrow Wilson that a willingness to
consider changing the Constitution should not be perceived as
disloyalty to it.

Review Questions

COMPLETION

1. In Great Britain, public opinion and interest-group pressure are

   directed at a _____.

2. While indirect influence is dispersed widely across British society,

   _____ are highly concentrated.

3. The separation of powers, as used in Ladd's discussion, refers

   especially to the _____.

4. The inefficiency inherent to a system involving the separation of
   powers is compounded by the fact that Congress and the White

   House are often _____.

5. The defeat by the Democrat-controlled Congress of FDR's court-

   packing plan is impressive testimony to the _____.

6. Reformers seem to overstate the _____ in the American system.

7. Ladd would consider a constitutional amendment that would make

   appointing members of Congress as cabinet members a _____

   rather than a _____.

TRUE/FALSE

1. Public opinion does not really play a role in Britain's budget process since it is a parliamentary democracy.
2. The greatest virtue of the fiscal 1986 budget was that it made everyone somewhat unhappy.
3. Woodrow Wilson's criticisms of the separation of powers are quite applicable today.
4. Congressional reforms of the last twenty years have done much to overcome the problems caused by the separation of powers.
5. Margaret Thatcher is better able to get her programs passed into law because her party has a larger margin of majority in parliament than did President Carter's in Congress.
6. It is not clear that the United States has been badly served by the division of authority, the sharing of responsibility, and the slowing of action that separation of powers encourages.
7. The British prime minister, unlike the U.S. president, need not be concerned about either her cabinet or the legislature (Parliament).
8. Ladd feels the Constitution should not be tampered with.

MULTIPLE CHOICE

1. The key effect of separation of powers is
   a. ineffective government.
   b. dispersion of power among government officials.
   c. endless and bitter feuds among the branches.
   d. a judiciary unresponsive to public opinion.
2. Which of the following best characterizes the president's budget proposal?
   a. the first step in the budget process as outlined by the Constitution.
   b. a binding result of legislative compromise.
   c. a document given little heed by Congress.
   d. a set of suggestions carrying a lot of weight.
3. Woodrow Wilson's critique of the separation of powers did not include which of the following?
   a. It leads to a weak government.
   b. It leads to an inefficient government.
   c. It forces the president to conduct foreign policy virtually unassisted by Congress.
   d. It creates a cumbersome government.
   e. It does not provide for political accountability.

4. Separation of powers refers
   a. to the autonomy of the three branches of government.
   b. especially to the independence of the executive and legislative branches.
   c. even to divisions within the legislative branch itself
   d. all of the above
   e. only *a* and *b*

5. Proposals for reforming the present system have included
   a. changing the terms of congressmen to four years.
   b. replacing our system with one modeled after Great Britain's.
   c. electing president, vice president, and congressman on the same ballot.
   d. all of the above
   e. only *a* and *c*

6. According to Ladd, large federal budget deficits can best be explained by
   a. inability of government—caused by the separation of powers—to react coherently to a problem.
   b. incompetent government leaders.
   c. disagreement within the parties as to what should be done.
   d. special interest dominance of the legislative process.

7. Which of the following does Ladd consider possible ways of improving the current system?
   a. lengthening the terms of representatives to four years.
   b. making former presidents members of the Senate *ex-officio*.
   c. allowing the president to appoint members of Congress to his Cabinet.
   d. all of the above
   e. only *b* and *c*
   f. only *a* and *c*

ANSWER KEY

Completion

1. small, disciplined group of officials   p. 296
2. direct authority and control   p. 297
3. executive and legislative branches   p. 306
4. controlled by opposing parties   p. 305
5. strength of American commitment to separation of powers   p. 313
6. incapacities for action   p. 314
7. permitted option, requirement p. 316

True/False

1. F   p. 296
2. T   p. 303
3. T   p. 304
4. F   pp. 306–7
5. F   p. 306
6. T   p. 314
7. F   p. 314
8. F   p. 315

Multiple Choice

1. b   p. 295
2. d   p. 299
3. c   p. 304
4. d   p. 306

5. e   pp. 308–9
6. c   p. 314
7. e   pp. 308, 315

ESSAY QUESTIONS

1. What are some reasons why a unitary form of government like that of Great Britain might be preferred to a system of separation of powers? What are some of the limitations of the unitary or parliamentary system of government?
2. One of the charges frequently leveled against the separation of powers is that it is not sufficiently responsive to the public. Evaluate this charge in light of the Reagan presidency.

Further Investigation

Polsby, Nelson W. *Congress and the Presidency.* 4th ed. Englewood Cliffs, N.J.: Prentice Hall, 1986.

Examines the relationship between the executive and legislative branches in both theory and practice.

Burns, James MacGregor. *Deadlock of Democracy.* Englewood Cliffs, N.J.: Prentice Hall, 1963.

One of the most enduring books on the subject. Burns' thesis is that the result of the separation of powers is a government unable to act.

Sundquist, James L. *Constitutional Reform and Effective Government.* Washington, D.C.: Brookings Institution, 1986.

Like Burns, Sundquist thinks the separation of powers needs some reform.

Light, Paul. *Artful Work: The Politics of Social Security Reform.* New York: Random House, 1985.

The reform of Social Security required collaboration between the White House and the Congress. Light describes how this was accomplished.

Applying Political Science

1. Visit the local office of your congressman or U.S. senator and discuss with the staff what if any benefits result from the separation of powers for your district? Does the representative bargain with the president? Also ask the staff what differences they think

would result if some of the reforms discussed by Ladd in this chapter were implemented.

2. The separation of powers principle is applied in varying degrees in local governments. Visit your city council or county government and observe the relationship between the executive and legislative branches at this level. Determine the extent to which the national model of separation of powers exists here. What lessons can you learn from this comparison about the allocation of power in different institutional arrangements? To what extent does the local division of powers meet the objections of Lloyd Cutler and the other critics of separation of powers as reviewed by Ladd?

11 | Federalism

Overview

American Federalism stemmed from the desire of the founding fathers to form a union where power is assigned both to a central government and to governments of the states. The Constitution provides an explicit guide to the provisions of federalism. These provisions can be divided into five categories: those relating to the powers of the states, to the powers of the national government, to the restrictions on states, to federal guarantees to states, and to interstate relations. While the Constitution provides an explicit guide to its provisions, it has always been dynamic, as exemplified by the controversy over who should set speed limits. Determining where responsibilities and authority begin and end for each of federalism's two levels is one of the most demanding tasks in the American federal system.

In the early nineteenth century, the states were more powerful and jealously guarded their prerogatives. The idea of states' rights fluorished and is exemplified by the doctrines of nullification and secession. But the Civil War established beyond debate the permanence of the federal union and the preeminence of the national government. In addition, the Civil War marked the beginning of the transition to the new age of industrialization and technology. These changes created a greater need for an expanded national government with powers to establish regulatory legislation.

The nationalization of American politics grew following World War I and reached new levels with the New Deal. In this era the national government claimed responsibility for smoothing out business cycles, preventing excessive unemployment, promoting economic growth — in short, for maintaining and extending prosperity. By enlarging the grants-in-aid program, the national government was able to pursue its goal of extending prosperity. Use of federal grants continued to increase until Ronald Reagan took office.

Federalism is a politically "charged" subject that divides the parties. Although Ronald Reagan's "New Federalism" has not gotten very far, it does not mean that the idea of shifting greater responsibility to state and local governments is doomed to failure. Others believe that only the national govern-ment is equipped to deal with these problems and all that federalism needs to provide is more effective administration. Given these divergent viewpoints, it is easy to see why federalism remains controversial.

Key Terms and Concepts

federalism

selective incorporation

nullification

dual federalism

categorical grants

revenue sharing

confederal

Fourteenth Amendment

secession

states' rights

pluralism

"boundary disputes"

Chapter Outline

Problems of federalism

The 55 m.p.h. speed limit is a good example of conflicts that arise under this system.

Many states resent the federal government imposing such a speed limit on them.

Where national and state governments responsibilities overlap, it is often difficult to sort them out.

Domain of the states

Few matters were originally seen as requiring uniform national action.

Most were subject to the *police powers* of the states.

Cars obviously weren't around in 1789.

When they did come along, state governments enacted laws dealing with them.

Setting speed limits is a function of the states.

National action

Congress saw an exception to this rule as necessary when it made the 55 m.p.h. speed limit in 1973–74 to deal with the Arab oil embargo. Some objected.

Concern for the energy problem outweighed concern for the states.

Congress didn't actually set the speed limit.

States now receive a significant portion of highway funds from the federal government.

States were told they would not receive funds if they failed to set their speed limits appropriately.

It worked.

Politics and perceptions

The energy situation changed by 1986.

OPEC had lost clout.

Oil prices were down.

Public opinion less staunchly favored the speed limit than it once had. More drivers sped.

States were weaker in enforcing the law.

Constitutional federalism is dynamic, modified continually by historical experience and public opinion.

Federalism: An enduring American innovation

Samuel Beer states that "at Philadelphia in 1787 . . . the Americans invented federalism."

The European schools of political thought, on which the framers depended, ignored the issue of federalism.

Federalism was a necessary consequence of the founders' consensus that there should be a strong national government and that the states should continue to have major political roles and power.

Since 1787, approximately twenty countries have adopted federal systems.

Constitutional provisions of federalism

There are five categories of constitutional provisions of federalism.

Powers of the states

The Senate preserves power of the states because each state, despite its population, has an equal voice.

Each state is constitutionally allowed to determine how its members of the electoral college will be chosen.

States play a key role in amending the Constitution.

After Congress has proposed amendments to the Constitution by a two-thirds vote, the amendments are submitted to the state legislatures, where at least three-fourths of the legislatures must ratify them.

Legislatures of two-thirds of the states represent enough to call for a convention to propose amendments.

The Tenth Amendment provides, "The powers not delegated to the United States by the Constitution, nor prohibited by it to the states, are reserved to the states respectively or to the people."

Supreme Court interpretations of this amendment have varied with time.

Powers of the national government

"The Congress shall have power . . . to make all laws which shall be necessary and proper for carrying into execution the foregoing powers, and all other powers vested by this Constitution in the government of the United States, or in any department or officer thereof."

The Constitution and the laws made under it are "the supreme law of the Land," and it requires state judges to uphold these provisions, "anything in the Constitution or laws of any state to the contrary notwithstanding."

The Constitution imposes a number of prohibitions on states.

Five post-Civil War amendments impose further prohibitions on the states.

The Constitution also guarantees the states certain things such as uniformity of taxes levied by Congress.

It also states that "full faith and credit" shall be given by every state to the laws and actions of every other state.

Evolution of American federalism

Most government activity before the Civil War was at the state and local levels.

The idea of states' rights flourished.

The doctrine of nullification, that states could review federal laws and even declare them null, was proposed by John Calhoun.

Secession meant that a state could withdraw from the union if its demands were unacceptable.

Dual federalism stressed the powers reserved to the states and the limited mandate of the national government.

McCulloch v. *Maryland* (1819) was a victory for the advocates of a broader national role.

The Civil War and its aftermath

The Civil War marked a transition to a larger role for national government.

Doctrines like nullification and secession died with the Confederacy.

The Fourteenth Amendment eventually gave "roving authority" to the feds "to invalidate state statutes."

The U.S. shifted from a rural, localized society to an industrial, interconnected one.

The industrial revolution led to demands for greater national government involvement in regulatory legislation.

The New Deal years

World War I marked an era of further federal expansion.

Increases in government tend to reflect sociopolitical eras rather than the programs of a particular administration.

Under FDR, the federal government expanded much further.

It assumed welfare functions.

It also took responsibility for the business cycle and its ramifications.

Interdependence created problems of a national character.

Federalism became cooperative instead of dual.

Federalism in the modern era

Technology has made possible a national cultural life.

Public opinion is becoming more uniform nationally.

Beginning in the 1950s, claims of national citizenship challenged racial discrimination.

The attack on segregation became an attack on federalism.

Federalism had made it possible for states to perpetuate racial discrimination.

As the claims of national citizenship have grown stronger, and the role
of the national government has been enlarged, states have been left
in an awkward position.

They have been left with a feeble, largely administrative status.

The volume of new national legislation testified to the erosion of
the states' position.

Supreme Court decisions have also enlarged the role of the federal
government.

Grants-in-Aid

Before the Depression, Congress made grant funds available for only a
few clearly national functions such as the building of roads.

During the Depression, various new grant programs were added to
cover additional services.

Expanded use of federal grant programs continued until some
authorities concluded that there were about five hundred of them
when Reagan took office.

The Reagan administration has halted this steady increase.

Types of grants

There are four types of grant-in-aid programs.

Categorical grants are funds provided for a particular category
of service.

Project grants are funds provided for various grants to projects.

Block grants are funds provided to state and local governments for
services in broad program areas.

Revenue sharing was the system of federal granting with the fewest
strings.

States and municipalities could use their revenue-sharing monies
as they saw fit.

Reagan phased out this type of grant.

Overload of the federal system

The two parties disagree on the proper role of the national
government in federalism.

There is a growing consensus, however, for the findings of the
Advisory Commission on Intergovernmental Relations (ACIR).

It believes that federalism swung too far to the national side during
the sixties and seventies.

It maintains that the national government should take full
responsibilities for some programs, such as Aid to Families with
Dependent Children (AFDC), and should phase out others better
handled by state and local governments.

Others admit that administrative problems have developed but
maintain that a strong centralized government is best equipped to
meet the demands of an increasingly nationalized society.

The Reagan proposals for a new federalism

President Reagan urged a "new day" for federalism.

The new federalism would swap Medicaid for AFDC, leaving
states with responsibility for the latter.
The idea did not go far because of the political tension that resulted
from mixing two sets of objectives.
The administration sought to get budget cuts and transfer duties to
states simultaneously.
Despite new federalism proposals being on the backburner, states have
gained influence through Reagan's block-grant setup.
The equity issue
States vary in resources.
No system for new national-state relations will be viable if it does
not provide for fiscal equalization among states of unequal
resources.
The future of federalism
The built-in lobby of state and local officials provides a good
safeguard for the existence of federalism.
There is also an intellectual argument for federalism.
It promotes freedom.
It preserves pluralism.
It allows for experimentation.
State and local governments are closer to the people and perceived
as more responsive to their needs.

Review Questions

COMPLETION

1. Setting speed limits is a _____.
2. Southern governors like Orval Faubus and George Wallace

proclaimed their _____ to continue to discriminate against
blacks.

3. South Carolinian John C. Calhoun loudly espoused the _____.

4. Using the _____ as its basis, the Supreme Court selectively incorporated key provisions of the first eight amendments making them
applicable to the states.

5. Article II, Section 1, delineates a state role in _____.

6. The Supreme Court case _____ is celebrated as advancing the
cause of the advocates for a broader national role.

7. Dual federalism stressed the reserved powers of the _____

compared with the limited mandate of the _____.

8. Today, _____ countries have federal systems.

106

1. Federalism makes experimentation and policy innovation more difficult.
2. In the modern world, the federal system is found only in the United States.
3. The doctrine of nullification allowed states to invalidate federal laws and was accepted practice during the early republic.
4. In *McCulloch* v. *Maryland* (1819), Chief Justice John Marshall and the court came down on the side of states' rights.
5. National supremacy was not firmly established in this country until after the Civil War.
6. Early laws concerning automobiles were enacted at the national level.
7. States' rights were established after the Civil War as part of the Reconstructionist period.
8. The Supreme Court has been an advocate of limited national power.
9. Grant-in-aid programs began during World War II with the ration tickets program.

MULTIPLE CHOICE

1. The four types of grants-in-aid include
   a. categorical grants, project grants, block grants, and research grants.
   b. categorical grants, research grants, block grants, and revenue sharing.
   c. research grants, block grants, Medicaid, and revenue sharing.
   d. revenue sharing, categorical grants, block grants, and project grants.
2. The _____ Amendment requires that no state deny to its citizens the right to vote.
   a. Twenty-sixth
   b. Thirteenth
   c. Fifteenth
   d. Nineteenth
3. Nullification has been associated with the South and its struggle
   a. to maintain slavery.
   b. to increase its cotton industry.
   c. to maintain the presidency.
   d. to have General Lee surrender.
4. The prohibitions against the states listed in Article I include
   a. they cannot pass any "bill of attainder," but may pass "ex post facto law."
   b. they may pass "bill of attainder," but not pass "ex post facto law."
   c. they cannot pass any "bill of attainder" or "ex post facto law."
   d. none of the above

5. Congress passed legislation to lower the maximum speed limit to 55 miles per hour
   a. to increase highway safety.
   b. in the national interest of encouraging fuel conservation
   c. in 1977.
   d. all of the above.
   e. both *a* and *b*.

6. Which of the following has been phased out under Reagan?
   a. revenue sharing
   b. block grants
   c. categorical grants
   d. project grants
   e. none of the above

7. Revenue sharing was initiated under President
   a. Eisenhower.
   b. Kennedy.
   c. Johnson.
   d. Nixon.
   e. Reagan.

8. Most of the largest nations in the world have
   a. unitary systems.
   b. communist systems.
   c. widely varied systems.
   d. federal systems.

9. Proponents of the doctrine of dual federalism saw the system as composed of two tiers:
   a. national government supreme and state governments subordinate.
   b. the state and federal governments acting cooperatively.
   c. the states and the national government in a competitive relationship.
   d. the federal government and local government bypassing the state's.

ANSWER KEY

Completion

1. state function   p. 320
2. states' rights   p. 338
3. doctrine of nullification p. 331
4. Fourteenth Amendment p. 339
5. the selection of president p. 326
6. *McCulloch* v. *Maryland* p. 331
7. states; national government p. 331
8. approximately twenty   p. 325

True/False

1. F   p. 355
2. F   p. 325
3. T   p. 331
4. F   p. 332
5. T   p. 331
6. F   p. 320
7. F   p. 331
8. F   p. 339
9. F   p. 340

Multiple Choice

1. d	p. 343	
2. c	p. 329	
3. a	p. 331	
4. c	p. 329	

5. b	p. 320
6. a	p. 346
7. d	p. 346
8. d	p. 325
9. c	p. 331

ESSAY QUESTIONS

1. Based upon your reading of the period before the Constitutional Convention, why was federalism a necessary part of the founders' plan? What are examples of federalism in the U.S. Constitution, in our national politics, in our culture?
2. Professor Ladd argues that the two world wars nationalized American politics. What was the consequence of this change for federalism? Describe the relationship between the states and federal government today.

Further Investigation

Advisory Commission on Intergovernmental Relations. *An Agenda for American Federalism: Restoring Confidence and Competence.* Washington, D.C.: Government Printing Office, 1981.
Final volume of an eleven-volume set on federalism.
Elazar, Daniel J. *American Federalism: A View from the States.* 2d ed. New York: Crowell, 1972.
A widely cited study that includes an analysis of political culture in the American states.
Pressman, Jeffrey, and Wildavsky, Aaron. *Implementation.* Rev. ed. Berkeley: University of California Press, 1980.
Examines the ways in which intergovernmental relations and bureaucratic politics complicate the implementation of federal programs in Oakland, California.
Reagan, Michael O., and Sanzone, John G. *The New Federalism.* 2d ed. New York: Oxford University Press, 1981.
Examines the history of federalism in the United States, questioning traditional definitions of federalism, and describes how American federalism works in practice.
Sharkansky, Ira. *The Maligned States: Policy Accomplishments, Problems, and Opportunities.* New York: McGraw-Hill, 1972.
Emphasizes the strengths and accomplishments of state governments.

Walker, David. *Toward a Functioning Federalism*. Cambridge, Mass.:
Winthrop, 1981.
> The author, from his vantage point as executive director of the
> Advisory Commission on Intergovernmental Relations, provides an
> assessment for contemporary federalism and proposals for
> improving it.

Applying Political Science

1. The United States is not the only federal country. Canada also
   practices federalism. Read about Canadian government to see the
   similarities and differences between American and Canadian federalism.
2. One way to understand the complex network of government relationships is to study a single policy area and ascertain what the national, state, and local governments are doing in that area. Take
   medical care—what are each of the areas of government doing
   here? Inquire of local health care providers, public health agencies,
   and interest groups. Why has the process not been simplified? A
   second area to examine would be elementary and secondary
   education.
3. As you will have noted from the further investigation readings,
   some observers believe the state and local governments are enjoying
   a resurgence. Develop a set of hypotheses that would support that
   argument and then try and find out whether they are true.

12 | Public Opinion

Overview

Democracy and public opinion go hand in hand; democratic representatives must know the opinions of their constituency in order for democracy to operate properly. Various ideas circulate as to the role of public opinion within a democracy. It is also difficult to ascertain precisely what the public's stand on any given matter is, as exemplified by its ambivalence and even conflicting positions on abortion. Some critics advocate the expansion of public opinion while others see many dangers inherent in mass public opinion. Often, public opinion is seen as a manifestation of manipulation by specially trained people to advance their personal interests. The public is viewed as helpless and too susceptible to demagoguery. Elections have been criticized for relying too heavily upon advertising and other techniques to convince voters to elect a certain candidate or adopt a certain position.

In order for public opinion to hold a place in democracy, the public must be informed. Survey research has revealed that most people are not only unaware but also not interested in the specifics of policies. However, not all policies are suitable for referendum vote. Generally speaking, the public knows general values of public policy but is usually uninformed as to specifics of policy. These values remain constant over time, but the attitudes toward specific policies vary over time and appear inconsistent. To some degree public opinion is ambivalent, especially in respect to the role of government and the subject of a nuclear freeze.

The influence of polling has increased with the new technology of computers. Public opinion has become a statistical exercise. Polling has become especially important to social scientists, the media, and political campaigns. Polls are not always an accurate representation of the truth. The experience of the *Literary Digest* is an example of poor sampling that leads to an inaccurate poll. Respected pollsters now use random samples and well-designed questionnaires. However, it is still necessary to examine polls carefully before accepting their results. Polls are faced by unavoidable time and space

110

constraints, which limit their usefulness in some areas. Exit polls have been viewed as an obstruction to proper electoral processes. Sometimes polls are distorted by sponsors to show what is favorable to them. Question wording requires utmost care to assess opinion fairly.

Americans, although recently suffering from a crisis of confidence in the government, are generally proud of their country. The problems and events of the 1960s and 1970s were trying on the nation's confidence, but most people are satisfied with the United States and continue to have high national expectations.

Key Terms and Concepts

public opinion vs. private
    opinion
attitudes
sampling frame
core values
systematic polling
demographic groups
ambivalence

opinions
values
false consciousness
statistically random
nuclear freeze
exit polls
caveat emptor
random digit dialing

Chapter Outline

Complexity and importance of public opinion
    Public opinion must be respected in a democracy, even if it is sometimes subordinated to minority rights.
    Deciphering public opinion and translating it into public policy can be difficult.
    The issue of abortion demonstrates this point well.
    The public is often ambivalent in its opinions.
Public opinion and democratic government
    Public opinion is the aggregate of citizens' personal views on public matters.
    It is comprised of opinions, attitudes, and values.
The debate over role
    James Bryce foresaw an expanded role for public opinion in democracy.
        Perhaps it could even bypass the representative institutions.
        The advent of polling seemed to make this possible.
    Others, such as Walter Lippmann, warn of the dangers of rule by public opinion.
        The mass public is uninformed about the specifics on issues.
        There is confusion about the proper role of public opinion.

Can public opinion be manipulated?

Many argue that the public is too susceptible to demagogues like Hitler.

Those on both ends of the spectrum harbor such fears.

Some argue that the establishment can manufacture a "false consciousness."

Even supporters of democracy maintain that public opinion can be altered with good techniques.

Public relations specialists play an increasingly important role in elections.

Many see no difference between selling products and selling candidates.

They have no qualms about affecting public opinion about candidates through advertising techniques.

It is clear that public opinion can be manipulated to some extent, but the question about its degree of autonomy remains.

Properties of public opinion

Americans seem to know shockingly little about public affairs.

They are often unfamiliar with important public figures.

They seem to know little about specific policies.

Many Americans lack the factual information necessary to make rational public policy decisions.

One study concluded that most people respond randomly to questions about public opinion.

This held true only for the 1950s.

General values versus program specifics

Gallup polls reveal stability in public opinion.

The mass public has a consistent set of underlying values about the ends of public policies.

It rarely knows enough details to determine the best means.

Orthodox democratic theory prescribes two roles for the public and its leaders based on the above distinction.

Public opinion and national defense: A case study

Since World War II, Americans have had a consistent set of values about foreign policy.

They reject isolationism in favor of international leadership.

They prefer a policy somewhere between strength and stridency.

They are hesitant to commit troops to war.

Americans have consistently supported defense expeditures which allow such goals to be achieved.

Public opinion and inherent personal values

Tocqueville commented on the firmness of the American public in its public opinion.

Public opinion does not appear to be easily manipulated.

Public opinion on social issues: A case study
  Core values do not change but are applied in new ways.
    Individualism is an important and long-held American value.
    In recent years women have been applying it to themselves.
Ambivalence of opinions
  Americans often say they think government is becoming too big.
  Simultaneously, they seek resolutions to most problems from the
    government.
  Such attitudes are not fickle but ambivalent.
  Public officials must strike a balance between such conflicting im-
    pulses.
Competing goals and values: The case of foreign affairs
  The public overwhelmingly favors a nuclear freeze.
    The consensus quickly deteriorates when specific questions are
      asked.
  Americans possess many such contradictory wishes as the desire for an
    end to the arms race and a defense second to none.
Polling
  Social scientists find it useful for a variety of purposes, including
    better understanding voting behavior.
  The media have found polls extremely useful.
  Polls are heavily used in campaigning and lobbying efforts.
  Polling is based on the principle of sampling.
    The cheapest form of polling is the mail questionnaire.
      It is, however, slow and often yields a low rate of response.
    Most early polling was done in-person.
      Gallup and Roper still use this method extensively.
    Telephone polling is becoming the most used method.
    There are several methods of deriving a sample.
  The *Literary Digest* pioneered massive political polling by sending out
  "ballots" to its readers.
    Its polls were relatively accurate predictors of several presidential
      races.
    Its 1936 poll, however, was so far off that it discredited the maga-
      zine.
    Gallup and others were able to explain the reasons for the dis-
      crepancy between the *Digest* poll and the election results.
      They had developed scientific methods by which they could get an
        accurate sample by polling a small number of voters.
      The *Digest* poll relied solely on its readers — hardly a representa-
        tive and random sample.
Problems in polling
  The 1936 election forever changed polling techniques.
  Statistical methods developed then have proven quite sound over the
    years.

Still, polling is not a science, and its findings can be inaccurate.
The press is often guilty of gross oversimplification of polls.
Exit polls used by television networks have been controversial because some claim that their projections discourage many citizens from voting.
Political distortions
Polls can be employed selectively to prove only certain points a politician or organization wants to make.
Politicians and pollsters sometimes read more into the findings of polls than is actually there.
Questions in the polls themselves can be loaded and thus skew the results.
The difficult task of question-wording
Formulating questions to get accurate results is always a challenge.
Double-barreled questions pose two questions in one, making it impossible to know how the participants actually feel about either question.
When the level of information on a topic is low, even slight differences in the wording of a question can affect the results.
Polling is useful but limited in what it can achieve.
Solutions to polling problems
Legislation does not appear to be a legitimate solution.
Journalists need to learn more about polls in order to use them better.
The general public should be aware of potential abuses in polling.
The polling industry should better police itself.
How Americans view their society
President Carter argued that Americans faced a "crisis of confidence."
There was definite national self-dissatisfaction after Vietnam, Watergate, and soaring inflation.
Lack of confidence in the leaders of the country reached its apex in 1980.
What the public was saying
There are different levels and results of public criticism.
Polls during the sixties and seventies discovered a mood of frustration, not a lack of confidence in the institution or loss of legitimacy for the system.
Strong foundations of confidence exist, as demonstrated in a 1981 poll.
There is even broad support across the demographic spectrum.
The confidence of black Americans in their country is especially striking.
Slumps and winning streaks
Like baseball teams, countries and politicians have slumps and winning streaks.
Like baseball fans, citizens can be fickle.

The sixties and seventies were much like a losing streak.
With a moderate winning streak in the eighties, public confidence
has reversed dramatically.

Review Questions

COMPLETION

1. _____ have become a staple of political assessment and commentary in every advanced industrial society.
2. The problem with the *Literary Digest* polls was the _____.
3. The principle source of misleading results from a survey is a problem in the area of _____.
4. The public often displays _____ in its attitude toward government.
5. _____ requires the presence of public opinion that reflects the people's needs and interests.
6. Elmo Roper expressed the opinion that in judging the common man "we _____ the amount of information he has; we _____ his intelligence."
7. If a respondent is relatively uninformed, his opinion on many governmental questions may be highly _____.
8. _____ polling has become the dominant tool for opinion measurement.
9. _____ is the idea that the public is manipulated into views that are not its own.
10. Exit polls are viewed as detrimental to the _____ because they may convince some voters that their vote doesn't count.

TRUE/FALSE

1. Public opinion is usually clear, fixed, and unambiguous.
2. Candidates are the only political actors using polls.
3. No state has officially banned exit polls.
4. It is easier to conduct a poll when the public is uninformed.
5. During the Vietnam War, a majority of the populace believed that U.S. military expenditures were either at about the right level or lower than they should be.
6. Over half the U.S. adult public couldn't name Mikhail Gorbachev as the head of the USSR early in 1986.

7. On abstract policy issues, the public's opinions often haven't taken clear form.
8. Different polling techniques are used to sell products than are used to sell political candidates.
9. All pollsters use exactly the same methodology.
10. Women's views of their position in American society have been undergoing important changes.

MULTIPLE CHOICE

1. _____ felt that Americans were engaged in infinitely varying the consequences of known principles rather than in seeking new principles.
   a. Phillip Converse   d. Lou Harris
   b. George Gallup   e. V. O. Key
   c. Alexis de Tocqueville
2. How citizens respond to questions pertaining to abortion is probably most affected by
   a. the wording of the   respondent.
      question.   c. the sex of the respondent.
   b. the party affiliation of the   d. the age of the respondent.
3. _____ concluded, "You can't fool all the people all the time."
   a. George Washington   d. Abraham Lincoln
   b. Gerald Ford   e. Andrew Jackson
   c. Jimmy Carter
4. _____ advanced the idea that the public is manipulated into views that are not really its own.
   a. Herbert Marcuse   d. James Bryce
   b. Harwood Childs   e. Michael Kaye
   c. Walter Lippmann
5. Public opinion is expressed through
   a. letters to newspaper editors.   d. all of the above
   b. rallies.   e. none of the above
   c. elections.
6. Polls have become increasingly important to
   a. social scientists.   d. all of the above
   b. the media.   e. none of the above
   c. political campaigns.
7. Advances in sampling techniques are attributed to
   a. the *Literary Digest*. d. the CBS network.
   b. George Gallup.   e. Alfred Landon.
   c. James Bryce.

8. Public opinion can be inaccurately measured if
   a. the whole country is not in-
      cluded in the sample.
   b. questions are worded
      poorly.
   c. interviewers are very careful
      and accurate in recording
      responses.
   d. all of the above
   e. none of the above

9. A _____ Americans are proud to be Americans.
   a. few
   b. small number of
   c. slight majority of
   d. full three-quarters of
   e. very few

10. The current crisis of confidence in government can be traced to the
    events of
    a. the Arab-Israeli conflict.
    b. World War II.
    c. the 1960s and 1970s.
    d. the OPEC oil embargo.
    e. none of the above

ANSWER KEY

Completion

1. Polls   p. 382
2. sampling frame   p. 386
3. question wording   p. 392
4. ambivalence   p. 378
5. Democracy   p. 361
6. overestimate; underestimate
   p. 372
7. unstable   p. 370
8. Systematic polling   p. 382
9. False consciousness   p. 366
10. electoral process   pp. 389–90

True/False

1. F   p. 362
2. F   p. 383
3. F   pp. 389–90
4. F   p. 393
5. F   p. 374
6. T   p. 369
7. T   p. 393
8. F   p. 367
9. F   p. 374
10. T   p. 376

Multiple Choice

1. c   p. 374
2. a   p. 361
3. d   p. 368
4. a   pp. 365–66
5. d   pp. 382–83
6. d   pp. 382–83
7. b   pp. 386–87
8. b   pp. 392–93
9. d   p. 397
10. c   pp. 398–99

ESSAY QUESTIONS

1. It is commonly assumed that the successful operation of a democracy is based upon an informed public that is knowledgeable about

public affairs and participates regularly in politics. To what extent does the American public meet these criteria?

2. Public opinion polls may not be all they appear to be. Describe the uses and misuses of polls in American politics. If you were advising a friend or associate about what to look for in a poll, what would you say?

Further Investigation

Abramson, Paul R. *Political Attitudes in America*. San Francisco: W. H. Freeman, 1983.
Examines attitude formation and change.

Almond, Gabriel A., and Verba, Sidney, eds. *The Civic Culture Revisited*. Boston: Little, Brown, 1980.
Building upon their earlier work, these authors and others reexamine their findings about political culture and attitudes in several countries and from different theoretical perspectives.

Greenstein, Fred I. *Children and Politics*. New Haven: Yale University Press, 1965.
Benchmark study of the political socialization of children.

Greenstein, Fred I. "Personality and Politics." In *The Handbook of Political Science*. Vol. 2. Edited by Fred I. Greenstein and Nelson W. Polsby. Reading, Mass.: Addison-Wesley, 1975.
Excellent review essay on the relationship between personality, public opinion and political behavior.

Jennings, M. Kent, and Niemi, Richard. *Generations and Politics: A Panel Study of Young Adults and Their Parents*. Princeton: Princeton University Press, 1981.
Reports the results of two separate national surveys on the attitudes of adolescents and their parents, allowing the authors to examine change and continuity in attitudes and behaviors.

Key, V. O., Jr. *Public Opinion and American Democracy*. New York: Knopf, 1961.
Although over twenty years old, this remains one of the most insightful treatments of public opinion available.

Lippmann, Walter. *Public Opinion*. New York: Free Press, 1965.
Thoughtful treatment of what public opinion is, how it is formed, and how it works in a democracy.

Lipset, Seymour Martin, and Raab, Earl. *The Politics of Unreason: Right-Wing Extremism in America, 1790–1977*. 2d ed. Chicago: University of Chicago Press, 1978.
Traces the history of right-wing extremist groups and examines the bases of support, opinions, and consequences of these movements.

Sears, David O. "Political Socialization." In *The Handbook of Political Science*. Vol. 2. Edited by Fred I. Greenstein and Nelson W. Polsby. Reading, Mass.: Addison-Wesley, 1975.
Useful short summary of the field of political socialization.

Applying Political Science

1. How do children learn about politics and government? When do they acquire a sense of nationalism, respect for authority, etc.? After reading Greenstein and Sears, arrange to interview a group of schoolchildren in your area and replicate some of their questions.

2. It is frequently argued that Americans are nonideological pragmatists who prefer the middle of the road. Why is this the case? Discuss this topic with your fellow students and persons in your community and attempt to determine why so few people are strong liberals or strong conservatives (to say the least of extreme liberals or extreme conservatives).

3. Follow up on a poll reported in your local media. After reading a little about how polls should be conducted, compare the local one against the commonly held standards for sample design, question wording, and interpretation. Was there room for an alternative interpretation of the data in the case you are studying?

4. During the 1984 presidential election, there were some significant discrepancies in the pre-election polls. How would you explain these discrepancies? What things should you look for when assessing the accuracy of polls?

13 | Interest Groups

Overview

Interest groups are people organized to further some common political interest. Interest groups lobby to accomplish their goals. Americans have a strong propensity to form and join interest groups; the United States has more voluntary associations than any other nation. Tocqueville, writing 150 years ago, explained this propensity to join in terms of individualism.

Interest groups vary in size, purpose, and approach. There are more than three thousand interest groups officially registered, with many more that are sporadic in activity or local in orientation. The regulations controlling interest groups are embodied in the Federal Regulation of Lobbying Act of 1946. Even though the act is full of loopholes, many groups voluntarily comply with its registration requirements. While not inherently undesirable, the efforts of interest groups and their lobbyists can conflict with the public interests. Ethical questions arise when former government officials such as Michael Deaver leave prominent government posts to assume lucrative positions as consultants and lobbyists.

To Madison, interest groups were factious, and the most common and durable source of factions is economics. In the 1780s, he described the conflict between interest groups as essentially a conflict between rich and poor. This interpretation remains valid today. Most interest groups revolve around economic interests. State and local governments also lobby the federal government. Public interest groups, which try to further a general interest rather than a specific one, also exist. The number of public interest groups has grown as the federal government has expanded. Also the organization of interest groups outside the traditional areas of business and labor has expanded; there are many womens' groups, education interest groups, and even some for the poor and minorities.

Interest groups use a variety of resources to accomplish their goals. Size is an important factor in influence. Financial resources can also be very important. The way interest groups use money differs depending on their purpose. Organization can be a valuable resource. The intensity of the issue can be another factor in interest group activity and success. Striking alliances also increases the chances of influencing legislation.

Although each interest group has its own tactics and strategies for getting what they want done, several tactics prevail. The 1981–1982 attempt to amend the Clean Air Act is a typical case of interest group tactics. Group alliances took place on both sides. Coalitions were built, allies grouped together, information was provided by the groups to the congressmen, grass-roots lobbying took place, and public opinion was mobilized. Business and labor were in favor of amending the act, and environmentalists opposed amendment. Because Congress was so divided, nothing was changed and the environmentalists, in effect, won the battle. Sometimes interest group conflicts do not attract public involvement, lack an opposing group, or are focused on the executive branch and the judiciary rather than the legislature.

The conditions for active group participation include education, free time, sources of information, and a stable and high economic position. The United States has these characteristics along with diversity, individualism, a decentralized government, and autonomy of labor and politics. These factors have fostered an abundance of interest groups in the United States. Madison saw interest groups as inherent in liberty. They are also in some ways desirable and inevitable. The presence of interest groups can be problem causing because they may overpower the rights of individual citizens, group tyranny can result, a power elite may develop, and groups often do not compete equally. The poor, minorities, and other resource-poor groups are underrepresented by interest groups. The president and political parties may compensate for this inequity in political power by looking out for their interests.

Key Terms and Concepts

interest groups
public interest
PACs
EPA
amicus curiae
conflict of interest

lobbying
factions
direct mail
grass-roots lobbying
iron triangle

Chapter Outline

The Deaver case and lobbyists
    Michael Deaver's journey from government appointee to private
      lobbyist serves as a good case study of interest groups and lobbyists.

An interest group is an organization formed to advance shared political interests.

Lobbyists represent such groups.

While lobbying is viewed as a legitimate activity, the Deaver case raises questions as to what the ethical bounds of the practice should be.

After leaving the White House Deaver set up his own public relations firm, with connections to former colleagues undoubtedly as a primary asset.

Lucrative contracts with several foreign governments drew attention to Deaver's firm.

Critics charged him with violating conflict-of-interest laws.

A special prosecutor was appointed by the Justice Department.

In-and-outers

The number of lobbyists multiplied from 4,000 in 1977 to 10,000 in 1985.

Former members of Congress, its staff, and the executive branch are in high demand as lobbyists.

Former local officials are also going on to lobby city hall.

Senate Judiciary Committee chairman Strom Thurmond attempted to pass legislation restricting potential lobbying activities by former government officials.

His bill met much opposition.

Eventually a weaker version of Thurmond's bill was passed.

A nation of joiners

Tocqueville explained the propensity to join groups in terms of individualism.

Joining together to attack common problems expresses a sense of individual responsibility and self-confidence.

A nation of interest groups

Interest groups come in a variety of sizes and purposes.

It is impossible to know how many interest groups exist in the United States because only those that operate regularly are required to register.

Many groups only intervene sporadically.

Churches and social organizations sometimes act as interest groups.

Most large businesses and corporations and many small businesses occasionally function as interest groups.

Types of interest groups

Federal regulation regarding lobbying is embodied in the 1946 Federal Regulation of Lobbying Act.

The legislation is full of loopholes, yet many groups still choose to comply with it.

Over three thousand groups are registered, since nearly every trade and professional association has policy interests.

Interest groups operate at the state and local level as well as at the national level.

Tens of thousands of individuals and groups spend hundreds of millions of dollars each year in efforts to shape public policy.

The most common and durable source of faction

Interests are disproportionately represented.

Madison saw the unequal distribution of property as the most enduring faction.

The prime source of organized interests is economics.

Conflict in the 1780s was between rich and poor.

Madison's interpretation of interest groups is still valid.

The lion's share of interest groups involve economic interests.

In 1983, four-fifths of all interest groups registering as lobbyists had predominantly economic interests.

Government lobbying government

The federal aid programs of the 1960s and 1970s have resulted in more active state and local government lobbying.

The federal government also lobbies itself.

Public interest groups

A public interest group is one that seeks a collective good.

Examples are environmentalists, consumer advocates, and governmental reformers.

The special nature of their claim is what spurs the organization of public interest groups.

The growth of public interest groups is a product of recent social changes.

Public interest groups are increasing in other countries as well.

Expanding sector coverage by interest groups

There are many women's interest groups.

Almost every conceivable dimension of education has formal representation.

The poor and minorities have very few groups to represent them.

Interest group resources

Size is an important factor in influence.

Big groups also have greater diversity.

Splits between leadership and rank-and-file membership are common in large groups.

Money is another key resource.

It can compensate for small numbers.

It is used in a variety of ways.

Some groups have large official staffs.

Others spend much money on publicity.

Some make large campaign contributions.

PACs bring lots of private money into electoral campaigns.

Organization

Sophisticated formal organization can be a group resource.

Use of direct mail is increasing.

Connections are very helpful in getting one's case to be heard by the right people.

Intensity of interest

Legislators avoid criticism, which is why legislation that brings out strong feeling is so often passed.

The defeat of gun control legislation is a prime example of lawmakers' attempts to placate interest groups.

Sometimes groups will donate funds to defeat a legislator who opposes their interests.

Groups with socially accepted goals have greater chances at striking alliances and seeing success.

Tactics and strategies of interest groups

Interest groups try to influence legislators to pass laws, impose or remove regulations, fund programs, change tax codes, commit the country to some new objective, etc.

Tactics by which interest groups accomplish their goals differ.

Legislating for the environment: a continuing interest group struggle

The Clean Air Act exemplifies the continual battle between environmental groups and business over environmental issues.

Its goals seem straightforward, but the act itself is highly complex.

The argument about the legislation centers around the means for achieving the objectives set forth in the act.

Groups formed alliances on both sides of the issue.

Such alliances are essential to successful lobbying efforts.

Lobbyists find allies where they can, often resulting in unusual coalitions.

Interest groups provided information and policy guidance.

Both sides actively sought to cultivate grassroots support.

They also employed polls on their behalf to show public support for their respective positions.

Stalemate

The conflict ended in a stalemate, thus preserving the status quo and benefiting the environmental groups.

In the 1980s, environmental groups have only been able to preserve past gains.

There is no longer enough support to enact much new environmental legislation.

Acid rain has become a controversial environmental issue which pits different regions against each other.

Some environmental legislation, such as amendments to the 1974 Safe Drinking Water Act, were passed in the mid-1980s.

Contrasting types of interest group efforts
    Many issues involve narrower objectives.
        Often issues are too narrow to attract much public involvement.
        Sometimes issues are too complicated for the general public to
           understand.
    Massive mobilization of oppposing interest groups is uncommon.
        Conflict often occurs between groups in a coalition as they
           formulate policy.
    Lobbying may center in the executive branch and judiciary.
        Interest groups may initiate or support litigation.
        They sometimes try to influence judges' philosophies.
        They can lobby judges through *amicus curiae* briefs.
Groups and American democracy
    Americans are involved in more voluntary associations than any other
        people.
Conditions for active group participation
    America has the necessary education, sources of information, and
        economic position.
    Diversity, individualism, decentralization, and autonomy are important
        conditions for such participation.
Groups and group power
    Interest groups are inevitable.
        Madison felt that liberty provided for factions.
        Groups experience competition.
    Interest groups are desirable.
        They are the primary means by which popular sovereignty is
           realized.
        Groups can be mediating structures.
    Groups can also cause problems.
        Interest groups by nature align them against the rights of citizens.
           Progressives sought to purge excessive interest group influence
               from political parties and government.
        People harbor at least three fears about interest groups:
           They could become a power elite.
           They could dominate specific policy areas.
           Some interests are better organized than others.
        Madison foresaw the possibility of group tyranny and rather
           successfully prevented it by instituting checks and balances.
        However, the separation of powers has also ironically benefited the
           interest groups.
           While government as a whole is beyond the control of any
               group, its many parts are susceptible.
           Expansive government leads to interest groups.
           National policy is the combination of the special interests.
           Groups do not compete equally.

Representation is not necessarily equal with interest groups.

The economically privileged enjoy greater group representation than do the poor.

Businesses organize so they have more influence.

Political parties and the president represent those under-represented by interest groups.

Review Questions

COMPLETION

1. Tocqueville viewed _____ as explaining the American propensity to join interest groups.
2. Madison, in *Federalist Paper* 10, wrote that the most common and durable faction has been the unequal distribution of _____.
3. Of the interest groups filed with the U.S. House of Representatives in 1983, most consist of _____ [type of group].
4. There has been a rise in the number of _____ interest groups because of the growth of a new stratum of middle-class political activists.
5. The battle of the Clean Air Act amendment was between the _____ and the _____.
6. Sometimes poll findings are _____ to fit in with the lobbying effort.
7. The principal charge against Michael Deaver was that he violated _____ laws.
8. _____ was the political movement in the early twentieth century that sought to purge excessive interest group influence from political parties.
9. Judges can be lobbied through the use of _____ briefs.
10. Businessmen have a disproportionately large place in the interest group process because they have the _____ means to sustain organized group action.

TRUE/FALSE

1. Interest groups only lobby congressmen.
2. Interest groups are not required to reveal how much money they expend in lobbying efforts.
3. Michael Deaver is one of the first former presidential advisers to become a successful Washington lobbyist.

4. Group leaders always try to accomplish the wishes of the rank-and-file members.
5. Interest groups receive federal funds to lobby.
6. Underprivileged groups are well represented by many interest groups.
7. The debate over the Clean Air Act centered around the standards to be enforced rather than the goals of the act.
8. Bipartisan alliances are common on controversial measures.
9. The financial stakes of narrow group objectives are sometimes very large.
10. Madison favored suppression of interest groups.

MULTIPLE CHOICE

1. Large interest groups tend to be more _____ than smaller groups.
   a. ineffective
   b. heterogeneous
   c. disorganized
   d. homogeneous
   e. centralized
2. Interest groups try to influence legislators to do which of the following?
   a. Pass laws
   b. Remove regulations
   c. Fund programs
   d. Favor their interests
   e. All of the above
3. The coalition of environmentalists for the Clean Air Act controversy was called
   a. Clean Air Working Group.
   b. National Environmental Development Association/ Clean Air Act Project.
   c. Friends of the Atmosphere.
   d. Environment Coalition.
   e. National Clean Air Coalition.
4. Which of the following is not a reason why polling is an important part of lobbying efforts?
   a. It informs legislators of what their constituency wants.
   b. It influences public opinion by the wording of the questions.
   c. It informs the public of the issue and the consequences.
   d. It discourages the opposing group.
   e. All of these support polling as a part of lobbying.
5. The "10-5-3" was
   a. never passed.
   b. sponsored by trade unions.
   c. an accelerated depreciation plan.
   d. an example of two strongly opposing groups fighting to pass a new law.
   e. one of President Carter's policy objectives.

6. Interest groups and their active involvement in the political process are
   a. inevitable.
   b. a continuing source of problems.
   c. desirable.
   d. a result of liberty.
   e. all of the above

7. The group least likely to be represented by interest groups is
   a. businesses.
   b. labor unions.
   c. educational concerns.
   d. environmental concerns.
   e. minorities.

8. The AFL-CIO is an example of a
   a. business affiliation.
   b. labor union.
   c. coalition of interest groups.
   d. citizens' group.
   e. PAC.

9. The group in favor of amending the Clean Air Act wanted to do so because
   a. they couldn't understand the regulations.
   b. the regulations were too expensive to enforce.
   c. they wanted higher standards to be set.
   d. no one was following the regulation guidelines.
   e. they thought the regulation was unfair to the handicapped.

10. Which of the following did not note that Americans were very involved in interest groups and voluntary associations?
    a. Alexis de Tocqueville
    b. Gabriel Almond
    c. Sidney Verba
    d. Alexander Hamilton
    e. James Madison

ANSWER KEY

Completion

1. individualism   p. 406
2. property   pp. 409–10
3. business corporations   p. 411
4. public   p. 413
5. environmentalists; business-labor coalition   pp. 423–24
6. manipulated   p. 428
7. conflict of interest   p. 404
8. Progressivism   p. 437
9. *amicus curiae*   p.433
10. financial   p. 440

True/False

1. F   p. 432
2. F   p. 409
3. F   p. 405
4. F   p. 418
5. F   p. 418
6. F   p. 414
7. T   p. 423
8. T   p. 427
9. T   p. 432
10. F   p. 436

Multiple Choice

1. b   p. 416
2. e   p. 422
3. e   p. 425
4. d   p. 428
5. c   p. 432

6. e   pp. 436–37
7. e   p. 414
8. b   p. 416
9. b   p. 424
10. d   p. 434

ESSAY QUESTIONS

1. Interest groups are frequently criticized but rarely praised. Why is this so? What are some of the most important positive functions of interest groups? Why has it been so difficult to limit them?
2. Professor Ladd argues that interest groups differ in resources and in the strategies they employ. Explain what he means and discuss the implications of how interest groups differ in their successes in politics.

Further Investigation

Bauer, Raymond A., et al. *American Business and Public Policy: The Politics of Foreign Trade.* 2d ed. Chicago: Aldine, Atherton, 1972.
  Detailed study of the approaches and effectiveness of interest group lobbying.

Berry, Jeffrey M. *Lobbying for the People.* Princeton: Princeton University Press, 1977.
  Public interest lobbies, which have become increasingly important, are the focus of this book.

Dahl, Robert A. *Who Governs?* New Haven: Yale University Press, 1961.
  Examines the relationship among interests, groups, and power in New Haven, Connecticut. Dahl maintains that it is the competition between contending groups that limits the power of any single group.

Haider, Donald H. *When Governments Come to Washington: Governors, Mayors and Intergovernmental Lobbying.* New York: Free Press, 1974.
  State and local governments are also interest groups. Haider describes how they lobby the federal government.

Malbin, Michael J., ed. *Parties, Interest Groups, and Campaign Finance Laws.* Washington, D.C.: American Enterprise Institute for Public Policy Research, 1980.
  Examines the ways interest groups attempt to influence elections.

Olson, Mancur. *The Logic of Collective Action: Public Goods and the Theory of Groups.* Cambridge: Harvard University Press, 1968.

Uses economic theory to explain interest group behavior.

Ornstein, Norman J., and Elder, Shirley. *Interest Groups, Lobbying, and Policymaking.* Washington, D.C.: Congressional Quarterly Press, 1978.

Using three case studies, the authors analyze interest group activity in influencing government policy and legislation.

Wilson, James Q. *Political Organizations.* New York: Basic Books, 1973.

Examines several different types of interest groups to generate a theory of how they attract members, organize themselves, and attempt to influence politics.

Applying Political Science

1. Identify a local interest group with representatives in Washington (examples would include teachers, farmers, students, universities, and colleges) and find out what communication channels exist between the lobbyist and local affiliates. Ask for examples when the local group wanted something from Washington and vice versa. Why does the local group feel it necessary to have this type of representation?

2. Attend a public hearing on a proposed law, zoning change, or policy question and compare the two sides of the question in terms of organization, resources, and lobbying. Afterward, follow up with the interests and inquire about why they were there and what they plan to do.

3. Choose a sphere of public policy and compile a list of interest groups in that area. Examples would include manufacturing, agriculture, maritime, and health. Who would be the likely allies in most policy disputes? Why?

14 | Voting and Elections

Overview

The 1986 elections exemplified the many factors involved in the partisan struggle. Despite claims made by both parties, the results of the election revealed little variance in voter attitudes from the last six years. As in most off-year elections, the appeal of local candidates played the major role, and the Democrats regained control of the Senate.

Voting is essential to democracy. The American electoral system is unique. Until the Civil War, the states exclusively decided who could vote. In our early history most states imposed property ownership as a condition for adult white male suffrage, thereby limiting eligibility to about one-half to three-fourths of the adult white male population. During the Jacksonian era, voting restrictions were relaxed to permit nearly all white males to vote. In 1865, the Thirteenth Amendment gave citizenship to blacks, but through a variety of methods, including poll taxes, literacy tests, grandfather clauses, and white primaries, Southern blacks were denied the right to vote. It was not until the 1960s and the civil rights movement that large numbers of blacks were able to vote. Suffrage was extended to women in 1920 with the passing of the Nineteenth Amendment. In 1971, the age requirement was set at eighteen nationwide.

Although virtually all Americans are eligible to vote, many fail to do so; voter turnout has been steadily dropping since 1960. This decline in turnout has confounded many experts because it has occurred at a time when voting restrictions have been liberalized. In addition, the overall level of education has risen, which usually indicates a greater likelihood of voter participation. Concern about low turnout arises because certain groups may be excluded from representation. Other countries may actually have even lower turnout but because of differences in measurement the United States may appear to have the lower rate. Voter participation in the United States is low for a variety of reasons unrelated to dissatisfaction with the present election or political situation. Two major reasons for the decrease in participation are the weakening of political parties and the scale and remoteness of the governmental process.

The people most likely to vote are better educated, older, and of higher socioeconomic status. They also are more likely to be Republicans or persons immediately affected by changes in policy.

No set of election rules is politically neutral. The United States has chosen a single-member, simple-majority, single ballot system. Although this system has the potential to produce big imbalances between the proportion of votes and legislative seats, it avoids the major problem with proportional representation, which is the fracturing of legislatures to the point where governing is impeded. The American system is a two-party system; third parties cannot be stable because of our election structure. America is unique because of its direct primary system.

Elections are held so often and campaigns last so long that our politics can be seen as an "endless campaign." Campaigning begins as early as two years before the general election. Stamina and money are needed to win an election. During the 1970s campaign finance was significantly reformed. However, loopholes remain. Some who want further reform maintain that campaign spending is too high, but a comparison of campaign costs with other political communication expenditures reveals that campaign spending has not grown disproportionately. The rise in the number of political action committees (PACs) is a direct result of the reforms of the 1970s. New methods and modern technology have also changed American elections.

Key Terms and Concepts

suffrage	white primaries
"endless campaign"	single-member district
simple-majority	single-ballot
proportional representation	direct primaries
PACs	FEC
campaign spending	

Chapter Outline

The 1986 election
  Republicans sought to maintain the control of the Senate they gained in 1980.
    They lost control; Democrats now have a 55–45 majority.
  Although either party would certainly have claimed a message of support from voters, the results were so close that no real mandate can be found.

As in most off-year elections, the appeal of local candidates decided most races.

Primary outcomes determined a party's chance of winning a race in many cases.

Democratic control of the Senate, no matter how slight, still has important and tangible ramifications.

Democrats also control the House, as they have in every session of Congress except one since 1928.

Republicans fared well in gubernatorial races, picking up a net gain of eight seats.

Expanding the franchise

Until the Civil War, states decided who could vote.

The Constitution only says that those able to vote for state representatives must also be able to vote for national congressmen.

Senators, until 1913, were selected by state legislatures.

The president is elected by the Electoral College.

Initially the vote was also restricted to adult, white, male property holders.

That did include one-half to three-quarters of all adult white males.

The vote broadened during the Jacksonian era to virtually all white males.

Extending the vote to blacks

In 1865 the Thirteenth Amendment gave citizenship to blacks.

In 1870 the Fifteenth Amendment gave all citizens the right to vote regardless of race, color, etc.

The South nullified this provision through several devices.

Poll taxes, which blacks could not afford, were levied.

Literacy tests, which blacks could not pass, were administered as prerequisites to voting.

Only whites were allowed to vote in Democratic primaries.

In 1944 white primaries were ruled unconstitutional in *Smith* v. *Allwright*.

Civil Rights Acts of 1957, 1960, 1964, and 1965 dramatically increased black registration and voting.

In 1975 the Voting Rights Act as extended has permanently banned literacy tests.

Coverage was also extended to language minorities.

Extending the vote to women

Women's suffrage did not come until 1920.

America was the first country to extend the vote to women.

Achieving the vote
  The Twenty-sixth Amendment lowered the voting age to 18
    throughout the country.
  Universal suffrage has come only within the last 25 years.
Participation in American elections
  A low proportion of eligible voters actually vote.
    Turnout has been steadily dropping since 1960.
    Turnout in voting for House members is even lower.
A confounding decline
  Turnout has dropped when it should have risen.
    Laws have been changed to enhance participation.
    Education has risen, which should have resulted in an increase in
      participation, but still turnout has dropped.
  Other countries have higher rates of turnout.
Is voter turnout a problem?
  Decline in turnout means that some groups may not enjoy full
    representation.
  Low turnout upsets the balance of power in American democracy.
  Statistical dissimilarities make it difficult to compare the United States
    with other countries and tend to make turnout appear lower than it
    really is.
    American registration laws result in a substantial proportion of the
      voting age population not being registered in any given election.
    Other countries measure turnout as a percentage of registered voters
      that voted.
    Any situation in which significant numbers of people are not
      counted among registered voters makes turnout appear higher
      than it really is.
  Many people who are not registered do not register because they are
    not interested in voting.
  Others of the nonregistered are unable to vote because of lack of
    citizenship, incarceration, institutionalization, etc.
  Nonvoting has been overstated in the United States.
Voter participation across history
  Electoral participation has always been low.
  Some nonvoting is unrelated to dissatisfaction with democratic perfor-
    mance or with the parties and their leaders, but stems from the as-
    surance that the election will not disturb the status quo.
    The differences between American parties is less drastic than the
      difference between opposing parties in other countries.
    Some Americans don't vote because they know that the structure of
      government will remain the same.
  Voter turnout in the late nineteenth century was higher than it is now.
  Voter fraud was rampant in the late 1800s.

Sources of diminished voter turnout
 Political parties are weaker.
  They can no longer mobilize the electorate.
  They aren't as vigorous as they were.
 People feel that government is big and distant.
  This feeling is likely to persist.
Who votes?
 High socioeconomic people are more likely to vote than those with lower socioeconomic status.
 Education has a substantial effect on the probability that one will vote.
  Education increases interest.
  Education increases one's capacity to understand the complexity of government.
 Those immediately affected by government are highly likely to vote.
 Turnout is lowest at the beginning of adult life, increases to a plateau in middle age, and then declines in old age.
  College students are more likely to vote than their less-educated peers.
 Voters are slightly more Republican than the general population.
 On issues, voters tend to reflect the entire population.
  Only unopinionated people tend to be underrepresented by voters.
Other forms of political participation
 The United States holds more elections for more offices than any other country.
 Elections are not the only way Americans participate politically.
  As noted earlier, citizens are very active in interest groups and volunteer associations.
  Again, participation is related to socioeconomic status and education.
The structure of elections
 No set of electoral mechanics is politically neutral.
Translating votes into seats
 Allotment of seats can vary drastically even with the same popular vote if different mechanisms are used.
The American electoral system
 Most U.S. elections are under a simple-member district.
  An area is divided into districts.
  Each district chooses only one representative under such a system.
  A few U.S. elections, such as for some city councils, involve plural-member districts.
 U.S. elections are also generally by simple majority on a single ballot.
 Some states have run-off primaries in which the two top contenders are voted on again.
  Some see such primaries as discriminatory.

England is the progenitor of the single-member simple-majority
system.

Most other democracies have some form of the plural-member proportional representation system.

Which system is best?

Single-member simple-majority systems can produce big imbalances
between the proportion of votes and seats won by a party.

Proportional representation fractures legislatures by producing so
many parties that governing is difficult.

It may also contribute to government instability.

To determine which system is best requires examination of electoral
goals.

The single-member system is best for a viable government.

Third parties

In a single-member system third parties are penalized.

In Britain, third parties form alliances and win.

Primary elections

America is unique because of its direct primary system.

In closed primaries only voters registered as party members can participate.

In open primaries any voter can cast a ballot.

Voters might vote for the candidate that their party can most
easily defeat.

Presidential primaries choose delegates to national parties' presidential nominating conventions through elections.

In presidential caucuses, party members publicly declare themselves
for one presidential candidate or the other.

Campaigns

Because of the abundance and duration of political campaigns,
America is seen as being involved in an "endless campaign."

Length of campaigns

Events of the 1984 presidential campaign began twelve to twenty
months before the election.

The first formal step of the Republican presidential nomination (for
1988) was well underway in the spring of 1986.

Unknowns can still win office by campaigning relentlessly, as did
Samuel Gejdenson.

Some view the endless campaigning necessary to win office as a
good test of political zeal.

Others view it as a potential barrier to qualified office seekers.

Money and campaigns

Without substantial funding, parties and candidates cannot reasonably
make their appeals to the electorate.

Until the 1970s, the law governing campaign expenditures was the
Corrupt Practices Act of 1925.

It set limits of $25,000 for Senate campaigns and $10,000 for House races.

In the early 1970s, Congress reformed regulations regarding federal elections.

The Federal Election Campaign Act of 1970 required the submittal of detailed financial reports and allowed for donation on tax forms.

Additional campaign finance legislation in 1972 set spending and contribution limits for presidential candidates, provided public funding for presidential candidates, and set up the Federal Election Commission (FEC).

Individuals are limited to $1,000 contributions to any candidate, $20,000 to any party's national committee, $5,000 to any other political committee, and no more than $25,000 total contribution per year.

Presidential elections are now conducted with public funding.

At preconvention stage, candidates can get fifty percent public financing if requirements are met.

Candidates not of a major party who get at least five percent of the popular vote are entitled to funds commensurate with their share of the total vote.

In nonpresidential campaigns private sources dominate.

Nineteen states provide public subsidies for state-level contests.

Are campaigns too expensive?

One estimate puts expenditures on state and local elections at $550 million for 1983–84.

Federal expenditures were approximately $1.15 billion for the same time period.

Some claim this is too much.

Others counter with comparisons of campaign costs to money spent on items such as lipstick.

Such claims are irrelevant.

A valid comparison is with the increase in costs of public affairs communications.

In early American history, parties played the decisive role in political communications.

Today it is not so.

Networks spend far more than parties.

Why then weaken the parties and candidates by limiting what they can spend?

Is one party disadvantaged?

On most counts the parties are balanced in campaign financing.

Democrats, however, enjoy a modest edge in money contributed by PACs.

Republicans enjoy a huge advantage over the Democrats when it comes to "institutional fundraising."

This is due to Republican party leaders capitalizing on a transition period.

They solicited more small individual contributions.

Democrats have since followed suit.

Some feel the Democratic party is at a serious disadvantage because of its class base.

Political action committees

The 1970 campaign reforms spurred the rise of PACs.

Past use of funds from corporations was banned.

The 1971 FECA permitted the use of corporate funds and union funds for political purposes.

PAC funds tend to favor incumbents.

Campaign techniques and technicians

The increasing use of television has greatly changed American elections.

Direct mail has aided in fund-raising.

The use of polling has increased.

The reliance on campaign consultants, etc., may produce candidates better able to campaign than govern.

Polling experts are now invaluable presidential advisers.

Media advisers are now key to political technology.

A more manipulative view of politics is developing.

Review Questions

COMPLETION

1. Southerners ignored the mandates of the _____ Amendment when they denied the vote to blacks following the Civil War.

2. A public announcement of one's intent to support a candidate takes place at a _____.

3. _____ primaries require that voters be party members.

4. The United States has a _____ district, single-ballot electoral system.

5. The _____ electoral system facilitates the forming and stability of third parties.

6. Federal matching grants cover _____ the costs of the prenomination phase of an election and _____ the costs of the general election phase, within limits.

7. A candidate not of a major party must attract _____ percent of the popular vote in order to be eligible for federal grants for campaign costs.

8. Pat Cadell and Richard Wirthlin are examples of _____ who became important presidential advisors.

9. Congressional races, especially in off-years when no presidential contest is occurring, are decided substantially on the basis of the relative _____.

10. Every biennium, _____ [number] House of Representative seats are contested.

TRUE/FALSE

1. Democratic congressional candidates receive more money from PACs than do Republicans.
2. Universal suffrage is unique to the past twenty-five years.
3. Voter turnout in the past was much greater than it is now.
4. On issues, the active voters mirror the views of the entire population.
5. Single-member simple-majority electoral systems fracture the legislature.
6. The Federal Election Campaign Act of 1971 set up the FEC.
7. Parties dominate political communication in the U.S. today.
8. No PAC can give a candidate more than $2,500 in any election.
9. Modern laws have sought to increase participation in elections.
10. Low rates of voter turnout are common to all democracies.

MULTIPLE CHOICE

1. Political parties are _____ able to mobilize the electorate than/as they were in the past.
   a. better
   b. less
   c. just as
   d. not at all
   e. much better

2. Which of the following is not a method by which Southerners denied the vote to blacks?
   a. literacy tests
   b. poll taxes
   c. direct primaries
   d. All methods eliminated blacks from voting.
   e. None of these methods prevented blacks from voting.

3. Voter turnout, according to official figures, is highest in which of the following countries?
   a. the United States
   b. Great Britain
   c. Switzerland
   d. Australia
   e. West Germany

4. The last time the GOP held a majority in the House was
   a. 1952
   c. 1958
   b. 1928
   d. 1972
5. The United States chooses its party nominees through
   a. closed primaries.
   d. direct primaries.
   b. party machinery.
   e. nomination by the current
   c. self-nomination.
   officeholder.
6. Which factor seems most important in indicating the likelihood that
   someone will vote?
   a. education
   c. income
   b. occupation
   d. gender
7. The six FEC commissioners must _____
   a. serve six-year terms.
   d. serve only while the presi-
   b. be from the same political
   dent that appointed them is
   party.
   in office.
   c. not be a member of any
   e. never run for office after
   political party.
   their term as commissioner
   is over.
8. Most of the political funds in the United States are
   a. raised through a special tax
   d. raised by the candidate.
   on voters.
   e. raised by foreign govern-
   b. raised by the parties.
   ments wishing to overthrow
   c. from federal grants.
   the American government.

Completion

1. Fifteenth   p. 450
2. caucus   p. 470
3. Closed   p. 469
4. single-member   p. 465
5. proportional representation   p. 466
6. half; all   p. 476
7. 5   p. 476
8. campaign pollsters   p. 484
9. appeal of the candidate
   p. 445
10. 435   p. 470

True/False

1. T   p. 479
2. T   p. 450
3. F   p. 458
4. T   p. 458
5. F   p. 465
6. F   pp. 474–75
7. F   p. 474
8. F   p. 482
9. T   p. 459
10. F   p. 455

ESSAY QUESTIONS

1. Who votes in American elections? How has this changed over time? What possible explanations exist for the general decline in turnout?
2. American elections are in some important respects different from elections in other democracies. Describe the impact of the following elements on American electoral politics: primary elections, length of campaigns, frequency of elections, and campaign technology.

Further Investigation

Abramson, Paul R., et al. *Change and Continuity in the 1980 Elections*. Rev. ed. Washington, D.C.: Congressional Quarterly Press, 1982.
> The best of the books written on the 1980 election; incorporates theory and data in an interesting and insightful way.

Alexander, Herbert E. *Financing Politics: Money, Elections, and Political Reform*. Washington, D.C.: Congressional Quarterly Press, 1980.
> Examines the amount of money spent in campaigns, how it is typically spent, and its impact on elections and government. The author also proposes a set of reforms.

Campbell, Angus, et al. *The American Voter*. New York: Wiley, 1960.
> In what has become the benchmark for voting studies, the four authors of this book report on the 1956 and 1960 elections and propose a model of electoral behavior that is still largely in use a generation later.

Fiorina, Morris P. *Retrospective Voting in American Elections*. New Haven: Yale University Press, 1981.
> Proposes an alternative view on how voters use issues and information when deciding how to vote.

Key, V. O. *The Responsible Electorate: Rationality in Presidential Voting, 1936–1960*. Cambridge: Harvard University Press, 1966.
> In response to some evidence that voters did not behave rationally or with sufficient information, Key examines data that lead him to the opposite conclusions.

McGinnis, Joe. *The Selling of the President, 1968*. New York: Pocket Books, 1969.
> Fascinating account of the behind-the-scenes work done to package Richard Nixon in his 1968 campaign for the presidency.

Niemi, Richard G., and Weisberg, Herbert F., eds. *Controversies in American Voting Behavior*. 2d ed. Washington, D.C.: Congressional Quarterly Press, 1984.

    Excellent set of articles that cover many of the most important research questions in the area of elections and voting behavior.

Wolfinger, Raymond E., and Rosenstone, Steven J. *Who Votes?* New Haven: Yale University Press, 1980.

    Using a very large national sample, the authors examine the correlates of turnout and the impact of voting requirements in the United States.

Applying Political Science

1. Interview a random sample of your classmates and inquire about who voted in the most recent general election. What were some of the reasons why some individuals did not vote? Identify a non-campus sample of people your own age. Interview these persons to see who voted and why. Were the college students more likely to vote? Why or why not?

2. Interview two candidates or their campaign managers. What themes did the candidate present in his or her campaign? Why? How important were issues, partisanship, and candidate image in their campaign?

3. Select a recent local ballot issue or referendum. How did the campaign on this issue differ from the candidate campaigns? What seemed to be the deciding factor in the outcome? Why? What are the advantages and disadvantages of this form of voting?

15 | Political Parties

Overview

Since the last major realignment of party loyalties in the 1930s, political scientists have discussed what could bring about the next realignment. During the 1980s we have experienced a definite shift of party preferences among different groups and regions, and there has been a net change in the partisan balance of power. While Republican gains have been significant, however, no new majority party has emerged.

Party identification in the United States is much more casual than in other countries. Several factors, ranging from present cultural ties to past party policies, can affect voters' party preference. Because these factors send conflicting messages to the voter, party allegiance is not very strong in the U.S. Voters often switch allegiances, with many regions today voting very differently from the way they did thirty years ago. Shifts are usually gradual; baseline party strength is determined by the generational makeup of the electorate. Yet sometimes entire groups convert to another party rather suddenly, such as blacks in the sixties and southern whites in the seventies and eighties.

Democrats have traditionally enjoyed an edge among the poorer socioeconomic classes because their programs are more specifically targeted at such groups. But while there is a relationship between income or occupation and party preference, it is not overwhelming.

Perhaps the most striking trend of recent years is dealignment, as voters become less devoted to parties in general. Several factors might account for this, including voter ambivalence, a more educated and affluent electorate, and the weakening of political party organizations.

The political climate has changed in recent years, but not as drastically as some experts purport. Many Democratic leaders agree that their party had become intellectually stagnant by 1980, offering many of the same ideas from forty years earlier. American voters, always pragmatic in their approach to politics, were simply looking for something new in 1980.

Political parties themselves are a relatively new political institution in the history of the world. Edmund Burke was one of the first to foresee and support them, while Washington warned against them. They first emerged in the U.S. as a result of a split between Thomas Jefferson, who established the Republican party, and Alexander Hamilton, who set up the Federalist party. They have played an integral role in American democracies ever since. While there are parties in some nondemocracies, they serve a vastly different function than in the U.S. and Europe.

The American system is unique in that it consists of only two parties. Single member districts, where representatives are determined by a simple majority, are largely responsible for such a system. The fact that Americans are not very ideological also encourages a two-party system. And the affluence and economic mobility present in the U.S. have minimized discontent and thus the call for change.

American parties, unlike their European counterparts, are undemanding "creatures of compromise," with the two parties vying for the support of many of the same groups. The majority of voters don't vote a straight ticket, and the majority of politicians don't vote a party line, at least at the national level. The decentralization of power and the separation of the legislative and executive branches allow and encourage independent voting behavior.

Party reform in recent years, particularly among Democrats, has been aimed at broadening the democratic base within the party. The recommendations of the McGovern-Fraser Commission, which were implemented at the 1972 convention, did much to include minorities and women to a greater extent. They also triggered a flood of presidential primaries and generally weakened the role of party leaders. Criticism of the new regulations brought about the Hunt Commission, which tried to increase the involvement of party leaders in the process. Discontent remained in the party even after the 1984 election, however, but the subsequent changes in procedures have only been minor.

Key Terms and Concepts

single-member districts
winner-take-all system
accommodative parties
party discipline
party identification
party cohesion
realignment
dealignment
majority party
political machines

direct primary
open primary
generational experiences
group conversions
straight ticket
party reform
McGovern-Fraiser Commission
Hunt Commission

Chapter Outline

Introduction
  Democrats emerged from the Depression as the majority party through
    the New Deal *realignment*.
  Many have debated what could bring about another realignment.
  Realignment can mean many things, including a shift of partisan
    loyalties among social groups, a net change of partisan balance of
    power, and a new majority party.
    Only the first two have occurred during the 1980s.
      There has been a definite shift in partisan loyalties of different
        regions and demographic groups.
Republican gains
  The GOP has also experienced a net gain.
    It is stronger than at any time since the Depression.
  Partisan balance of power has not been stable over the last fifty years.
  Events, policies, and candidates can raise or lower a party above or
    below its base-line support.
  Democrats and Republicans are about even in support now.
    This represents a large gain for the Republicans.
  In polls, Republicans are rated higher by the public for handling cer-
    tain issues while Democrats get the edge for others.
  A shift in partisan balance of power does not necessarily represent a
    new majority party.
    Republicans have done well in recent presidential elections.
    Democrats have done well outside the presidency.
      Many claim this is a result of Americans' attraction to the separa-
        tion of powers.
      Others attribute this to the institutional advantages of incum-
        bency.
  Neither party is ascendant at present.
The nature of party identification
  In the U.S. the strength of a party is determined by how many voters
    identify with it.
  Polls suggest that party attachments do persist through time for many
    voters.
    Analysts now conclude, however, that party identification is much
      more fluid than previously perceived.
    They have also developed more complex models of what influences
      party preferences.
      Parties, issues, and candidates interact in influencing a voter's al-
        legiance to party or preference of a candidate.
Forming, and changing, party loyalties
  Ladd has developed seven sets of factors which can influence a voter
    in forming and changing party loyalties.

Like the tendency to "root for the home team," voter allegiance to
parties also exists.

Voters often remember their party as the party of yesterday's
hero—a political figure with whom they particularly identified.

Voters are also reasonably comfortable with and even enthusiastic
about their party's current candidates.

Past cultural ties can be very important in determining a voter's
party loyalty.

Catholics have traditionally belonged in the Democratic fold.

Protestants have often been identified with the Republican party.

Present cultural ties are also important.

Past party policies can also greatly influence voters.

Present policies are, of course, important as well.

When these seven factors coincide for voters, they usually feel a
strong allegiance to their party.

For many voters, however, the stimuli point in different directions.

Cross pressures

Most voters are subject to cross pressures.

Many southern whites swung over to the Republicans in the 1970s.

By 1985, there were more Republicans among white southerners.

Such a quick shift of voter allegiance is exceptional.

Usually the stimuli are more mixed, and old loyalties prevail.

Realignment is a continuous process involving many groups.

Changing group alignments

Experiences voters have while formulating their political opinions
(generational experiences) are very influential in determining their
political views later in life.

Polling data support this.

The Democrats' margin over Republicans is highest among those
who came of age politically at the height of the Democrats'
New Deal ascendancy.

Republicans have gained the advantage with those coming of age
under Reagan.

The long string of Democratic dominance has had lasting effects because of the generational experiences it created for so many voters.

Republicans could enjoy such fruits in the future if they continue with
their current trend.

Group conversions

Parties can live off of favorable generational groups even when they
aren't attracting new voters.

Base-line party strength is determined in part by the generational
makeup of the electorate.

This changes only very slowly with time.

Party popularity can rise or fall below this level with current political and economic experience.

An exception to this slow process occurs when a party is able to convert an entire group.

Black Americans and the Democratic party

The shift of blacks to the Democratic party was not a result of generational replacement.

The 1964 presidential election was the turning point.

Because the different parties' attitudes toward civil rights issues, a massive, immediate partisan swing occurred.

Hispanic Americans' party preferences

As a voter bloc, this group is more complex.

Florida's Cuban population is predominately Republican.

The Mexican population of the Pacific states is more heavily Democratic.

White southerners and the Republican party

Southern whites are the only other critical group to shift party loyalties in the last fifty years.

The large Democratic lead among southern whites had totally disappeared by 1984.

Young white southerners are heavily Republican.

Other regions have virtually reversed the allegiances of thirty years ago as well.

Religious and ethnic groups and the parties

Most group shifts are more gradual.

The case of Protestants and Catholics is fairly typical.

As immigrants poured into the country, Protestants tended to become Republicans and Catholics often became Democrats.

As cultural differences between the two groups have lessened in the twentieth century, so have party loyalties—but only slightly.

The Republicans have made gains in both groups, narrowing the gap.

Socioeconomic groups and the parties

The support that Democrats gained among the relative "have nots" during the New Deal persists today.

Democrats are more inclined to tax and spend for social welfare programs.

Republicans tend to concentrate on limiting government and taxes.

While there is a relationship between income and party support, it is hardly overwhelming.

Dealignment

Recent shifts in party support have been marked by an overall dealignment.

Voters today have made party identification a more casual matter than at perhaps any time in the history of the country.

Only a minority of voters continue to vote a straight ticket.

Such a dealigned electorate can be very volatile.

A couple of explanations are usually given for this dealignment.

One asserts that a more affluent and highly educated public feels less of a need for parties.

Another emphasizes the weakening of political party organizations, particularly with mass communications assuming many former duties of the parties.

Another explanation is often overlooked.

Americans have become ambivalent about public policy.

Changing political climate

Public opinion has evolved, but not to the point of narrowly defined conservatism.

In 1980, many Democrats agreed that their party had become intellectually stagnant, relying on the old ideas of the New Deal.

Their inability to handle inflation became a particular concern to Democratic leaders.

Democrats suffered overwhelming losses in the 1980 elections.

Americans have always been politically pragmatic, supporting whichever approach seems to work.

The 1982 elections reaffirmed the message of 1980.

A surprisingly high percentage of voters viewed the Republicans as better able to handle the economy.

Voters expressed support for continuing the Reagan experiment.

By 1984, an overwhelming majority of voters felt that the Republicans were better able to insure a strong economy.

The birth of political parties

The American party system is one of the world's oldest, yet the party as an institution is relatively young.

The collapse of artistocratic society and the growth of classical liberalism made parties possible.

The principle of popular sovereignty encourages common people to band together in parties.

Edmund Burke and the early argument over parties

Political parties did not emerge without some difficulties.

Some viewed parties as evil and contrary to the national interest.

Edmund Burke recognized that parties would be a necessary connection between citizens and government.

He believed a politician could be loyal to both his party and his own political convictions.

Development of parties in the United States

Madison recognized that factions would emerge, but he did not foresee the development of political parties.

Several of the founding fathers, including Thomas Jefferson, viewed factions and parties as evil.

Even after parties formed, many were not sure that parties were a needed part of democracy.

The first party conflict stemmed from the division between
Jefferson and Hamilton on how the new government should be
run.
They and their supporters made the party division very obvious
on the national level, but not on the state level.
A core democratic function
Parties have at least three functions.
They facilitate representation.
They also provide the populous with a mechanism for popular con-
trol of government.
They link candidates for the many different elective offices in an
understandable and meaningful way.
They help establish coherent policy in an incredibly complex
government.
Parties in nondemocratic countries
In totalitarian states like the Soviet Union, the party is used to edu-
cate, mobilize, and communicate.
In such a setting, parties do not compete for public support, nor do
they serve the same purposes as in a democratic society.
Characteristics of the American party system
Even among democracies, the American party system is distinctive.
A two-party system
Most democratic countries have multi-party systems.
America's single-member districts and winner-take-all electoral system
stops third parties from power or wide support.
The majority of Americans are not ideological.
American political thought is based on classical liberalism, which
has not given radical or reactionary parties much of a foundation
to build upon.
American society has aided the two-party system.
Economic and social mobility have minimized discontent and thus
the call for change.
Parties of accommodation
The two-party system has led to accommodative parties.
The parties are not ideological and are quite similar.
Both parties try to appeal to a broad section of the public.
Political parties in the United States do not demand a great deal from
voters or party members, unlike the Communist party.
Loose and undemanding alliances
Most American party ties are usually informal and very loose.
There are no formalities or criteria for party membership.
Some states have "open primaries," which allow voters to vote for
either party without declaring party affiliation at all.
Even among party leaders there is little cohesion or party discipline.
Members of Congress rarely vote strictly along party lines.

The separation of the executive and legislative branches allows elected officials to behave independently.

Another reason for lack of party cohesion is the decentralization of power in the U.S. system.

The system creates individualists.

American tradition considers independent voting a virtue.

Weak party organizations

Political machines and party bosses are rare.

Voters determine a party's nominee through primaries.

Party reform

The goal of party reform has often been to make the institution more democratic.

The Democrats' McGovern-Fraser Commission outlined two options to increase internal party democracy:

Proportional representation among delegates at caucuses and conventions nominating presidential candidates.

Presidential primaries.

Commission guidelines led to a proliferation of primaries.

This weakened the organization Democratic party.

Republicans were also affected by the reforms.

Because of criticism of the McGovern-Fraser reform, the Hunt Commission made new recommendations.

It tried to bring party officials back into the candidate selection process.

It moved away from the proportional system and closer to the winner-take-all system.

These new rules helped Mondale win the Democratic nomination over Hart and Jackson.

In light of the 1984 results, some felt the system was not fair and needed to be reformed again.

Despite such discontent, the Democratic National Committee made only a few changes of the rules for the 1988 convention.

The new regulations slightly expanded the number of party officials who can serve as delegates.

They also relaxed rules restricting primary participation to Democrats, thus almost encouraging open primaries.

They also lowered the percentage of the vote that a candidate must have in a primary to receive delegates.

The reforms were a conscious effort to achieve some stability.

Review Questions

COMPLETION

1. During Franklin D. Roosevelt's presidency in the 1930s, the _____ emerged as the country's majority party.
2. The partisan balance of power has been _____ over the last half-century.
3. Political scientists now think that party identification is considerably more _____ than it has been portrayed.
4. The current trend of generational experiences benefits the _____.
5. The two cases of critical group conversion during the last half-century involve _____ and _____.
6. One manifestation of the diminished strength of party ties is the high frequency of _____ voting.
7. Weak party loyalties characteristic of the contemporary electorate leave it inherently _____ than electorates used to be.
8. Vogel argues that a _____ distinguishes the American approach to questions of political economy.
9. In his farewell address, Washington warned against the harmful effects of the _____.
10. Jefferson was the architect of one of the world's first fullfledged parties: _____.

TRUE/FALSE

1. The New Deal realignment began after World War II as there was a major shift from Republicans to Democrats.
2. During the Reagan years, Republicans have emerged as the new majority party.
3. The GOP today is stronger than at any time since the Great Depression.
4. The Democrats have enjoyed a majority in the U.S. House of Representatives continuously since 1955.
5. For most voters, the different stimuli influencing party loyalty point in the same direction.
6. The shift of black voters to the Democratic party was a gradual shift in support through generational replacement.
7. Income plays a greater role today in determining party preference than at any time since the Depression.

8. Most Democrats insisted that the 1980 elections were largely a fluke.
9. Parties are among the oldest political institutions in the world.
10. Edmund Burke warned against the evil of parties.
11. Parties also exist in nondemocracies.
12. Most democracies operate with some type of multi-party system.

MULTIPLE CHOICE

1. Which of the following is not one of the commonly used meanings of realignment?
   a. major social groups changing their partisan loyalties
   b. a significant net change in the partisan balance of power
   c. the emergence of a new majority party
   d. assimilation of third party ideas into one of the two major parties
   e. all are commonly used meanings

2. In recent polls, Republicans have generally received better marks for all but which of the following?
   a. dealing with the Soviet Union
   b. keeping the country prosperous
   c. providing jobs for the unemployed
   d. controlling inflation
   e. national defense

3. In the U.S., party strength is gauged by the number of
   a. registered members a party has.
   b. people who identify themselves with a party.
   c. citizens who vote for party candidates.
   d. party members who participate in caucuses and conventions.

4. Which of the following would be the best example of a generational experience?
   a. a child seeing anti-war riots on television
   b. a student attending college and majoring in political science
   c. an older couple becoming alienated with its elected officials
   d. a college student getting involved in a Reagan campaign

5. How does a party best enlarge its base?
   a. by attracting disproportionate numbers of new voters
   b. by building new coalitions
   c. by stimulating the economy
   d. by running dynamic and charismatic candidates

6. Dealignment is best defined as
   a. voters switching back to their original party.
   b. voters becoming apolitical.
   c. voters' tendencies to make party identification a casual matter.
   d. the dissolution of coalitions.
   e. both *b* and *d*.

7. Which of the following has been suggested as an explanation for dealignment?
   a. American ambivalence
   b. American apathy
   c. an affluent, highly educated public
   d. all of the above
   e. both *a* and *c*

8. Which of the following best illustrates resolute pragmatism among voters?
   a. they supported the Reagan experiment even when the economy wasn't doing well in 1982
   b. they supported the New Deal reforms because they seemed to work
   c. they elected a Democratic president in the wake of Watergate
   d. they supported Eisenhower even though the majority of voters were Democrats at the time

9. According to Gallup polls, in which year did voters feel that the Republicans could better insure a strong economy?
   a. 1980
   b. 1982
   c. 1984
   d. both *b* and *c*

10. The first stirrings of party were in the policy conflict between
    a. Madison and Adams
    b. Jefferson and Madison
    c. Hamilton and Jefferson
    d. Hamilton and Washington
    e. none of the above

11. Which of the following could not be cited as a valid explanation for our electoral system being a two-party system?
    a. single-member election districts
    b. the winner-take-all system
    c. American ambivalence
    d. most Americans are not highly ideological
    e. national wealth and economic mobility enjoyed by Americans

12. The two political parties can best be described as
    a. doctrinal
    b. strongly programmatic
    c. deeply committed to conflicting economic policies
    d. creatures of compromise

ANSWER KEY

Completion

1. Democrats   p. 493
2. far from stable   p. 494
3. fluid   p. 499
4. Republicans   p. 508
5. blacks, white southerners
   p. 510

6. split ticket   p. 514
7. more volatile   p. 515
8. resolute pragmatism   p. 517
9. spirit of party   p. 523
10. the Republican   p. 523

True/False

1. F   p. 493
2. F   p. 494
3. T   p. 494
4. T   p. 497
5. F   p. 504
6. F   p. 509

7. T   p. 514
8. F   p. 516
9. F   p. 523
10. F   p. 522
11. T   p. 525
12. T   p. 526

Multiple Choice

1. d   p. 432
2. c   p. 496
3. b   p. 498
4. d   p. 507
5. a   pp. 508–09
6. c   p. 514

7. e   p. 515
8. b   p. 517
9. c   p. 519
10. c   p. 523
11. c   p. 526
12. d   p. 527

ESSAY QUESTIONS

1. A noted political scientist, E. E. Schattschneider, once argued that democracy would not be possible without political parties. Do you agree or disagree? Why?
2. American political parties are sometimes accused of being the same wine in different bottles. To what extent is this accusation correct? What are some of the ways the parties are similar? What are the important differences between the parties?

Further Investigation

Downs, Anthony. *An Economic Theory of Democracy.* New York: Harper, 1957.

Provides a compelling argument for the middle-of-the-road, moderate stands the parties take.

Ladd, Everett Carll. *Where Have All the Voters Gone? The Fracturing of America's Political Parties.* 2d ed. New York: Norton, 1982.
  Draws a connection between the health of the parties and the level and type of participation.

Lengle, James I. *Representation and Presidential Primaries: The Democratic Party in the Post-Reform Era.* Westport, Conn.: Greenwood Press, 1981.
  Summarizes the best available data on participation in presidential primaries, the representativeness of those participants, and the impact of different types of rules on election outcomes.

Polsby, Nelson W. *Consequences of Party Reform.* New York: Oxford University Press, 1983.
  Reviews the recent party reforms and what they have done to political parties, elections, and governance.

Ranney, Austin. *Curing the Mischiefs of Faction: Party Reform in America.* Berkeley: University of California Press, 1975.
  Integrates the Democratic party reforms of the 1970s into the broader questions of parties and democratic government.

Rosenstone, Steven, Behr, Roy, and Lazarus, Edward. *Third Parties in America.* Princeton: Princeton University Press, 1984.
  Examines the incentives and disincentives for third parties in America.

Schattschneider, E. E. *Party Government.* New York: Holt, Rinehart and Winston, 1942.
  An early book on the nature and function of parties. Draws an explicit connection between parties and democracy.

Shafer, Byron E. *Quiet Revolution: The Struggle for the Democratic Party and the Shaping of Post Reform Politics.* New York: Russell Sage Foundation, 1983.
  Thorough examination of the Democratic party reforms and reformers of the past fifteen years.

Sundquist, James L. *Dynamics of the Party System.* Washington, D.C.: Brookings Institution, 1973.
  Examines the early history of parties and some of the reasons we have the kind of parties we do.

Applying Political Science

1. Much of what you have read says political parties are organizationally weak. Is this as true in your area as it appears to be elsewhere in the country? Decide what things would be important to make parties organizationally viable and then set out to see the extent to which they exist in your town or community.

2. Your reading has taught you about the concept of party identifica-

tion, or the sense of affiliation most people have with a political party. If you were to ask yourself the question, Generally speaking, in politics do I consider myself a Democrat, a Republican, an independent, or what? how would you answer? Why do you consider yourself Republican, Democratic, or independent? Have you ever changed party identification? If so, when and why? What is the party identification of your parents? Did they ever talk to you about why they consider themselves part of one party or the other? The next time you talk to your parents, ask them these questions and attempt to determine the roots of their party identification as well as your own.

16 | The Media

Overview

People that expect to govern themselves can hardly do so without information on political officials, policies, and events. But the press can never be a neutral source of vital information. It is instead a social, economic, and political institution whose organization and resources make it very powerful.

Because of the increased remoteness and complexity of government, the press has become a central institution in this nation. With its increased importance, the press itself has become the subject of much study. Advanced technology has made it possible for the news media to reach mass audiences and thereby potentially influence public opinion. The press has become a profitable and powerful industry.

In the United States the press is for the most part a private business. In most democracies, newspapers and magazines are privately owned, but radio and television, especially in Europe, are commonly government enterprises. The American "electronic press" in contrast, is largely privately owned and operated. Government regulation of the print media is minimal, but the regulatory reach of government is substantial in the case of radio and television, because the airwaves are a finite public resource. The Federal Communications Commission grants and renews broadcast licenses, and it imposes such regulatory standards as the equal time rule and the fairness doctrine.

Contemporary technology for news dissemination, including radio and TV broadcasting, cable television, and the printing of newspapers in locales around the country by satellite transmissions, all have contributed to a concentration of news resources. With this concentration has come greater attention to the power of the press and greater concern over its possible abuses.

The press and government are bound closely together in the United States. Journalists have unusually open access to government officials. They form an important part of the group with whom political figures have regular contact. Journalists are themselves part of the political community, not distant reporters on it. The press has come to play an especially important role in

158

the American electoral process. The news media, not the parties, are for most voters the main source of information about candidates, and they may shape campaigns.

Although the press has been charged with having a liberal bias, research conducted on reports does not substantiate this criticism. Studies do suggest, however, that journalists are now more likely to see themselves in an adversary relationship with the central institutions, including government, and to stress exposure of the latter's shortcomings. Some students of the press worry that these professional norms have contributed to the rise of an excessively cynical view of political life.

Key Terms and Concepts

FCC
First Amendment
actual malice
fairness doctrine
participant model
ethics
Freedom of Information
    Act-1974

bias
press liberalism
cynicism
sensationalism
yellow journalism
neutral model

Chapter Outline

Introduction
    In early American history, government was local and personal.
        It has become remote and complex.
        Our information about it now comes mostly through mass media.
    The press has emerged as a central player in our society.
        It is concerned about its image.
        In polls, the media have generally been given high marks for believability, accuracy, competence, etc.
            People were critical of intrusiveness and some other practices, however.
    We need to scrutinize the news media as we do government.
Communications resources and democracy
    Examining the resources available to the press helps us analyze the power of the press.
        Press resources matter, and even enforcement of the First Amendment cannot solve all the problems.
        Only with developments in transportation and communications has the press been able to reach mass audience.
            Fifty million Americans tune into TV.

Newspapers and magazines also circulate to millions.

Large audiences generate enormous advertising revenues.

Such funds allow for a greater number of journalists than ever before.

They earn much better salaries than in years past.

The profession has risen in prestige.

Freedom of press is no longer enough to ensure pluralism in the news media.

Organization of the press

The press plays an important public-sector role.

Citizens must have information to decide issues.

In America there is agreement that the press should be privately owned and operated with the fewest possible government regulations.

The natural interplay of market forces will assure a variety of communications media that are in competition with each other and will report as fairly as possible.

The American press is private enterprise.

A small amount of radio and TV stations are public.

In Europe telecommunications are seen as more of a national utility.

Regulation

Federal Communications Commission regulates and permits electronic licenses.

Licensing is necessary because there are a limited number of airwaves.

TV stations get licenses renewed every five years.

There are few cases of license denial.

The FCC has established criteria for license renewal.

Equal time is required for political candidates in every office and every party.

The fairness doctrine requires that stations allow reasonable time for expression of opposing views on controversial issues.

Right-of-rebuttal provisions require that stations allow individuals an opportunity to respond to personal attacks.

Libel law

In Britain, persons can collect money in damages from newspapers if information printed is found to be untrue.

Consequently, British media don't "go public" until facts are watertight.

In the United States, "actual malice" must be proven, i.e., reckless disregard of the truth.

The British press is subject to other additional laws not present in the U.S.

Growing regulation

As late as 1960 there were virtually no national media in the U.S.

Most papers and television stations were locally owned.

An FCC regulation prohibiting ownership of more than seven TV or seven FM and seven AM radio stations simultaneously was partly responsible for this.

Three television networks handle news today.

USA Today, New York Times, and *Wall Street Journal* are examples of national newspapers.

National news magazines like *Time, Newsweek, U.S. News & World Report* also attest to the centralization of American media.

Evolution of the press

As parties took shape, so did newspapers.

Parties used newspapers to communicate their interpretation of political events.

They gave new dignity and color to American journalism.

Both the Federalists and their opposition had newspapers by 1791.

Newspapers rapidly assumed a key role in American political life.

Development of an independent press

The press changed greatly after the Civil War.

New printing technology reduced costs.

Electronic transmitters facilitated news gathering.

The size of newspapers increased.

The controlling audience for the American press shifted from partisan groups to a mass audience.

Joseph Pulitzer was a key figure in this development.

He bought the bankrupt *St. Louis Dispatcher* in 1878.

In 1883, he bought the *New York World* and dedicated it to uncovering and exposing fraud and evil.

The search for larger audiences gave rise to yellow journalism.

Competition between William Randolph Hearst and Pulitzer was sensationalistic.

Hearst even created a war in Cuba.

The rise of professionalism

Journalists wanted their own norms, ethical standards, and intellectual standards, to describe things as they saw them, with objectivity and factual detail.

Programs to teach journalists were developed.

By 1912 there were more than 30 schools.

With these developments came an increase in journalistic independence.

Radio and television

The first commercial radio station was started in 1922, and by 1925 there were more than 575 stations.

They were used for political purposes, e.g., fireside chats with
Roosevelt.

They were less influential than newspapers.

There was no TV news until the 1960s.

In 1963 news broadcasts were extended from fifteen to thirty
minutes.

As news became highly profitable, networks devoted much greater
resources to it.

News broadcasts command very large audiences, with the average
American watching twenty hours of television a week.

Television's share of the total news audience has risen sharply.

The number of people who list TV as their prime source of news
has risen from 29 percent in 1954 to 66 percent in 1982.

When there is conflict among stories, Americans indicate they are
more inclined to believe TV news versions than newspapers,
radio, or magazines.

The press and the institution of government

Press envelops the government in the U.S.

Reporters not only receive government press releases, but also have
tremendous personal contact with government officials.

The press and political parties

Reporters often act as "talent scouts," conveying judgments of candidates to the public.

They call the race.

They expose weaknesses.

The press role in campaigns is both a cause and consequence of
weakening political parties.

Political parties can no longer compete with the press as sources of
information on candidates and the progress of electoral campaigns.

Political parties are now subordinate structures in the whole process
of communication.

The press and the president

The press and politics are centered in Washington, D.C.

The press spotlights the presidency.

It makes the president seem larger than life.

It also shows his weaknesses.

Journalists are never rewarded for "favorable coverage," only for
exposing the bad.

The president manages the press for his benefit.

The press and government pluralism

The press can be seen as a fourth branch of government.

It represents both an opportunity and a problem for politicians.

It may advance their candidacies but may not reflect what the politician wants reflected.

Many fear that the inclination of the press to probe for weaknesses is eroding popular confidence in the governing process.

The press helps to disperse power further.

The media, politics, and responsibility

With the press playing such an influential role in American politics, its own political outlook is important.

Surveys show the press is liberal in ideology and tends to support Democratic candidates.

On social issues, the press is more liberal than the public at large.

More important than the opinions of the press is its behavior.

Research shows the liberal bias is not evident in the actual reports.

Research in the 1980 campaign also revealed no bias in the selections of stories.

Story selection is as important as actual writing.

The press often allies itself with liberals.

There is no agreement on whether or not bias exists in the media's coverage of news.

Political cynicism

Political cynicism is more of a concern than press liberalism.

Negativism and cynicism are fostered more by professional outlook than by political ideology.

Paul Weaver argues that especially TV news people see politics as a game for individuals to acquire personal gain.

Therefore, the task of the press is to expose politicians' bad tendencies.

This structure bias encourages an excessively manipulative view of politics.

The press, according to Michael Robinson, injects a negativistic, anti-institutional bias.

New professional norms

Negativism may be a result of a new set of professional norms.

The old normative model was "neutral," with sensationalism and bias viewed as the worst journalistic sins.

In the new "participant" model, sins are news suppression and superficiality.

Weaver modifies and extends this model.

The "liberal" tradition is characterized by preoccupation with facts and events, indifference to the ideological point of view.

The "partisan" or investigative tradition is not as neutral and more critical.

The public feels the press has a constitutional obligation to be as objective as possible.

What to report: a case study

A 1983 incident involving some missing State Department files and a television station's decision on whether or not to report them caused controversy within the journalistic community.

The reporter and his editor chose not to report them because the government had not lied.

They felt they might compromise national security by airing the documents.

Other journalists felt they should have been made public because it is a reporter's responsibility to report.

Still others would not have looked at the documents.

Review Questions

COMPLETION

1. In the United States, revenue is generated through _____.
2. The U.S. agency charged with regulating broadcasting is the

   _____.
3. The number of television and radio stations is limited because there

   are only so many _____.
4. In libel suits one must prove _____ in order to win.
5. The American press is protected from an overprotective government

   by the _____.
6. The *Gazette of the United States-1789* reflected the political views

   of the _____ party.

TRUE/FALSE

1. In the United States and in Europe, telecommunications systems are privately owned.
2. The FCC renews licenses to broadcast every three years.
3. The equal time doctrine requires stations to give political candidates equal time on the air.
4. The press devotes a disproportionate amount of coverage to the presidency.
5. The Times Mirror study found that the public ranked Ronald Reagan higher than Dan Rather in believability.
6. Despite his conservative views, a majority of reporters surprisingly voted for Richard Nixon in 1972.

MULTIPLE CHOICE

1. The rivalry between newspaper magnates Hearst and Pulitzer developed into
   a. the merging of the *Boston Globe* and the *Louisville Sun-Times*.
   b. the Cuban war.
   c. yellow journalism.
   d. a penny press.

2. Yellow journalism has to do with
   a. the color of ink used in the Sunday edition.
   b. excessive sensationalism.
   c. the low-life reporters during the end of the nineteenth century.
   d. the electronic media.

3. The *Red Lion Broadcasting* case dealt with
   a. libel.
   b. unlicensed operation.
   c. right of rebuttal.
   d. equal time.

4. The case of *New York Times* v. *Sullivan* established that a "public official" seeking libel must prove that
   a. it was a false statement.
   b. it was defamatory.
   c. it was made with "actual malice."
   d. he had lost office because of it.

5. Newspapers in the early years were
   a. called the party press.
   b. called the penny press.
   c. headed by people against the king.
   d. used to incite riots.

6. Who said, "You furnish the pictures and I'll furnish the war"?
   a. Grover Cleveland
   b. William Randolph Hearst
   c. Philip Freneau
   d. John Fenno

7. The Federal Communications Commission grants and renews licenses to broadcast and imposes regulatory standards such as
   a. equal time.
   b. the fairness doctrine.
   c. all of the above
   d. none of the above

ANSWER KEY

Completion

1. advertising   p. 543
2. FCC   p. 547
3. air waves   p. 547
4. actual malice   p. 549
5. Freedom of Information Act   p. 549
6. Federalist   pp. 551–52

True/False

1. F   p. 546
2. F   p. 547
3. T   p. 548
4. T   pp. 559–60
5. F   p. 539
6. F   p. 564

Multiple Choice

1. c p. 553
2. b p. 553
3. c p. 548
4. c p. 549

5. a p. 551
6. b p. 553
7. c p. 547

ESSAY QUESTIONS

1. What impact, if any, do the news media have on American public opinion and politics? Be sure to cite examples to support your case.
2. Describe the most important phases in the evolution of the American press and mass media. What impact did the changes in ownership, orientation, and medium have on the news and its audience?

Further Investigation

Crouse, Timothy. *The Boys on the Bus.* New York: Ballantine Books, 1972.

An inside and entertaining look at how the press covered one of the presidential candidates in the 1972 election.

Epstein, Edward J. *Between Fact and Fiction: The Problem of Journalism.* New York: Random House, 1975.

Uses case studies such as Watergate and the Pentagon Papers to look at how the press handles big stories.

Gans, Herbert. *Deciding What's News.* New York: Vintage Books, 1980.

What is news? Who says what is news? This book examines these questions.

Graber, Doris. *The Mass Media and American Politics.* Washington, D.C.: Congressional Quarterly Press, 1981.

Provides an overview of the role the media play in our political system.

Hess, Stephen. *The Washington Reporters.* Washington, D.C.: Brookings Institution, 1981.

Interesting book that examines the backgrounds, beliefs, and behavior of the reporters who cover national government.

Patterson, Thomas F. *The Mass Media Election.* New York: Praeger, 1980.

Examines the impact of television on election campaigns.

Ranney, Austin. *Channels of Power: The Impact of Television on American Politics.* New York: Basic Books, 1983.

There is no doubt that television has changed American lives and politics. Ranney assesses some of the most important ramifications for elections and government.

Simmons, Steven J. *The Fairness Doctrine and the Media*. Berkeley: University of California Press, 1978.
  Carefully examines the Federal Communication Commission's equal time and fairness requirements.

Applying Political Science

1. Select three newspapers and carefully monitor their presentation of the news for a one-week period. In your list of things to look for include which subjects received the most favorable location (front page, inside, second section, etc.), the length given to the major stories, and the accuracy of the headline and opening paragraph. Also monitor the syndicated columnists to determine whether they tend to select the same topics and identify if you can which reporters seem to lead the "pack." If you can, compare your information on newspaper coverage with the nightly news coverage. Do the same stories get top billing? Are important stories not covered by television, newspapers?

2. Accepting the premise that television is the primary source of news, how well informed are reporters about politics and current events? If there is a department or school for broadcast journalism on your campus, then interview faculty and students to see what, if any, work they do to learn about the subjects they will be reporting. If your university does not have a broadcast journalism department, then arrange to interview one of the reporters from a local television station about his or her background in journalism.

3. To what extent do people pay attention to the news? Conduct an experiment with the other students in your apartment, dormitory, or house. After a group of them have watched the news, ask them which parts they watched with greatest interest and why. Also ask a few fact questions to see whether they recall much about the news program they just watched on TV.

17 | Civil Liberties and Civil Rights

Overview

There is little disagreement that discrimination should be eliminated from laws, but there is controversy as to how far we should go in remedying past injustices. The Supreme Court has narrowly ruled that quotas and hiring goals are acceptable, but that plans which protect newly hired minorities to the point of necessitating layoffs of more senior white employees go too far. The debate still rages, especially concerning the fixing of racial quotas. Proponents of quotas point out that such systems are the only real way that affirmative action can have any positive effect in America. Opponents point out that quotas frustrate choice by merit.

In a signal case involving quotas, *Regents of University of California* v. *Bakke*, the Supreme Court was sharply divided. Four of the justices felt that quotas were unconstitutional. Four felt that they were constitutionally permissible. The controlling justice in this case, Lewis Powell, decided the issue by maintaining that although ethnic background could be considered in assigning state benefits, explicit quota systems were unconstitutional. The issue of quotas has not been fully resolved, in part because both sides are right.

Civil rights and liberties have been part of the American heritage since the very beginning. The Constitution explicitly guarantees them, reflecting their central role in democratic government. They are given unusual status, protected from factional strife and even majority rule. Although there is legitimate disagreement about how equal rights and equal protection should be achieved, the rights themselves cannot be overturned even should the vast majority favor such an outcome.

The term "civil rights" refers to those rights which are meant to protect segments of the community that have been subject to categorical discrimination. "Civil liberties" refers to the rights of citizenship of isolated individuals.

An excellent example of the struggle to obtain civil rights can be seen in the black civil rights movement, especially since World War II. Although the system of segregation had long been in conflict with the American ideals of liberty and equality, the movement to stop them did not make much progress until after World War II. The groundwork for the civil rights movement was laid by the large-scale movement of blacks to the North and into the cities before World War I. Such changes made political organization easier and more productive.

Signs of change in civil rights began in the late 1950s and early 1960s with the Court's decision in *Brown* v. *Board of Education of Topeka*, direct-action protests against segregation led by Martin Luther King, Jr., and several national laws forbidding the segregation of public facilities and protecting the voting rights of blacks. Public attitudes regarding this change in racial policy have been increasingly supportive. Educational opportunities for blacks have greatly improved over the last decade, as have managerial opportunities for black employees, black voter representation, and political opportunities for blacks. However, other statistics show that unemployment remains proportionally much higher for blacks, and black income continues to lag far behind the income of whites.

The civil liberties of the accused have also undergone dramatic change in the recent past. Through selective incorporation the Court has guaranteed those accused of state crimes the protections provided in the Bill of Rights. For instance, in *Mapp* v. *Ohio* in 1961, the Court held that any evidence seized illegally could not be entered in a state court against a defendent. In *Gideon* v. *Wainwright* all defendants were guaranteed the right to an attorney. Finally, in 1966, the Court held that incriminatory statements made by defendents who had not been informed of their rights and had voluntarily decided to waive them could not be admitted in a court of law. This proscription applied equally to federal and state courts. The Court, in recent years, has consequently qualified these rights to a degree, but they still appear to be mainstays of the American legal system.

Court rulings have helped to eliminate *de jure* segregation, but *de facto* segregation still exists where sections of cities are predominately black or white. Busing has been upheld by the Court as a legitimate method for eliminating *de jure* segregation but not *de facto* segregation. It remains a controversial issue.

One of the most important rights in a democracy is the right to freedom of expression. Even this right is not unlimited: it must be balanced against competing rights and societal objectives. Our nation has curtailed an individual's right to express himself politically, particularly in times of war or during periods of national tension. During the communist scare of the early cold war, for example, leaders of the Communist party of the United States were imprisoned for advocating the overthrow of the U.S. government. However, later in the same decade the Court held that for speech to constitute a "clear and present danger" it must be closely tied to incitement of illegal action.

Another problem involving free speech that has plagued the Court is pornography. A majority of the Court has consistently held that pornography is not a form of protected speech, but some justices believe it should receive absolute protection. Other justices are concerned that society not ban important works of art that might include elements offensive to the sensibilities of some. The present decision of the Court, promulgated in *Miller* v. *California*, allows communities some say in determining what is pornographic but also requires that the banned literature or film be without serious social value and that it depict some behavior specifically outlawed by statute.

Women are the most recent group to contend for civil rights in America. They typically receive less than equal pay and benefits for equal work. Although there are now federal laws that require equal pay for equal work, it has not proven to be an easy chore to classify jobs in terms of their worth so that women may receive such pay.

The president is the major governmental actor in the field of civil rights. He and his attorney general introduce legislation involving civil rights policy, enforce existing legislation, and set the tone for civil rights in their administration. They are aided by the Commission on Civil Rights, which monitors the performance of the federal government in fulfilling its civil rights obligations and makes recommendations concerning possible improvements. The Equal Employment Opportunity Commission exists to eliminate employment discrimination against minorities. The Congress, especially some of its committees, plays a significant oversight function in the field of civil rights. Most importantly, the courts seek to protect the civil rights of all minorities and often take action when other branches of government are stalemated.

There are a number of private groups interested in the fields of civil liberties, the rights of blacks and other ethnic minorities, and the rights of women. The major private organization responsible for the protection of civil liberties in America is the American Civil Liberties Union, which through court action and other means attempts to limit government intrusion against individuals. There are a number of organizations that have worked for the achievement of civil rights for blacks and other minorities. Among them are the National Association for the Advancement of Colored People, its now independent Legal Defense and Education Fund, the National Urban League, the Southern Christian Leadership Conference, Operation PUSH, and the Leadership Conference on Civil Rights. Groups engaged in women's rights are NOW (National Organization of Women) and the National Women's Political Caucus.

Key Terms and Concepts

civil rights

civil liberties

categorical discrimination

Fourteenth Amendment

Bill of Rights

Gideon v. *Wainwright*

American creed
selective incorporation
de jure segregation
de facto segregation
affirmative action
exclusionary rule
quotas
Smith Act
community standards
obscenity
comparable worth
Civil Rights Act of 1964
Voting Rights Act

Mapp v. *Ohio*
Miranda v. *Arizona*
Brown v. *Board of Education
of Topeka*
*Regents of University of
California* v. *Bakke*
Equal Employment Opportu-
nity Commission
American Civil Liberties
Union
National Association for the
Advancement of Colored
People

Chapter Outline

Ending racial discrimination
    The issue of how this should be brought about is very controversial.
        People generally agree that discrimination should be eliminated
            from existing legislation.
        They disagree as to whether additional positive steps need to be
            taken.
    As with many controversial issues, it has been left to the courts to re-
        solve this one.
        In *Sheet Metal Workers' International* v. *EEOC*, the Equal Employ-
            ment Opportunity Commission sued a local union for racial dis-
            crimination.
            The Supreme Court narrowly upheld the decision of a lower
                court, which ordered the union to increase its non-white mem-
                bership to 29 percent by a given date.
            In arguing for the minority, Justice White argued that the Court
                had never endorsed quotas and should not do so.
                He called them a "kind of racially discriminatory hiring prac-
                    tice."
        In another case involving the protection of newly hired black
            teachers from layoffs in order to attain a proper percentage of
            black faculty, the Court narrowly ruled against the school board
            policy.
            Justice Powell argued that such discrimination is valid to achieve
                hiring goals, but not when considering layoffs.
    The Court is quite divided on such issues.
        One cause of such controversy is the distinction between affirmative
            action and racial quotas.
        Affirmative action has more support among the justices than quotas
            do.

Regents of University of California v. *Bakke*

  Allan Bakke was denied admittance to medical school despite his credentials being stronger than those of many minority applicants who were accepted.

  He eventually sued the school, charging that its policy was illegal.

  The California courts upheld Bakke's assertion.

  The Supreme Court also sustained Bakke's position in a highly unusual 4-4-1 split.

    Fifty-seven *amicus curiae* were filed with the Court — an unprecedented number.

    A lengthy *New York Times'* editorial declared that "both sides are right. . . ." but thought in the national interest for Bakke to lose the case.

The Constitution, majority preferences, and basic rights

  Civil liberties and civil rights are a key element in contemporary public policy in the United States.

  The Declaration of Independence and the Bill of Rights are examples of this country's commitment to civil rights and liberties.

  The Constitution contains explicit policy statements in these areas.

Civil rights are basic political entitlements without which democracies could not exist.

Civil rights questions are different from political policy considerations because majority preferences are not the basis for decision.

There can be legitimate disagreement about how civil rights policy should be formulated.

Civil rights are often stated as absolutes and therefore have a tendency to clash with other rights.

  In such cases, the will of the majority should rule.

If a group can claim that they are being denied a basic right, it tends to further their cause.

Securing basic rights

  Civil rights often refer to a segment of the population that has encountered categorical discrimination (e.g. blacks).

  Civil liberties refer to the denial of rights of citizenship to isolated individuals or small groups.

Extending rights

  Changes in these areas have resulted from increasing expectations and demands.

    The civil rights movement was particularly strong in the sixties.

    The women's movement was more active in the late seventies and early eighties.

  Tocqueville wrote that America was founded and flourished in perfect freedom, yet this perfect freedom has undergone considerable expansion since that time.

Curbing racial discrimination
   In race relations, rising expectations produced dramatic change.
      Black soldiers returning home from World War II still found them-
      selves excluded from most public facilities and the decision-
      making of government.
      They were also victims of extreme racial violence.
Assertion of American values
   The sources of this rapid transformation in race relations are complex.
   Conflict between the American creed and the reality of American race
      relations was not new but became important during this period.
   Demographic changes were another source of the rapid change in race
      relations.
   At the start of World War I, industrial opportunities started a black
      migration from the South that continued after the war.
      In the North, blacks did not encounter segregation.
      Concentrated urban black populations were much less likely to be
         victims of violence.
      Northern blacks also began to move to the cities.
   These changes made black political organization easier and sparked
      the political effort to improve race relations after World War II.
Signs of change
   The courts in *Brown* v. *Board of Education of Topeka* (discussed in
      Chapter 10) were among the first to signal a change in national
      racial policy.
   Martin Luther King, Jr., the most influential black leader, led early
      protests in the South against segregation and other discriminatory
      practices.
   The Civil Rights Act of 1964 and the Voting Rights Act of 1965 em-
      powered the federal government to ensure the desegregation of
      public facilities and the voting rights of blacks.
   Public attitudes have been increasingly supportive of efforts to guar-
      antee civil rights to deprived minorities.
Substantial gains in civil rights
   There are several indications of the success of recent civil rights
      policy.
      Segregation has been eliminated.
      De jure segregation no longer exists.
      Black voter participation has increased dramatically, as has the
         number of black officeholders.
      Educational opportunities for blacks and whites are beginning to
         equalize.
      Finally, an increasing number of blacks are entering managerial oc-
         cupations.
   Unfortunately, however, the income of black families remains con-
      siderably smaller than that of white families.

Unemployment statistics also remain considerably higher for blacks than whites.

Extending the rights of the accused

The constitutional protections accorded persons accused of crimes have been greatly enhanced by court decision applying the Bill of Rights to the states.

Selective incorporation

The Bill of Rights was enacted to protect states and individuals from a list of actions that the national government might take.

However, by the advent of the Civil War, it was clear that state governments could also deny individual freedoms.

To correct this oversight, the Fourteenth Amendment was passed.

It prohibited states from abridging the privileges or immunities of citizens and from denying them life, liberty, or property without due process of law, or denying any person equal protection of the laws.

In the late nineteenth century, the Court began to enforce compliance with these broad and sweeping requirements.

Today almost all prohibitions against the national government contained in the Bill of Rights apply as well to state governments through the Fourteenth Amendment.

This process is known as selective incorporation.

In *Gideon* v. *Wainwright* (1963), the Court guaranteed the right to counsel in state courts.

In *Mapp* v. *Ohio* (1961), the Court required that the exclusionary rule barring the use in trial of unconstitutionally seized evidence be required of the states.

In 1966, the Court made the Miranda rules binding upon federal and state courts alike.

These rules require that a suspect be advised of his right to remain silent and obtain counsel.

Competing values collide

Pursuit of civil rights often means that attainment of one worthy objective may cause serious problems for the attainment of another.

In *Brewer* v. *Williams*, for example, enforcement of exclusionary rule guarantees seems to jeopardize the administration of justice.

As a result, the Supreme Court has created exceptions to an absolute imposition of the exclusionary rule.

Civil liberties decisions are still being made within the general framework laid down by Miranda, Mapp, and Gideon.

From *de jure* to *de facto* segregation

Although *Brown* v. *Board of Education of Topeka* abolished *de jure* school segregation, it did not abolish *de facto* segregation.

De jure segregation is written into law.

De facto segregation exists because some schools serve neighborhoods which are made up almost entirely of one race or another.

Since *Brown*, the Court has upheld school busing as a remedy for *de
jure* segregation.

The Court has also held that there is no constitutional protection
against *de facto* segregation, striking down some remedies to cure
such segregation.

Freedom of expression

Freedom of expression is necessary to a democratic society.

The courts have been forced to balance freedom of expression with
other interests.

When the government of the United States faces a serious threat, it is
more willing to enact restrictions on political speech.

Restrictions on speech were established during both the Civil War
and World War I.

The Smith Act made it possible to convict subversives advocating
the violent overthrow of the government.

In 1951, the Court upheld the conviction of several Communists
under this act.

In subsequent cases, the Court moved away from this decision.

Obscenity and community standards

The Court has continually held that obscenity is not protected by the
First Amendment.

Defining obscenity is difficult.

Some justices feel that all forms of speech, including obscenity, are
entitled to absolute protection.

Others believe what is and is not considered obscene should reflect
community standards as long as those standards do not wipe out
great works of art or the expression of acceptable works of
literature.

A 1986 report of a special commission appointed by the U.S. Attorney
General urged Congress and state legislatures to strengthen provisions of obscenity laws.

The report caused considerable controversy.

Men and women in the labor market: The issue of "comparable worth"

Women's rights are an important element of the American civil rights
movement.

Female workers make less than their male counterparts in the same
positions.

The distinction between "equal work" and "comparable work" is important.

Key actors in civil liberties and civil rights policy

The president may initiate civil rights legislation, appoints key Justice
Department civil rights personnel, and administers civil rights
programs.

The Justice Department is charged with enforcement of national civil rights laws and setting broad policy directives for civil rights administration.

The Commission on Civil Rights monitors the performance of the federal government in the administration of civil rights and makes recommendations to the president to improve federal performance.

The Equal Employment Opportunity Commission is charged with eliminating discrimination in employment practices nationwide.

The judiciary committees of both the House and Senate are the chief congressional committees with jurisdiction over matters involving civil rights and liberties.

Courts have been major actors in the shaping of American civil rights and liberties, especially when the other branches of government are immobilized.

Interest groups

Interest groups play an important part in civil liberties, the rights of blacks and other ethnic minorities, and women's rights.

The American Civil Liberties Union is the major interest group in the field of civil liberties.

The ACLU frequently files cases against governmental action that seems to restrict civil liberties.

The oldest civil rights group in the U.S. is the National Association for the Advancement of Colored People (NAACP), which works to stop racial discrimination in all areas of national life.

Other groups involved in civil rights activities are the National Urban League, the Southern Christian Leadership Conference, Operation PUSH, and the Leadership Conference on Civil Rights.

The two organizations most active on behalf of women's rights are the National Organization for Women (NOW) and the National Women's Political Caucus.

Review Questions

COMPLETION

1. Many of the protections of the Bill of Rights apply to state governments as well through the _____ Amendment.

2. _____ led early direct action protests in the South against policies of segregation.

3. _____ segregation is the segregation that exists due to neighborhoods that are made up of predominantly one race.

4. The _____ warnings require police officers to inform criminal suspects of their rights under the law.

5. In *Gideon* v. *Wainwright* the Supreme Court held that _____ must be provided by the state for all indigent defendants accused of a crime.
6. The Supreme Court struck down the Jackson Board of Education's affirmative action plan because it dealt not only with valid hiring goals but also with _____.
7. The process by which the guarantees of the Bill of Rights have been gradually applied to the states is known as _____.
8. Justice William O. Douglas felt that pornographic speech should be _____.
9. The main reason that civil rights and liberties cannot be absolute is _____.

TRUE/FALSE

1. The Constitution is very explicit regarding civil rights and civil liberties.
2. The National Association for the Advancement of Colored People is a government organization founded in 1909.
3. Despite *Brown* v. *Board of Education of Topeka* de jure segregation has not been alleviated.
4. The "clear and present danger" doctrine only applies in times of war.
5. The exclusionary rule bars the introduction of illegally seized evidence into criminal trials.
6. Selective incorporation refers to the process by which busing was introduced as a remedy of segregation.
7. Even pornography is considered protected speech under the First Amendment.
8. The income of the average black family continues to lag behind the income of the average white family.
9. The Fourteenth Amendment was passed to guarantee criminal suspects their civil liberties.

MULTIPLE CHOICE

1. Marvin confesses to a crime without having been informed of his right to an attorney. His case would probably be most interesting to
   a. the Department of Justice.
   b. the NAACP Legal Defense Fund.
   c. Operation PUSH.
   d. the American Civil Liberties Union.
   e. the National Socialist party.

2. Civil rights are different from civil liberties in that
   a. there is no distinction.
   b. civil liberties are only for criminals.
   c. civil rights have been won through court opinions; civil liberties were granted in the Bill of Rights.
   d. civil rights are only for minorities; civil liberties are for everybody.
   e. civil liberties involve isolated individuals while civil rights have to do with ethnic groups.

3. A major reason for the rising expectations that led to major civil rights gains in the post-World War II era was
   a. demographic change.
   b. a rise in the ratio of black income to white income.
   c. an increase in black politicians.
   d. the passage of the Fourteenth Amendment.
   e. Truman's civil rights policies.

4. Juan is fired because he is Mexican-American. His case could probably best be handled by
   a. the National Organization for Women.
   b. the House Committee on the Judiciary.
   c. the Equal Employment Opportunity Commission.
   d. the Justice Department.
   e. the Commission on Civil Rights.

5. Traditionally women who have done comparable jobs to men have earned
   a. 30 percent of their salaries.
   b. 40 percent of their salaries.
   c. 110 percent of their salaries.
   d. 75 percent of their salaries.
   e. 60 percent of their salaries.

6. Court-imposed busing has been
   a. upheld in cases of de jure segregation but struck down in cases of de facto segregation.
   b. upheld in cases of de facto segregation but struck down in cases of de jure segre-gation.
   c. mostly favored by blacks and whites.
   d. upheld in cases of both de facto and de jure segregation.
   e. generally a poor means of segregating schools.

7. Majority rule has no role in deciding what rights should be granted to individuals or groups. It does, however, have something to say about
   a. how long a period those rights should be granted.
   b. under what conditions those rights can be denied.
   c. what rights are necessary to democracy.
   d. how those rights should be achieved.
   e. when requested rights really are rights and not just political desires.

178

8. In *Miller* v. *California*, the Court determined that
   a. we know pornography when we see it.
   b. pornography is constitutionally protected.
   c. no work regardless of its merit should be exempt from being banned.
   d. community standards have a role in the determination of what is pornography.
   e. state law need not specifically define the behavior in question to label it pornographic.

ANSWER KEY

Completion

1. Fourteenth   p. 598
2. Martin Luther King, Jr.   p. 593
3. De facto   pp. 606–07
4. Miranda   p. 601
5. an attorney   pp. 598–600
6. layoffs   p. 580
7. selective incorporation   p. 598
8. protected by the First Amendment   p. 611
9. that they tend to conflict with other important societal objectives   p. 585

True/False

1. T   p. 583
2. F   p. 620
3. F   p. 606
4. F   pp. 609–10
5. T   p. 600
6. F   p. 598
7. F   pp. 611–12
8. T   p. 596
9. F   p. 598

Multiple Choice

1. d   pp. 619–20
2. e   p. 585
3. a   pp. 588–89
4. c   pp. 618–19
5. e   p. 614
6. a   pp. 606–07
7. b   p. 585
8. d   p. 612

ESSAY QUESTIONS

1. From the very beginning the question of civil rights for blacks has been an important part of American politics. Summarize the important constitutional and political changes that have extended civil rights to black Americans.
2. Some observers argue that the courts are entrusted with the responsibility of guarding civil rights and civil liberties. Yet, as we know, all members of Congress and the president swear to uphold the Constitution. Are the courts more likely to become involved in civil liberties or civil rights questions than the other branches? Why? Is this a good idea?

Further Investigation

Berger, Raoul. *Government by the Judiciary*. Cambridge: Harvard
University Press, 1977.
Reviews the history of the Fourteenth Amendment and its present
applications. Argues that the original meaning should be followed
by the courts.
Dwarkin, Ronald. *Taking Rights Seriously*. Cambridge: Harvard University Press, 1977.
America is a country committed to political and other rights. This
book examines what rights are, how they relate to government, and
what happens when they come into conflict.
Friendly, Fred W. *The Good Guys, the Bad Guys and the First Amendment: Free Speech and Fairness in Broadcasting*. New York: Vintage
Books, 1975.
An examination of the rules governing broadcasting and their impact on the news and the First Amendment.
Hamilton, Charles V. *The Bench and the Ballot: Southern Federal
Judges and Black Voters*. New York: Oxford University Press, 1973.
Useful summary of the legislative and judicial actions taken to ensure black voting rights.
Kluger, Richard. *Simple Justice*. New York: Random House/Vintage
Books, 1977.
How the Court responded to more than a century of school segregation.
Levy, Leonard W. *Legacy of Suppression: Freedom of Speech and Press
in Early American History*. Cambridge: Harvard University Press,
1960.
Argues that those who adopted the Constitution and Bill of Rights
did not support a broad scope for freedom of speech, even in
politics.
Lewis, Anthony. *Gideon's Trumpet*. New York: Vintage Books, 1964.
Lewis's account of a convict's appeal to the Supreme Court establishing the right to legal counsel.
McClosky, Herbert and Brill, Alida. *Dimensions of Tolerance: What
Americans Believe About Civil Liberties*. New York: Russell Sage
Foundation, 1983.
Represents several years' worth of original research on public
opinion on this important dimension of American life.
Peltason, Jack W. *Fifty-eight Lonely Men*. New York: Harcourt, Brace
and World, 1961.
Insightful study of the federal district and circuit court judges in the
South who implemented the *Brown* decision.
Woodward, C. Vann. *The Strange Career of Jim Crow*. New York:
Oxford University Press, 1957.

Allows reader to sense the legal and institutional hurdles placed before Southern blacks.

Applying Political Science

1. If your local police department has a "ride-along" program, arrange to spend an evening with a local policeman. In addition to learning about police work, interview the officer about how he or she implements the Miranda warnings discussed in the text and what precautions are taken during search of automobiles and homes of defendents. Also ask about whether the Supreme Court rules have impeded police work.

2. Interview the editor or a senior writer for one of your local newspapers and ask about how they decide to print a story. Pose several hypothetical cases for them, including some involving possible libel, inconsistent informants, and the private lives of elected officials. Also discuss the editor's or writer's views on disclosure of sources in criminal or civil trials.

3. There has been a lot of discussion recently about the separation of church and state. Interview three local religious leaders and discuss what role organized religion should play in American government, i.e., display of religious symbols on public property, reference to deity on currency, prayer in public schools, or a ban on abortion. If possible, also interview someone from the American Civil Liberties Union and inquire about the same issues.

18 | Political Economy

Overview

Political economy is the use of government power to secure economic objectives. While the actual lasting impact that government actions can have on the economy is limited, government's role in the economy is nonetheless significant. For example, the Tax Reform Act of 1986 was a useful and needed piece of legislation that will undoubtedly influence the economy, although probably not as much as its sponsors would hope.

American policy makers generally agree that we want high economic growth, high employment, and low inflation. In the United States, as contrasted to other Western democracies, most attention is focused on how best to achieve these economic goals and objectives. In short, although policy makers agree on what we want, they differ sharply on how to secure it. Politicians rely heavily upon economists for economic theories intended to better secure what we want.

The Great Depression uprooted traditional ideas about economics, and politicians began seriously questioning whether the old ideas fit new economic conditions. In this context the prescriptions of British economist John Maynard Keynes gained popularity as a means to redirect government activity without altering our private-property-based economy.

Keynes maintained that the only way to achieve high employment and high economic growth while in the throes of a depression would be to have government assume the burden of promoting consumption rather than savings. The ultimate solution for recovery necessitated breaking the vicious circle generated by underconsumption in the private sector. Prior to the 1929 stock market crash, the wealthier members of society began hoarding much of their wealth, rather than reinvesting it in business enterprises. This action reduced the amount of money in the economy. As the rest of society recognized that the money supply was dwindling, large numbers of people began hoarding money they would otherwise have spent on goods. With less money flowing in the economy and little demand for goods and services, businesses closed, banks failed, prices for goods fell, and deflation dominated the economy. Individuals, fearing that the trying times would leave them with nothing, further reduced their levels of consumption. Then, in the face of this trend of underconsumption, people began losing their jobs. Unemployment then completed the circle, which continued to feed itself.

Keynes felt that if government stepped in and got money to those beset with problems, they would once again begin to spend rather than save. And as more people began to spend, the demand for goods would increase, business would pick up, people would go back to work, and prices would return to normal.

The economic theories expressed by Keynes generated substantial opposition, but still were implemented in part by Roosevelt. By Keynes's standards the government spending programs Roosevelt instituted were far short of what was needed to overcome the Depression. In fact, America did not fully recover until massive government spending began with our entry into World War II.

In Keynes's time there was widespread concern that government was not doing enough. Now there is a wisespread concern that government is doing too much. Over the last half century the government has grown to a point where its rate of spending has outstripped the growth of the economy. Along with this we are now witnessing our government's largest budget deficit in history. The size of the deficit, in turn, directly affects interest rates and inflation. The results of big government, however, are not all bad. Phenomenal growth in our gross national product (GNP), creation of new and varied job markets, and a higher or more affluent standard of living for the broadest portion of the population are some of the most prominent benefits provided by our expanded federal government.

The government's involvement in economic policy making also has implications for politics. Presidents and congressmen seeking reelection often claim that it is their policies that are responsible for providing a healthy economy. Their opponents would like voters to believe that the incumbent has either been entirely unsuccessful or has failed in some important areas of the economy. Hence, economic policy is not solely a means to achieve a prosperous and sound economy but also a help in furthering political goals.

There are three areas of economic policy — regulatory, monetary, and fiscal. Regulatory policy is concerned with prices and entry into the market. Most of government's attention has focused on prices in an effort to ensure orderly growth in developing industries. But businesses generally do not require regulation throughout their existence; hence, there is now a trend to deregulate stable industries like the airlines, trucking companies, utilities, and financial institutions, whose price levels can be dictated by market forces.

Government may use regulation to protect the health and safety of society and the interests of consumers. Examples of such regulations in this sense are pollution emission standards, vehicle safety standards, and advertising standards.

Monetary policy emphasizes the need to control the money supply and the interest rates in order to secure sound economic growth. The monetarists' contention is that steady, stable growth in the money supply will correspond to and sustain real economic growth.

Fiscal policy deals with those adjustments that the government makes in taxing and spending. In fiscal and monetary policy the government looks for solutions to the problem of how best to secure our economic objectives.

Who are the participants in making economic policy? The president is generally recognized as the primary actor in drafting economic policy, although he is aided by the Council of Economic Advisers, the Treasury Department, and the Office of Management and Budget. The president decides on an overall set of objectives, then develops an economic plan to achieve those objectives.

Next the president's economic proposals may require congressional approval. The plan is evaluated by various appropriation, finance, and budget committees, which usually make only minor recommendations and changes. After their work is finished, the proposal is sent to the floor of the House and Senate for final acceptance and incorporation into public policy.

The success of the policy, however, rests in hands of the other actors. The Federal Reserve System is a complicated structure responsible for monetary policy. The "Fed" was designed to be an autonomous entity that would regulate the money supply and discount rates; in a sense it is the central bank of the United States. Neither the president nor any part of his administration has any direct influence over the "Fed."

Various governmental departments, private business groups, labor groups, and even the lone consumer are important to the ultimate success or failure of any economic policy.

Key Terms and Concepts

political economy
gross national product
inflation vs. deflation
regulatory policy
stagnation
consumer protection
real economic growth
tax policy

consumption vs. saving
deficit
fiscal policy
monetary policy
prices and entry
monetarism
discount rate

Chapter Outline

Introduction
  Political economy is the use of governmental power to secure economic objectives.

Government is limited in what it can do to affect the economy.

One of its principal means of promoting its economic objectives involves tax policy.

Major new tax legislation was passed in 1985–86.

The intellectual case for tax reform

The 1986 tax reform reflected a consensus that there was need to repair the tax laws, which had become discriminatory among various businesses and industries.

There was a great range in real tax rates among different industries.

Deductions were allowed on income devoted to paying interest charges of all kinds.

A host of other items had deductions and exemptions.

The tax code contained its own spiraling paradox: High rates encouraged people to push for exemptions, and the exemptions made it necessary to raise the rates to maintain revenue levels.

Many experts concluded this system was economically inefficient.

They pushed for a broader tax base that would allow for cuts in the rate of taxation.

The Tax Reform Act of 1986

Despite the political promises necessary to produce such a piece of legislation, the bill reflected the intellectual arguments set forth above to a surprising degree.

The new act replaced the fourteen rates of individual income tax with two.

Many rates were cut and deductions were eliminated.

Both parties claim and deserve a portion of the credit.

President Reagan lent personal prestige and the resources of his administration to the effort.

Two young Democrats, Senator Bill Bradley and Representative Richard Gephardt, authored the first tax reform bill.

Bradley especially helped push the final measure through Congress.

Politics and economics

In the future, economists are likely to conclude that the new tax legislation both helped and hurt the economy.

They will also probably conclude that its impact on the economy was less than its sponsors had hoped it would be.

The government is limited in its ability to influence the economy, but it is the most responsive to public demands of any factor influencing the economy.

The electoral fate of administrations often rests on economic performance.

The 1984 economic recovery helped Reagan win reelection.

Politicians are guided by underlying economic philosophies.

Democrats and Republicans disagree on these philosophies.

It is important to understand the evolution of this debate.

Economic policy: 1930s to the 1980s

Economic debates often involve two questions:

What goals and objectives are to be advanced through government intervention?

How does the economy work, and how can an economic objective best be achieved?

In foreign countries disagreement is over objectives.

Because a general agreement on objectives exists in the U.S., the arguments center mostly on how to achieve them.

Politicians often look to economists for general guidance.

John Maynard Keynes and Keynesian Economics

Keynesian ideas became influential in America during the Depression of the 1930s and were associated with Franklin Roosevelt.

"Old economics" ceased to fit actual conditions.

A "new economics" was needed.

Keynes offered a solution to the crisis without abandoning capitalism.

He maintained consumption should be promoted rather than savings because the former stimulates investment and utilization of resources.

He thought government should generate consumption through public work programs to get money to the poor, financed through deficit spending if necessary.

The economic conditions of the 1930s necessitated some solution.

Unemployment in 1935 was 20.1 percent.

There was a decline in gross national product, with productivity, income, and consumption falling drastically.

Deflation occurred because a shrinking market forced prices down.

Lower prices are a disincentive to investing.

Given the role of the government during the 1930s, Keynes' proposal seemed a measured, sensible, prudent response.

It suited the country's needs better than any available alternative.

Most economists agree the amount of government stimulus was in fact too modest.

Spending for World War II was the ultimate remedy.

Shifts in the political economy: The post-Keynesian era

As conditions changed, economists and politicians came to search for another new economics.

During the New Deal, government presence was small and taxes low.

By the 1970s, government presence had become very large, making it difficult to argue that more government was the answer.

Taxes have risen.

Government spending has outstripped the growth of the economy.

Politicians have found it easier to increase expenditures than taxation.

Roosevelt intentionally created a federal debt to stimulate the economy during the Depression.

This debt rose sharply during World War II.

It is now roughly $2.1 billion.

Making the interest payments on the debt is now a problem.

Large federal deficits are a departure from Keynesian economics.

According to Keynes, government should:

Spend more than it takes in during a recession to stimulate demand.

Tax more than it spends when economy is booming to temper inflation and sustain growth.

Fiscal policy is this adjusting of taxing and spending levels.

Inflation has climbed to record levels over the last quarter-century.

It has replaced deflation as a major economic concern.

However, falling oil prices actually brought inflation in the industrialized world to a halt in the mid-1980s.

Still, the problem is no longer underconsumption but inflation.

Economic changes have brought gains as well as problems.

The problems have become large government, public expectations, difficult-to-manage revenues, expenditures, and inflation.

Some advantages have been accrued.

The GNP has experienced tremendous growth despite some recessions.

Many jobs have been created to accommodate the baby boom generation and the entrance of women into the labor market.

Affluence has increased, with U.S. per capita income being the highest among industrialized nations.

Public attitudes on political economy

The public perceives inflation as the greatest evil.

Inflation erodes savings and makes financial planning difficult.

The public questions government's ability to manage the economy.

Government's ability to control inflation has become more important to voters than its ability to curb unemployment.

Americans' opinions on who is responsible for inflation have also changed.

Most tend to hold government responsible for it now.

Ambivalence about government

A majority of Americans tend to criticize government for going too far in regulating economic life.

They also feel, however, that it should ensure that everyone has a good standard of living.

There are many examples of such ambivalence.

Political implications

Big government is no longer in, although no one advocates dismantling existing government programs.

Both parties want to promote economic growth and thereby win the hearts of the electorate.

The Reagan administration has used its own approach to handle the political economy.

It proposed to:

curb government growth and spending.

curb government regulation of business.

cut back federal tax levels.

curb inflation through competitive private economy and national money supply tied to economic growth.

The Democrats offered a different approach.

They felt that:

military spending should be curbed.

more vigorous federal regulations are needed in some areas.

Reagan's tax cuts have fueled an unacceptably large deficit.

economic growth requires intelligent federal planning.

Tools of economic policy

There are three broad groups of government policies dealing with economics: regulatory, monetary, and fiscal.

Regulatory policy: the push to deregulate

Deregulation has been the watchword of the late 1970s and the 1980s.

There are two types of regulation: prices and entry; and health, safety, and consumer protection.

In regulating prices and entry, government sets prices and determines which firms can enter which markets, thus promoting orderly growth.

In the eyes of many, deregulation was necessary in order to increase competition, improve service, and lower prices.

An alliance of liberals and conservatives emerged to enact deregulation legislation.

Conservatives favored deregulation of certain industries for ideological reasons.

Liberals favored certain deregulation because it was an unwarranted aid to business.

With such an unusual agreement among economists, liberals, and conservatives, deregulation made rapid progress.

The airlines, trucking, and railroad industries have been significantly deregulated.

It seems to be working since no one is calling for a return to the former regulations.

The other type of regulation deals with health and safety standards as well as consumer protection.

Congress passed more than fifty major pieces of legislation in the 1960s and 1970s designed to ameliorate the social impact of business.

There was no conservative-liberal alliance in support of deregulation in this area.

Liberals defended existing legislation and sought to extend it.

Conservatives favored a rollback or at least an end to new laws.

A rough equilibrium preserved existing legislation and prevented new legislation.

Fiscal and monetary policy: contending approaches among economists

Five general schools of economic thought prevail in this area.

Monetarists emphasize adjusting money supply and interest rates to control inflation.

Supply-siders would use across-the-board tax cuts to encourage people to work harder in absence of tax penalties and invest more in productive enterprises.

The "old time religion" is based on a belief in government austerity: Curb the profligacy of the democrats.

Other components include a tight money supply, a balanced federal budget, and a willingness to endure economic slowdowns to stop inflation.

The industrial policy advocates enlarging government's role in promoting conditions for growth, especially in new technologies.

Keynesian economics, though not nearly as prominent today as in the late 1930s to the 1960s, is still a major school of thought.

It proposes achieving full employment with a high and rapid level of growth in GNP by government management of demand.

Growth dividends can then enlarge social programs.

The economic policy-makers

The president is a key player.

Presidential popularity is affected by the economy.

Short-term economic policies are often pursued to stimulate the economy before elections.

As a result, there is an electoral rhythm to the national economy.

The president has little direct control over monetary policy.

The Federal Reserve System is another key player.

The "Fed" is the central bank of the U.S.

It has four components: the Board of Governors, the Federal Open Market Committee, twelve Federal Reserve Banks, and all of the member commercial banks.

The Fed is the center of a political storm.

Strong backing from the president is critical.

The Fed and the president have a symbiotic relationship.

The Council of Economic Advisers counsels the president.

The Treasury Department is by far the most influential Cabinet department in economic policy. \

The Office of Management and Budget assists the president in formulating a budget each year.

The Departments of Commerce, Labor, and Agriculture also play substantial parts.

Congress has a say in every area of fiscal policy.

    The Congressional Budget Act of 1974 enlarged the role of Congress in budget affairs.

Business groups such as the Chamber of Commerce of the United States have great influence in economic policy.

    The Business Roundtable is another group with great influence.

Despite declining influence, labor remains an important actor.

    The AFL-CIO has access and influence in economic policy due to the strength of its membership.

Review Questions

COMPLETION

1. _____ was the economic philosopher who said, "I come not to bury capitalism."
2. Governmental adjusting of taxing and spending levels is known as _____ policy.
3. In the Tax Reform Act of 1986 the base was *broadened* and the rates were _____.
4. For the last twenty years, the public has pinpointed _____ as responsible for inflation.
5. _____ is the leading monetarist economist.
6. _____ policy is the economic policy that has the greatest impact on short-term economic performance.
7. The United States was the only country to experience reduced inflation during the mid-1980s.
8. _____ economists put great weight on fiscal policy.
9. According to the Keynesians, a rapidly growing economy provides a _____, which is additional revenues that can be expended to enlarge social programs.
10. According to Tufte, personal income tends to _____ faster in election years than in years without elections.

1. The United States has followed the same economic philosophy consistently since the early 1800s.
2. The basic productive capacities of the United States were the same during the 1930s as they were during the 1920s.
3. The Roosevelt administration immediately implemented Keynesian prescriptions.
4. Deregulation was supported by both conservatives and liberals.
5. Economists all agree on how the economy is best to be managed.
6. Deregulation has generally worked.
7. The United States is the only country suffering from persistent high inflation.
8. Since the early 1970s, per capita income in the United States has continued to rise in real terms.
9. In recent polls, welfare programs are more deeply criticized than any other governmental service.
10. Because of the plethora of competing groups and interests, it has been impossible to pass meaningful tax reform.

MULTIPLE CHOICE

1. Keynesian economics does not include which of the following?
   a. Full employment is best advanced by promoting consumption rather than savings.
   b. Increased consumption stimulates greater investment.
   c. Society's resources are best used when production is low.
   d. Capitalism can work better than socialism because it allows more personal choice.
   e. all of the above
2. Over the last quarter-century, the rate of growth of government spending has _____ rate of growth of the overall economy.
   a. decreased faster than the
   b. increased faster than the
   c. decreased at the same
   d. increased at the same
   e. increased slower than the
3. Which of the following does not deserve credit for the Tax Reform Act of 1986?
   a. Ronald Reagan
   b. Dan Rostenkowski
   c. Bill Bradley
   d. Richard Gephardt
   e. all deserve credit
4. The Reagan administration tried to
   a. curtail growth of the government.
   b. curb the steady growth of federal domestic spending abroad.
   c. cut back governmental regulation of private business.
   d. all of the above
   e. none of the above

5. The Federal Reserve does not consist of which of the following?
   a. Bank of America
   b. Board of Governors
   c. Federal Open Market Committee
   d. twelve Federal Reserve banks
   e. all of these are components

6. The Treasury Department is
   a. a relatively uninfluential cabinet department.
   b. not usually involved in economic planning.
   c. never an influence on economic policy.
   d. not one of the original executive departments.
   e. none of the above

7. A 1986 dollar purchases _____ a 1960 dollar.
   a. less than
   b. much less than
   c. the same as
   d. much more than
   e. more than

8. Government policies in the economic area are considered
   a. regulatory.
   b. monetary.
   c. fiscal.
   d. all of the above
   e. none of the above

9. Which party has established a firm contemporary hold on the title "party of prosperity"?
   a. the Democrats
   b. the Republicans
   c. the Libertarians
   d. the Independents
   e. none of the above

ANSWER KEY

Completion

1. Keynes   p. 631
2. fiscal   p. 636
3. lowered   p. 626
4. government   p. 642
5. Friedman   p. 650
6. Monetary   p. 651
7. deflation   p. 633
8. Supply-side   p. 651
9. "growth dividend"   p. 655
10. grow   p. 656

True/False

1. F   p. 634
2. T   pp. 630–31
3. F   p. 634
4. T   p. 648
5. F   pp. 651–52
6. T   p. 649
7. F   p. 637
8. T   p. 640
9. T   p. 643
10. F   p. 624

Multiple Choice

1. c   pp. 630–32
2. b   p. 635
3. e   pp. 626–27
4. d   p. 645
5. e   pp. 656–57

6. e   p. 661
7. a   pp. 637–38
8. d   p. 646
9. e   p. 645

ESSAY QUESTIONS

1. To what extent can the president or congress influence economic activity? Why?
2. Macroeconomic policy is often a difficult area to understand because it involves so many different problems and possible responses. Briefly define the major economic problems of inflation, recession, deficit spending, and stagnation. What are the policy options the government has to deal with each of these problems? What are the political consequences of the problems and the responses?

Further Investigation

Congressional Quarterly, Inc. *Budgeting for America*. Washington, D.C.: Congressional Quarterly Press, 1982.
> A thorough review of the budgetary process, including the impact of economic projections and deficit spending.

Friedman, Milton and Rose. *Free to Choose*. New York: Harcourt, Brace, Jovanovich, 1980.
> Defense of free market and a limited role of government in economic matters.

Gilder, George J. *Wealth and Poverty*. New York: Basic Books, 1981.
> Compares Keynesian and supply-side economics, with a preference for the latter.

Maisel, Sherman J. *Managing the Dollar*. New York: Norton, 1973.
> Overview of the Federal Reserve and how it works.

Porter, Roger B. *Presidential Decision-Making: The Economic Policy Board*. Cambridge: Cambridge University Press, 1980.
> Examines economic policy making in the Ford administration.

Stein, Herbert. *Presidential Economics*. New York: Simon and Schuster, 1984.
> Stein, who has served as an economic advisor to several presidents, examines the impact the political process has on the economy and vice versa.

Tufte, Edward R. *Political Control of the Economy*. Princeton: Princeton University Press, 1978.

Examines the relationship between electoral politics and economic intervention.

Wildavsky, Aaron. *The Politics of the Budgetary Process*. 4th ed. Boston: Little, Brown, 1983.

Examines federal budget making from all sides.

Applying Political Science

1. Political economy is important not only for domestic politics but for international politics as well. Identify a local enterprise — agriculture, manufacturing, steel, autos, etc. — and discuss with the management of these enterprises the impact of government activities on their business. To what extent is foreign competition subsidized? Are there restrictive tariffs or trade practices for the good or commodity abroad? How could public policy better serve the international economic interests of this business?

2. Local governments often provide tax incentives as a means of securing economic growth. Interview your local economic development official and discuss the ways your locality is trying to stimulate growth. What are the costs and consequences of these efforts?

3. As you have learned in your reading, interest rates are not set by the Congress or the president; nevertheless, they are politically controversial. Interview a local banker, realtor, and contractor or car salesman and discuss the impact high interest rates have had on their business activity. Ask them who is to blame for this and what they would propose be done about it.

19 | Public Welfare

Overview

While welfare programs are usually understood as those targeted to help the poor, public welfare is actually a much broader concept. Among the many programs operating under this umbrella are the U.S. Department of Agriculture's farm assistance programs. They are a good example of how a program's objectives can be worthy yet extremely difficult to achieve.

Americans are committed to helping the truly needy but resent "welfare" because it connotes getting something without working. They prefer an individualistic approach in which equality of opportunity prevails, yet they are not entirely opposed to government intervention in order to create an atmosphere in which individual pursuits can be realized. They believe government should help the deserving poor but able individuals should help themselves.

Programs that fit into this public ambivalence have been hard to develop. Workfare programs seem to follow this philosophy but have proven impractical. In-kind payments now account for most welfare payments because they provide only for the necessities and are more difficult to misuse.

This strong ideological commitment to individual responsibility has slowed the growth of a welfare state when compared to European democracies. Still, the U.S. pays more for programs such as education because they provide equality of opportunity. The Great Depression changed attitudes and made possible the passage of the Social Security Act in 1935, and despite tremendous increases over the years, Americans still support the tax and its benefits.

Some welfare programs target specific segments of the population based on need, while others, such as Social Security, benefit all who contribute. Somewhat surprisingly, the public supports both kinds.

It was the Great Depression that first brought Washington into the welfare picture. Current programs can be distinguished by whom they benefit, who administers them, and who finances them. As previously noted, some are based on need while others benefit general sections of the population regardless of economic status. Some programs are administered exclusively by Washington, but more are jointly administered by federal and state governments. Financing is also a complex combination of national and state and local resources. Such a decentralized welfare program varies from state to state in benefits.

Sufficient levels of welfare spending can only be designated based on differing political values. It is clear, however, that welfare spending has increased dramatically over the years, regardless of how it is measured. The largest increases have come in the Social Security program.

Despite much talk of a Reagan Revolution, any reductions in welfare programs have been only modest during his administration. Spending under Reagan has generally followed trends begun during the Carter years. His attempts to significantly reform Social Security resulted only in minor modifications, and, despite much debate, the safety net remains generally unaffected. Even Gramm-Rudman-Hollings did not affect welfare programs much because it excluded so many of them from its scope. Reagan was only able to make adjustments within the boundaries set by national needs, resources, and expectations.

Americans generally agree on the objectives of welfare policy but debate the means vigorously. Democrats have traditionally looked more to government for solutions, while Republicans have turned to the private sector. Many proposals have been developed with few satisfactory results.

Even measuring poverty is controversial. Most statistics fail to include in-kind payments, thus skewing the findings significantly. Such measurements include many more people under the poverty line.

A strong president with a supportive public can play a decisive role in formulating welfare policy, but generally, presidents have less influence in this field than they do in foreign affairs or the economy. The departments that administer welfare programs play a significant role. Congress, however, is at the center of policy specification for welfare issues. Interest groups provide powerful lobbies for almost every welfare program.

Key Terms and Concepts

equality of opportunity
redistribution of wealth
nationalization
Department of Health and
   Human Services
Basic and Supplemental
   Educational Opportunity
   Grants
farm subsidies

helping the poor vs. welfare
payments-in-kind
New Deal
Family Assistance Plan
poverty line
mandatory production
   controls
Gramm-Rudman-Hollings

Chapter Outline

Introduction
    Welfare policies generally assist the poor.
    Public welfare is a broader concept.
        Farm assistance programs are an example of the many diverse efforts under the umbrella of public welfare today.
        The U.S. Department of Agriculture (USDA) has served the general welfare of the country, particularly through farmers, longer than probably any other government agency.
        Farm subsidies are the most expensive and controversial of its programs.
            Under such programs, farmers are guaranteed prices for certain crops and subsidized not to grow others.
            There has been a shift away from the philosophies upon which such programs are based.
            Still, farmers face increased competition from producers abroad.
                The U.S. actually experienced an agricultural trade deficit for the month of May 1986.
                The 1985 farm law attempted to make some helpful modifications, but a record amount was paid in subsidies in 1986.
        The program is an excellent example of many of the difficulties faced by government welfare programs.
        Often the goals are worthy but difficult to achieve.
        Programs often have unforeseen consequences.
Public opinion and welfare
    Some programs are intended to help the needy, while others target a great majority of citizens.
    Americans do not like the concept of welfare.
    They are, however, willing to help the truly needy.
    Welfare connotes getting something without working.
The American approach to welfare
    In the U.S. as well as other Western democracies, welfare spending has more often reflected what is possible than what is needed.
    There are two general approaches to welfare.
        One is a collectivist approach in which a centralized government intervenes to reduce economic inequality.
        The other rejects government intervention and equality of results in favor of equality of opportunity.
    The U.S. identifies more, but not entirely, with the latter approach.
        Americans have not been altogether hostile to governmental action.
            They support programs that provide an atmosphere in which individual pursuits can be realized.
            They also favor programs that help those who are in need despite their own best efforts.

"Helping the poor" versus "welfare"
  Americans support spending for the "deserving" poor.
  Among Americans, welfare tends to connote the avoidance of in-
    dividual responsibility and effort.
  Most Americans believe that hard work is rewarded in this country.
  Polls have revealed a definite ambivalence about welfare programs.
    One solution is workfare, but it has proven somewhat impractical.
    Another is payment-in-kind programs that replace cash payments
      with food stamps and medical and housing subsidies.
      This form of payment is now given by a two-to-one ration over
        cash.
Extending individual security and opportunity
  Strong ideological commitments to individual responsibility and to
    equality of opportunity rather than results have slowed the growth
    of the welfare state.
  Education funding has always been high in part because it extends op-
    portunity.
  The Great Depression brought about a change of attitudes and the
    passage of the Social Security Act in 1935.
    Social Security taxes have risen dramatically in recent years because
      of increases in benefit levels, yet most people feel that neither
      taxes nor benefits are too high.
    Roosevelt claimed that Social Security benefits were paid for by the
      workers, as opposed to welfare.
Minority versus majority welfare
  There are two kinds of welfare programs: those benefiting a poor
    minority of the population, and those benefiting all who contribute.
  Surprisingly, both kinds of programs have survived equally well.
Federalism and public welfare
  The Great Depression brought Washington into the picture.
    National funding grafted onto state central management.
    Today's welfare mix is a complex conbination of federal and state
      administration.
  American welfare programs are decentralized and vary from state to
    state.
  Debate over further nationalization is hot.
Welfare programs and policies
  There are three useful criteria for distinguishing welfare programs:
    whom they benefit, who administers them, and who finances them.
    Some programs are need based, while others benefit general sections
      of the population regardless of economic status.
    Some programs are administered exclusively by Washington, but
      more are jointly administered by federal and state governments.
    The same holds true for financing of programs.

Spending on welfare

Differing political values determine levels of sufficient welfare spending.

It is clear that the rate of increase has been substantial.

In raw numbers, the increase is enormous.

Even in constant dollars, per capita welfare spending increased 400 percent from 1950 to 1980.

It has increased faster than the economy has grown.

In 1950 it was eight percent of the GNP.

In 1980 it was just under 19 percent of the GNP.

The most dramatic increase in benefits has occurred in the Social Security program.

A "Reagan Revolution"?

Expenditure levels began to level off around 1975 as political leaders began to feel the need to impose checks.

Reagan won office campaigning against big government.

In office he attempted to cut back certain aspects of welfare programs.

In actuality, the changes have been mild, following trends begun during the Carter years.

Early proposals to modify the Social Security program were repelled by furious attacks from various sources.

A commission charged with investigating possibilities recommended some limited proposals that were enacted by Congress and resulted in additional revenue and a few modest cuts.

However, because it is an entitlement program, its costs will continue to soar unless Congress changes the formulas for automatic increases in benefits.

Reagan did not attempt to cut Unemployment Compensation.

There is much debate over whether or not Reagan's cuts have affected "safety net" programs, or programs for the needy, disproportionately.

Data reveal a moderate growth in such spending during the Reagan years, even when inflation is taken into account.

Spending has increased at a slower rate under Reagan than in the past two decades.

Gramm-Rudman-Hollings has had only a limited effect on welfare spending because so many welfare programs were excluded from its scope.

What limited potential impact the bill had for welfare expenditures was seriously endangered, if not nullified, by the Supreme Court decision declaring key segments of the bill unconstitutional.

The Reagan shifts were within boundaries established by national needs, resources, and expectations.

"How to do it"?

The parties have traditionally been split on the question.

Democrats are more inclined to turn to more government.

Republicans tend to look to the private sector.

Many members of both parties agree that spiraling medical costs can somehow be restricted without denying people the medical care they need.

Many agree that significant reform is needed.

The issue of how to help the poor without taking away their incentive to work has been debated endlessly without any satisfactory solutions.

Daniel Moynihan devised a proposal as an adviser to Nixon, but even he noted that it was flawed.

Measuring proverty and income

Even measuring poverty is difficult.

It has become a mixture of relative and absolute criteria that we use to measure poverty.

Poverty statistics are politically sensitive.

In-kind payments make it especially difficult to measure poverty.

Most poverty statistics exclude in-kind payments, making such data flawed.

When statistics are calculated in such a manner, it keeps a much larger group of people categorized below the poverty line.

The makers of welfare policy

As with other policy areas, the president is a key player here as well.

A strong president with a supportive public can play a decisive role in formulating welfare policy.

Such situations are exceptions rather than the norm.

Presidents have even less ability to affect policy in this field than they do in foreign or economic policy.

Interest groups and states detract from the president's ability to implement welfare policy.

The Department of Health and Human Services is the principle welfare agency of the national government.

Its 1984 budget was easily the largest of any department.

Its components include the Social Security Administration, the Health Care Financing Administration, and the Public Health Service.

The Department of Agriculture operates a number of programs including Food Stamps.

The Department of Housing and Urban Development deals with housing assistance for the poor, among other things.

The Department of Education administers programs that help the disadvantaged and low-income obtain education.

The Veterans Administration is also a major welfare agency.

ACTION is a federal voluntary action agency that mobilizes volunteers for service to those in need.

Congress is at the center of policy specification for welfare issues.

Its organization for dealing with welfare policy is surprisingly coherent.

Most issues are decided by the taxation and appropriation committees.

Some more specialized welfare issues are handled by other committees and subcommittees.

Interest groups are quite influential through their lobbying on welfare policy.

Each program seems to have its own interest group to lobby for it. They are part of the iron triangle.

Review Questions

COMPLETION

1. Americans believe in equality of _____, not equality of _____.

2. People are expected to get by and achieve their goals by _____ effort.

3. A program where people work for their welfare benefits is called _____.

4. _____ has been avoided in the United States because of a firm belief in the individual.

5. During the Great Depression the _____ was thought to have the duty to rid the nation of poverty.

6. Government had very _____ to do with welfare before the Great Depression.

7. The _____ directs the Food Stamp Program.

8. _____ was organized to tap the spirit of volunteerism in America.

9. A large concern in determining who lives under or above the poverty level is whether _____ are counted.

10. Under _____ a great number of welfare programs were excluded from automatic cuts.

TRUE/FALSE

1. The U.S. Department of Agriculture has only recently become an agency that deals with welfare.

2. The public accepts government intervention in welfare funding very reluctantly.
3. Anti-poverty measures are at times acceptable to Americans as a whole.
4. Americans are bothered by what the term "welfare" connotes.
5. Americans believe that America is a land that provides limitless opportunities to whoever is willing to work.
6. The education budget has always been lacking in funds.
7. Almost all of the major welfare programs are run by the federal government.
8. Presidents do not usually wield power to alter welfare programs drastically.
9. Pell Grants have to do with housing and urban development policy.
10. The budget for welfare programs in 1983 was smaller than the Defense Department's.

MULTIPLE CHOICE

1. Welfare benefits given instead of money are called
   a. handouts.
   b. in-kind payments.
   c. food stamps.
   d. real market value payments.
2. Benefits originally for the social security plan were considered
   a. bought and paid for as a pension plan.
   b. only another tax to be paid.
   c. a tax break for employers.
   d. another example of government increasing taxes.
3. Studies of opinions about social security benefits in 1983 point out that people generally think that levels of benefits are
   a. too low.
   b. too high.
   c. they did not know.
   d. about right.
4. The countertrends in the trimming or modifying of welfare expenditures came in the
   a. Reagan term.
   b. Ford term.
   c. Carter term.
   d. Have not occurred yet.
5. Which of the following is not one of the programs administered by the USDA?
   a. providing rural electric utilities with funding
   b. farm extension services
   c. Food Stamps
   d. farm subsidies
   e. all are administered by the USDA
6. To get food stamps you would face
   a. waiting for them by mail.
   b. substantial federal red tape.
   c. federal inspectors.
   d. local and state workers.

7. Which office administers the National School Lunch Program?
   a. Health and Human Services
   b. Department of Education
   c. Department of Agriculture
   d. Senate Subcommittee on Food and Nutrition

8. The Veterans Administration is a
   a. major federal welfare agency.
   b. result of volunteerism
   c. privately operated organization.
   d. trusteeship for veterans' families.

9. According to GNP figures, as the nation got wealthier,
   a. welfare spending went down.
   b. taxes went down.
   c. unemployment went down.
   d. welfare spending went up.

10. To provide the most accurate data concerning those near the poverty level line, we need the best possible information about
    a. hours worked and taxes paid.
    b. income distribution and standard of living.
    c. real value income and number in the family.
    d. standard of living and type of job one has.

ANSWER KEY

Completion

1. opportunity, results p. 672
2. individual p. 673
3. workfare p. 673
4. Collectivism p. 672
5. government p. 675
6. little p. 684
7. Department of Agriculture pp. 698–99
8. ACTION p. 701
9. in-kind payments pp. 693–94
10. Gramm-Rudman-Hollings p. 688

True/False

1. F p. 667
2. T p. 672
3. F p. 673
4. T p. 670
5. T p. 673
6. F p. 675
7. F p. 679
8. T pp. 695–96
9. F p. 700
10. F p. 697

Multiple Choice

1. b p. 673
2. a pp. 675–76
3. d p. 677
4. c p. 690
5. e pp. 667–68
6. d p. 699
7. c p. 699
8. a p. 700
9. d p. 685
10. b p. 692

1. How would you describe the American view on welfare? In what ways are Americans supportive of public assistance and why? What parts of public welfare are unpopular and why? Be sure to cite examples to support your answer.
2. How would you respond to the statement that most of what the government does it does for the middle class? Explain your answer.

Further Investigation

Derthick, Martha. *Policymaking for Social Security*. Washington, D.C.: Brookings Institution, 1979.
    Excellent overview of the history of social security, its financial problems, and its likely future.
Harrington, Michael. *The Other America*. New York: Penguin, 1981.
    Examines the nature and extent of poverty in the United States in the early 1960s.
Helco, Hugh. *Modern Social Politics in Britain and Sweden*. New Haven: Yale University Press, 1974.
    Provides a useful comparison to social programs in other democracies.
Moynihan, Daniel Patrick. *Maximum Feasible Misunderstanding*. New York: Free Press, 1969.
    The Community Action program of the War on Poverty required local participation in its administration. Moynihan analyzes this requirement and others of the War on Poverty.
Page, Benjamin I. *Who Gets What from Government*. Berkeley: University of California Press, 1983.
    As the title suggests, the book examines the beneficiaries of government programs and finds that it is not so much the poor but rather the middle class and well-to-do that benefit from government programs.
Schwarz, John E. *America's Hidden Success: A Reassessment of Twenty Years of Public Policy*. New York: Norton, 1983.
    Schwarz challenges the widespread view that the antipoverty and environmental policies of the 1960s and 1970s did not achieve their purposes.

Applying Political Science

1. Public programs are frequently criticized for waste and inefficiency. Visit your campus financial aid office and interview the director or assistant director about how the office attempts to collect loan pay-

ments and minimize waste. Select a comparable private sector loan agency and interview its management and evaluate its practices.

2. As your reading has demonstrated, the poor are not the exclusive beneficiaries of government programs. Select a policy area like agriculture, transportation, or education and attempt to identify who gets what from that program.

3. During the 1960s the federal government dramatically increased its involvement in public education. Several of those programs deserve your evaluation—Head Start, school lunch, and aid for special or handicapped education. Research the intent of these programs and then evaluate how those programs are used in your local school district.

20 | Foreign and Defense Policy

Overview

The national interest and morality are two sometimes conflicting criteria on which foreign policy can be based. As the issue of apartheid in South America makes clear, however, the difficulty is often in determining what constitutes a moral action or what is in our best interest. And even when there is a consensus on what these are, there is not always agreement on how they can be achieved.

In its early years, the nation was able to use its geographical location to avoid significant participation in the international affairs. As it became drawn into the arena of world affairs, however, the weaknesses of democracy in conducting foreign relations became apparent. It is clear that with the openness and freedom extant in a democracy, certain disadvantages are inherent.

After World War II, the U.S. began to fill the vacuum left by Britain in maintaining a balance of world power. Abandoning its unilateralist role, the U.S. soon adopted a policy of *containment*, aimed at preventing communist expansion. First set forth by George Kennan, the doctrine has guided U.S. foreign policy for the last four decades.

The United States saw the need to help the devastated nations of Western Europe for humanitarian reasons and for strengthening their economies to combat communism. Soviet acts such as the Berlin Blockade triggered the formation of NATO. Despite the harsher rhetoric of Secretary of State John Foster Dulles, the U.S. continued a cautious foreign policy during the Eisenhower years.

In the sixties, however, containment was probably misapplied in Vietnam. The war cost Americans thousands of lives and caused tremendous division at home, with the debate about its appropriateness continuing even today. Many agreed with both its objectives and its means, while others denounced it completely, and yet others were sympathetic to its objectives and in disagreement with the methods used to achieve them.

Vietnam resulted in a prudent and cautious foreign policy during the 1970s. The Soviet invasion of Afghanistan in 1979 and the Iranian seizure of a U.S. embassy reversed this trend, with containment again becoming the major theme as the U.S. reasserted itself in the 1980s. Still, there are divisions among Americans about various policies such as those concerning South Africa and Nicaragua. The Nicaraguan situation especially exemplifies the post-Vietnam American ambivalence about getting involved beyond U.S. borders. The public seems to fear both communist expansion and the prospect of increasing military involvement in the region.

Liberals tend to stress the problems facing humanity over the East-West conflict, while conservatives see the threat of Soviet expansion as the greatest problem. Both agree that the U.S. should be involved abroad, and they agree that military force is a necessary part of our foreign policy. Disagreements center around such issues as how much military power we need.

In actual dollars, the U.S. spends about as much now as it did at the peak of the Vietnam War, although, in relative terms, less was spent in the decade in between. As a proportion of GNP, military expenditures are down drastically from World War II.

The Soviets have increased their spending in the last two decades and probably now outspend the United States. But when NATO spending is compared to that of the Warsaw Pact, the West still spends more. Arms control is seen as an alternative to the arms race, but is also difficult to achieve because of the complexities and subtleties of the situation in which the Soviets and Americans find themselves.

While East-West relations often dominate U.S. foreign policy, there are many important issues that deal with North-South relations due to the disparity between the wealth of the Northern and Southern Hemispheres. In many less-developed regions, the population is growing at a rapid rate, and world population is up nearly two billion since 1960. The U.S. gives a substantial amount in aid and loans to Third World nations each year, but with some nations accumulating nearly insurmountable debts, many are saying the U.S. must do more.

Foreign affairs is the only policy area in which foreign governments participate. The president is the chief policy-maker, more so than in any other area, partly because of the constitutional powers he has. He also fills the practical need to represent the U.S. to other nations. Other actors have a difficult time stopping a determined presidential initiative in foreign policy.

In 1947 the National Security Council was created to assist the president in formulating foreign policy. Particularly since 1961, the national security adviser has had great influence with the president.

The Department of State has the broadest formal responsibilities in this area, but the Department of Defense has tremendous influence with its size. Its intelligence services are key to decision-making, although activities of agencies such as the CIA have been somewhat controversial over the years. Other departments and agencies also play smaller roles in the development of foreign policy.

In this area, Congress serves mostly as a check against the president, although the chairmen of key committees often exercise considerable influence. Ideological interest groups can also affect policy, particularly on broader issues. On more specific issues such as trade, development of weapons systems, and policies affecting ethnic groups, more specialized interest groups play a role. Even foreign governments actively lobby on certain issues.

Key Terms and Concepts

National Security Council

War Powers Act of 1974

national interest

apartheid

economic sanctions

clandestine activities

balance of power

containment

contras

arms control

Chapter Outline

Introduction
- U.S. foreign policy can be based on American self-interest and/or morality.
- It is not easy to determine to what degree actions are in our best interest or are moral.

South Africa and American national interests
- U.S. national interest would dictate somehow averting the establishment of any kind of pro-Soviet government in Pretoria.
- There is disagreement as to the efficacy of economic sanctions.
  - Some argue that economic sanctions would weaken the current government and hasten its fall.
  - They believe that could yield extreme violence and a Soviet dictatorship.
  - Others fear the current course will alienate non-Communist black leaders and thereby increase the chances of an eventual anti-West regime.
- Even when there is a consensus on what is the national interest, there is not always agreement on what should be done.

A foreign policy of morality
- Economic sanctions can be seen as a concrete step towards eliminating a practice that denies a majority of South Africans equality and freedom.
- Others argue that economic sanctions would actually hurt blacks more than whites and dissolve any moderate center.
- Sincere and intelligent people often disagree on matters of foreign policy.

Foreign and defense policy comprises the agreements, alliances, military and economic intervention, etc., undertaken to deal with the outside world.

Democracies and foreign affairs

In the early years, the U.S. was able to use its unique geographical location to remain aloof of international "interweaving."

Tocqueville foresaw the potential weaknesses of a democracy in dealing with foreign policy.

Democracies are not able to handle foreign affairs in ways that stable authoritarian regimes can.

Kissinger believes the U.S.S.R. is able to concentrate resources, making it a formidable adversary.

The democracies of the world experienced frustrations as they struggled to employ their superior resources against the dictatorships aligned against them.

Democracy demands freedom and openness.

Democracy opens the formulation of foreign policy to active political debate.

Administrations change with elections.

Foreign and defense policy since World War II

Foreign policy can be marked off into a few periods.

Emergence as a world power

Since World War II, the U.S. has increased tremendously in national power relative to Germany, France, and Great Britain.

The U.S. economy was actually revitalized by the successful war effort, as opposed to the European nations, which were devastated.

They tired of world leadership and turned inward to rebuild, leaving a leadership vacuum.

Before the war, the U.S. had been unilateralist, intervening only selectively in international affairs.

This was possible largely because Great Britain kept a balance of power in Europe and prevented any menacing hegemony.

Britain was no longer able to maintain this role after the war.

Containment

Balance of power politics suggest a certain amorality.

They did, however, sometimes have moral objectives.

Containment was the U.S. version of such politics.

It aimed at containing the Soviet Union and communist expansion.

It began with President Truman's request for economic and military aid to Greece and Turkey in order to implement the Truman Doctrine.

George Kennan made the intellectual case for such a policy.

He argued that the U.S. needed a policy of "long-term, patient but firm and vigilant containment of Russian expansive tendencies."

He called for countermeasures at strategic geopolitical points.
His vision of containment has provided the foundation for the
last four decades of policy.

The Marshall Plan and NATO

It was clear that devastated Europe needed help after the war.
Humanitarian considerations alone were reason enough for American aid.
The need for strong economies in the European democracies to
combat communism strengthened American resolve to aid European democracies.

The U.S. response was the Marshall Plan, which funneled over $12
billion into West European nations.

A military alliance developed along with Western European
economies.
Soviet actions triggered the formation of NATO.

Strong rhetoric, cautious policy

Dulles saw the policy of containment as "negative, futile, and immoral" because it conceded initiative to the Soviets.
He argued America should eliminate the threat of Soviet power.

Still, the U.S. continued with a cautious foreign policy during the
Eisenhower years.
Public opinion did not support an aggressive policy that could have
led to war.

Vietnam: The misapplication of containment

Contrary to the doctrine of containment, Vietnam was not an important strategic location.

Logistically, the war was a miscalculation that claimed the lives of
over 50,000 Americans.

It provoked bitter domestic division in the U.S. and, to a large extent,
shook the country's resolve to contain communist aggression.
Even now the debate continues.
A majority agree that we should not have become militarily involved.

Two questions are involved in the debate:
Were the objectives sound?
Were the means appropriate?

There are generally three positions:
Containment was a sound policy and Vietnam a necessary application of it.
Containment itself was a flawed policy.
The objectives were sound but this war was a misapplication of
the policy.

The long war resulted in a turning inward and an insistence on a
more prudent foreign policy.

Without abandoning the overriding objective of containment, Carter emphasized other aspects of American leadership.

Reassertion

Events such as the Soviet invasion of Afghanistan and the seizure by Iranians of the U.S. embassy and staff led to a reevaluation of American foreign policy.

According to one poll, by spring of 1980, most Americans felt too little was being spent on defense.

In January of 1980, the president announced the Carter Doctrine.

It proclaimed the Persian Gulf a vital U.S. interest and warned outside forces not to interfere with it.

With Reagan, American foreign policy's major theme again became containment.

Policy differences

Central America, like South Africa, is an area where Americans are divided.

Reagan has pushed for full-fledged economic and military aid for the *contras*.

Many Democrats have opposed this on the grounds that *contra* human rights violations make them unworthy of aid.

The public seems to fear both Communist expansion and the prospect of another Vietnam.

Liberal versus conservative internationalists

Both accept the underlying premise that the U.S. should be involved internationally.

Liberals stress problems facing humanity over the East-West conflict.

Conservatives see the threat of Soviet expansionism as the greatest problem.

Psychological assumptions about the Soviet leadership are inherent to this debate.

Conservatives like Nixon perceive a Soviet mentality that understands only enemy strength as a reason not to expand.

Liberals like Cyrus Vance believe there are areas of mutual interest that can compel the Soviets to act agreeably.

Military balance: How much is enough?

There is a consensus about the necessity of military force in the nation's foreign policy, but disagreement as to how much is required.

U.S. military expenditures

U.S. is spending much more today in actual dollars than ever before.

In constant dollars, expenditures are at about the same level as during the height of the Vietnam War.

Less money was expended in between these two peaks.

As a proportion of GNP, military expenditures are down drastically from World War II and the fifties, but up slightly from the post-Vietnam decline.

U.S.-U.S.S.R. expenditures

This comparison is critical yet difficult to make.

The Soviets do not share expenditure data.

Intelligence efforts yield some information, but it is difficult to transfer into terms used in the West.

Estimates say the Soviets have increased their spending significantly in the last two decades.

They are now spending more than the U.S.

NATO versus the Warsaw Pact

This is a more complete comparison.

The Soviets are in a weaker position in this context.

NATO allies spend far more than Warsaw Pact allies on defense.

Arms control

Arms control is an alternative to the arms race.

Reagan came to office with the view that arms control agreements of the seventies were basically not in the best interest of the U.S.

After having beefed up U.S. defense and having compiled huge deficits, Reagan began to explore new arms agreements with the U.S.S.R.

It is a complex and subtle system through which arms control can be achieved.

Distrust exists between the two nations and their leaders.

Each nation faces a unique set of pressures.

The Soviets seem to fear SDI.

Reagan wants cut-backs in the number of Soviet offensive missiles.

"North-South" issues

East-West relations have largely dominated U.S. foreign policy since World War II.

For many other nations, poverty is a much greater concern.

When viewed in righ-poor terms, we see North-South issues instead of East-West.

World population is up by nearly two billion since 1960.

Most rapid growth is in the less-developed regions.

The U.S. spends about $5 billion a year in economic aid to Third World countries.

Much is direct aid in the form of food assistance.

The U.S. also contributes to international financial institutions that loan money to Third World nations.

Some say that the amount, although substantial, is not enough.

Many of the Third World nations have accumulated almost insurmountable debts to developed nations.

Several have proposed rescheduling their debt repayments.

Many Western experts agree that something must be done.

The role of Third World nations in the East-West conflict complicates matters.

Foreign- and defense-policy-makers

This is the only policy area in which foreign governments participate.

There are many opportunities for them to influence decisions.

The President: Chief foreign-policy maker

Here the president's scope is greater than in any other policy area.

He has powers explicitly granted in the Constitution.

He is commander-in-chief.

He can make treaties with foreign governments.

He appoints those who make foreign policy decisions.

He fills the practical need to represent the United States in dealing with other countries.

He can claim to articulate transcending national interests.

He encounters fewer contending pressures than in any other area of domestic policy.

Critics allow him greater room to maneuver than they would on any domestic issue.

The current importance of the military in foreign relations makes the president's role as commander-in-chief very influential.

Congress has attempted to reassert its authority in recent years.

In times of crisis, however, the president is clearly the key player.

It is much more difficult for other players to stop a determined presidential initiative in foreign policy.

The National Security Council

Created in 1947 to assist the president in discharging his foreign policy responsibilities, this council operates in an advisory capacity.

It provides the president with an expanded corps of advisers on foreign policy.

Since 1961, the national security adviser has almost always had great influence with the president.

Kennedy used the NSC staff as his foreign policy team to fill a deficiency he perceived in the State Department.

Nixon especially expanded the role of the NSC with Kissinger.

The Department of State

State has the broadest formal responsibilities.

It operates embassies, missions, consulates general, and consulates around the world, among other things.

It includes many influential agencies such as the Agency for International Development.

The Department of Defense

DOD has the biggest payroll in the U.S.

Because of its sheer size, critics worry about the amount of influence
the DOD yields.

It has great economic muscle.

Politicians often fashion their remarks to get the support of the
military.

The jount chiefs of staff are also influential in advising the civilian
secretaries, the president, and Congress.

Intelligence services

Most intelligence work is done far from enemy lines.

The Defense Department collects more intelligence than any other
government agency.

Air Force Intelligence, its biggest unit, handles surveillance through
reconnaissance satellites.

The National Security Agency, second largest in total budget in the
U.S. intelligence community, handles code-breaking and code-
making.

The CIA accounts for only 10 percent of U.S. intelligence staff.

Most of its operations involve compiling available information from
published sources.

The clandestine activities of the CIA, however, have made it the
most controversial.

There are two kinds of such activities: spying and covert operations.

The "Bay of Pigs" was probably its greatest fiasco in the latter
category.

Americans have ambivalent feelings about foreign intelligence-
gathering.

They realize its necessity but tend to dislike clandestine activities.

In the 1970s, Congress tried to exert greater control over such activities.

By the 1980s, the pendulum had swung back.

The director of Central Intelligence also has general responsibility
for coordinating the entire U.S. intelligence community.

Other executive agencies with foreign-policy responsibilities

The Treasury Department, the Commerce Department, the Office of
the United States Trade Representative, and the Department of
Agriculture all play smaller roles in developing U.S. foreign policy.

Congress

In this area, Congress serves more as a check against the president.

The relationship between the two branches in this arena only draws attention when they are in disagreement, as was often the case during
the Vietnam War.

Chairmen of key committees often exercise considerable influence.

Interest groups

Because the benefits and costs of any particular foreign policy are usually widely distributed across the population, relevant interest groups are distinguished by ideological differences.

Some interest groups such as the *Committee on the Present Danger* deal almost exclusively with foreign policy, while others such as the AFL-CIO have broader interests but are also concerned with foreign policy.

Some issues pertain to more specific groups: issues over foreign trade, arguments over weapons systems, and issues involving ethnic concerns.

Virtually all sectors of the U.S. economy are affected by international trade.

The auto industry and its unions often unite in calling for protectionism.

Farmers lobby for increased sales abroad, sometimes in direct conflict with administration policies.

Businesses, unions, and states often lobby for the construction of certain weapons systems.

As the U.S. has become more involved abroad, ethnic groups have had greater impact on foreign policy.

The powerful voice of Jewish groups lobbying for Israel is probably the prime example of ethnic influence.

Many other ethnic groups have had significant influence as well.

Government is hardly helpless in its interaction with interest groups, with different elements within government sometimes pitting the various interest groups against each other.

This happened in 1977–78 when Carter lined up an impressively broad coalition of interest groups to fight for the passage of the Panama Canal Treaty.

As noted, foreign governments also actively lobby to influence American foreign policy.

Two factors encourage this: U.S. foreign policy affects other countries, and American democracy is quite open to lobbying.

Many hire lawyers and public relations firms to conduct their lobbying campaigns.

In many instances, political figures who formerly held prominent government positions are retained.

Foreign governments also use their embassies.

Review Questions

COMPLETION

1. The _____ appoints members of the Joint Chiefs of Staff.

2. _____ percent of all the intelligence community is employed by the Central Intelligence Agency.
3. According to a 1983 *New York Times* Poll, 77 percent of the people asked said that America should not have been involved in the _____.
4. President _____ had a very suspicious outlook concerning Soviet intentions in the world.
5. South Africa's system of racial segregation and discrimination is known as _____.
6. Issues of development, population control, and economic stability are all factors in _____ nations.

TRUE/FALSE

1. The Senate has sole responsibility in negotiating treaties on behalf of the United States.
2. The National Security Council is only an advisory body to the president; it does not make policy.
3. The CIA is the primary source of intelligence gathering by the United States.
4. The Treasury Department has a substantial role in foreign policy responsibilities.
5. A former government official would not be the best contact for a foreign lobbyist to make in Washington.
6. The Vietnam War had a major influence in the passing of the War Powers Act of 1974.
7. By 1976, the United States was spending less for defense than in 1955.
8. Political and economical issues in the Third World will most likely be seen only in the context of an East-West confrontation.
9. If a citizen favors a foreign policy of morality over a foreign policy of national interests, he supports economic sanctions against South Africa.

MULTIPLE CHOICE

1. Periodic changes in American government
   a. strengthen foreign policy by allowing new ideas.
   b. really do not alter foreign policy.
   c. hamper foreign policy execution.
   d. are often too insignificant to measure.

2. Under President Nixon, the NSC controlled the shaping of foreign policy more than which other two branches?
   a. The CIA and the State Department
   b. The Senate and the Defense Department
   c. The State Department and the Defense Department
   d. The CIA and the Agency for International Development

3. The National Security Agency (NSA) is a subgroup within the
   a. Department of State.
   b. Senate Intelligence Committee.
   c. CIA.
   d. Department of Defense.

4. Which of the following is considered to be the most powerful lobby among special interest groups in Washington?
   a. The Irish lobby
   b. The Jewish lobby
   c. The Veterans of Foreign Wars lobby
   d. The United Auto Workers lobby

5. Of the following, which country did not receive money from the Marshall Plan?
   a. Britain
   b. Hungary
   c. France
   d. West Germany

6. President Johnson committed how many troops to Indochina?
   a. 250,000
   b. 1,000,000
   c. 500,000
   d. 1,500,000

7. Increases in real costs for our nation's defense can be attributed to what factor?
   a. A more hostile Soviet Union
   b. Inflation
   c. Record deficits
   d. Congress's unwillingness to supply the money needed to spend on defense

8. When considering the situation in Nicaragua, Americans seem to
   a. fear communist expansion in Central America.
   b. fear a widening military struggle in the area involving the U.S.
   c. both of the above
   d. none of the above

ANSWER KEY

Completion

1. president   p. 738
2. Ten   p. 739
3. Vietnam War   p. 718
4. Nixon   p. 722
5. apartheid   p. 706
6. Third World   pp. 729–30

True/False

1. F   p. 741
2. T   pp. 732–33
3. F   p. 739
4. T   p. 741
5. F   p. 746

6. T   p. 719
7. T   p. 724
8. T   p. 731
9. F   pp. 707–08

Multiple Choice

1. c   pp. 709–10
2. c   pp. 733–34
3. d   p. 739
4. b   p. 745

5. b   p. 715
6. c   p. 717
7. b   p. 724
8. c   p. 721

ESSAY QUESTIONS

1. As Professor Ladd argues, containment has been the key to our superpower policy since World War II. What is containment? How have we applied it? Has it been successful? Be sure to cite examples to support your argument.
2. Foreign policy is not made by the president alone. Identify the important players in the foreign policy-making arena, what they do, and what their particular point of view is likely to be.

Further Investigation

Allison, Graham, *Essence of Decision*. Boston: Little, Brown, 1971.
    Presidential decision making in a foreign policy crisis, notably the 1962 Cuban missile crisis.

Fallows, James. *National Defense*. New York: Random House, 1981.
    Critical assessment of present defense policy.

Halperin, Morton H. *Bureaucratic Politics and Foreign Policy*. Washington, D.C.: Brookings Institution, 1974.
    How the military and diplomatic bureaucracies defend their policy interests.

Hilsman, Roger. *The Politics of Policy Making in Defense and Foreign Affairs*. New York: Harper & Row, 1971.
    Somewhat dated but thorough treatment of policy making in these areas.

Mueller, John E. *War, Presidents, and Public Opinion*. New York: Simon and Schuster, 1973.
    Analysis of the impact of foreign policy on presidential popularity and public opinion on war and foreign policy generally.

Sapolsky, Harvey M. *The Polaris System Development: Bureaucratic and Programmatic Success in Government.* Cambridge: Harvard University Press, 1972.

Case study of how the Polaris submarine system was developed.

Yergin, Daniel. *Shattered Peace: The Origins of the Cold War and the National Security State.* Boston: Houghton Mifflin, 1977.

Overview of the early cold war years and the policy of containment.

Applying Political Science

1. Ambassadors represent our country in foreign countries. How are they selected? What attributes does the president look for: ability to speak the language, prior experience in that country, formal training in international relations or diplomacy? Select three to five countries and then research how the present ambassador was appointed. You will need the help of your documents librarian to find the confirmation hearings for your ambassadors.

2. Dwight Eisenhower in his farewell address warned the country of the military-industrial complex. Select a major weapons systems proposed over the past ten years and attempt to identify whether such a complex exists and what impact it might have on present defense policy.

3. Select a foreign policy crisis that occurred in a previous administration for which you can obtain memoirs and other published documentation. Examples would include the Bay of Pigs and Cuban missile crisis in the Kennedy administration, Vietnam in the Johnson and Nixon administrations, the Mayaguez in the Ford administration, and the Iranian hostage crisis in the Carter administration. Did the president receive adequate information? Was there bureaucratic competition over policy? What mistakes were made? Based upon this case study, what would you advise a president about crisis management in the future?